BAYONETS:
AN ILLUSTRATED HISTORY

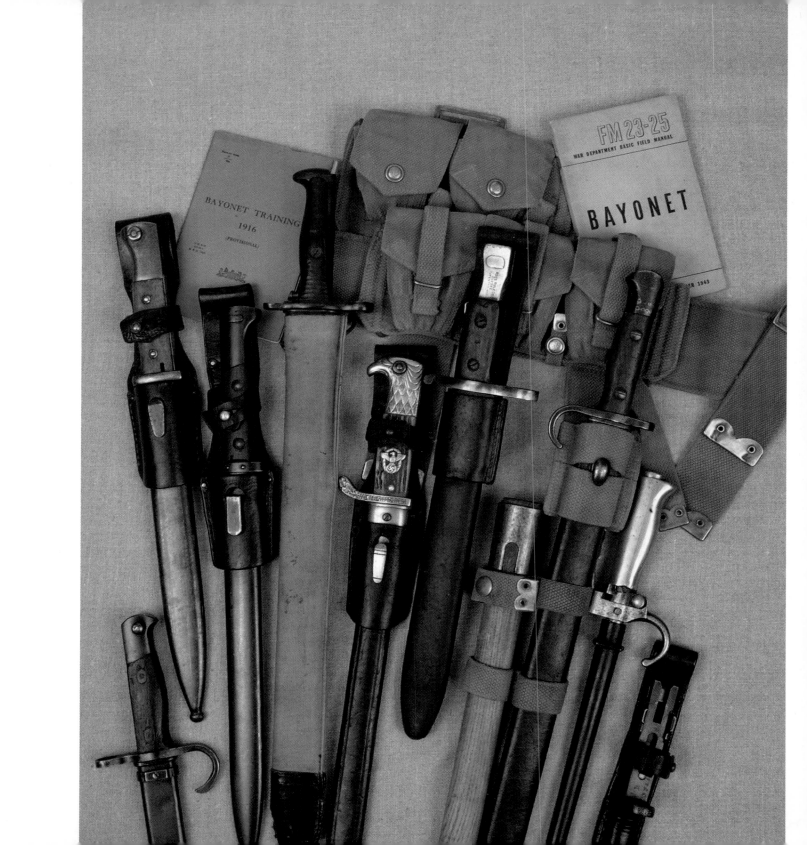

BAYONETS:
AN ILLUSTRATED HISTORY

Martin J. Brayley

D&C
David and Charles

**"In my training as a young officer I had received
much instruction in how to kill my enemy with a
bayonet fixed to a rifle."**
Bernard Montgomery
Memoirs of Field Marshal Montgomery

Acknowledgments
The author would like to thank the following individ-
uals and institutions for their assistance with the
production of this work: Caroline Wigley; Graham
Priest; Rog Dennis; Simon Forty; Bob Stedman;
Ed Storey; Jamie Mangrum; Royal Thai Embassy;
U.S. Embassy; Josef Inauen, Swiss Federal Military
Library; Annele Apajakari, Finnish Defence Forces;
Brigadier S.C. Sharma, Indian Army; Major P.A.
Williams, Australian Defence Staff; Major Per Olav
Vaagland, MA CofS Norwegian Army; Lt. Col.
Emilio Sarabia, Spanish Army; Martin S. Jakobsen,
Royal Danish Embassy; WOII Udo Sadrinna, Federal
German Army; WOII Cyrile Amichaud, French
Military Mission; Commander Juhani Karjomaa,
Finnish Defence Force; Colonel Eduardo Cunha Da
Cunha. Brazilian Army; Major P. Vagland, MA to the
Chief of Staff, Norwegian Army.

Martin J. Brayley
Martin Brayley works as a professional photographer and freelance
author. Martin served 24 years as a military photographer serving world-
wide from desert, jungle and arctic terrain to duties in Iraq and East
Timor. He has written eleven titles to date including *WWII British
Women's Uniforms; The WWII Tommy; Khaki Drill & Jungle Green; WWII
Allied Women's Services; WWII Allied Nursing Services; British Army 1939-
45 Northwest Europe; British Army 1939-45 Middle East & Mediterranean;
British Army 1939-45 Far East; The Home Front 1939-45;* and *British Web
Equipment of the First and Second World Wars.* Having a keen interest in
all aspects of military history, particularly the first half of the 20th centu-
ry, he is a dedicated militaria collector.

Contents

Foreword

Author's Notes

In the beautiful summer of 1986, a fresh-faced Naval rating arrived loaded down with cameras, tripods and miles of photographic film. A happy day was spent polishing, arranging and recording bayonets from my collection for posterity. Observation of an artist at work was an education in itself, and the clear black and white photographs produced are treasured to this day.

That photographer was Martin J. Brayley. Although the years went by and Martin produced, and published, many excellent photographic images of uniforms and equipment for his numerous projects, it was with delight that I heard he was to create a book on bayonets. Even better was the news that the pictures were to be in color, and that the subject was to be a survey of bayonets in general.

Not since the late Anthony Carter's *World Bayonets 1800 until the Present* (London: Arms & Armour Press, 1984) has there been an attempt to produce a non-specialist book of this type in England.

Well-known publications, such as John Watts and Peter White *The Bayonet Book* (Self-published, 1975), R.D.C. Evans and F.J. Stephens *The Bayonet: An Evolution and History* (Milton Keynes: Militaria Publications, 1985) and J.L. Janzen *Bayonets from Janzen's Notebook* (Broken Arrow: Cedar Ridge Publishing, 1987) are long out of print, so have become expensive collectors' items in their own right.

Here then is new material, photographed in "glorious Technicolor" by an acknowledged expert and long-term bayonet collector. If you are just starting the fascinating journey into the world of the bayonet then this is for you. If, like myself, you have reached more "mature" years, and you want to see images of weapons not published before then it suits you also.

Martin's coverage is a purely personal one. His insight as a professional military photographer, and the bearer of at least one of the models illustrated, is clear, accurate and engrossing. There is much to be learned between the covers of this book.

I am only too pleased to recommend this publication to budding and advanced collectors alike. It will soon become well thumbed in this household as it travels from shelf to desk in frequent usage.

Graham Priest
(Author of *The Brown Bess Bayonet, 1720–1860* (1986) and *Spirit of the Pike: British Socket Bayonets of the Twentieth Century* (2003).
Biddestone, June 21, 2004.

This reference is intended only as an introduction to the hobby of bayonet collecting. Rather than a catalog of all known bayonet types, which would take many volumes of this size. It illustrates the principal bayonets of select nations and key variations in design and development. With a few exceptions the majority of the bayonets illustrated are relatively easily obtained and, importantly, affordable for the average collector.

Bayonets are generally worn on the left side with the muzzle ring pointing to the rear, although there are exceptions to this rule. If photographed in the scabbard the right side of the bayonet would normally be shown. However, for illustrative purposes the left side of the bayonet has occasionally been shown alongside a correctly orientated scabbard.

Bayonets of a particular type or pattern designation may be mentioned in a number of national entries, but are not always illustrated. Bayonets that are illustrated within the work, either in their original nation or elsewhere as export or licensed items, are marked in **bold** text.

ABOVE Italian Carcano 1891 fitted to Carcano rifle

Introduction

"To attack with the bayonet effectively requires **Good Direction, Strength and Quickness,** *during a state of wild excitement and probably physical exhaustion. The limit of the range of a bayonet is about 5 feet (measured from the opponents eyes), but more often the killing is at close quarters, at a range of 2 feet or less, when troops are struggling corpse a corpse in trenches or darkness."*

Thus reads the opening paragraph of the 1916 Canadian Army manual *Bayonet Training*. Later sections go on to indicate the best targets for the bayonet point, the throat, face, chest, abdomen and thighs; or when an opponent was in retreat, his kidneys. A penetration of four to six inches was considered enough to incapacitate an enemy, any greater penetration may have made it impossible to withdraw the blade; making it necessary to fire a round to break up the obstruction.

Few bayonet-training manuals leave any doubt as to the wholly offensive nature of the bayonet. It was designed as a tool for killing, and in most cases little more than that. But despite their intended purpose the bayonet holds a fascination for collectors. Many are quite attractive in their shape and in the materials used, such as the British **1855** Lancaster bayonet with its brass hilt and scabbard fittings, and long pipe-back

LEFT Bayonet manuals. *Les Principes du Combat à la Baionnette*, a commercially produced French manual published during World War I; a World War II British training pamphlet *Small Arms Training, Volume 1 Pamphlet No. 12. Bayonet 1942*; *Tommy Gun Rifle and Bayonet*, a British World War II manual aimed at the Home Guard; American field manual *FM 23-25 Bayonet*; and a World War I Canadian manual *Bayonet Training 1916*.

ABOVE RIGHT British medical orderlies undertaking stretcher drill, c.1890. They carry the Lancaster 1855 bayonet as a dress sidearm.

RIGHT A British infantry instructor with the bayonet "training stick" used to instruct in the parry and point. From *Pamphlet No. 3 Rifle and Bayonet (All Arm) 1948*.

blade. A military quirk, the Lancaster later became the dress sidearm of the soldiers of the Medical Staff Corps, the very men required to tend to troops wounded by such weapons.

EVOLUTION

The sword and knife were the close-quarter weapons of soldiers for many centuries before the advent of the matchlock musket. Musketeers, protected by pikemen, would laboriously load their cumbersome pieces before discharging their shot, and repeating the whole process over again. In any melee the musketeer had to rely on using his musket as a club, or resort to any sidearm that may have been carried, such as a sword or a knife. It is not known exactly when the first knife was pushed into the muzzle of the musket to provide a short makeshift pike-type weapon; however, the idea rapidly evolved during the 16th century and the bayonet was born. The term bayonet has long been associated with the French town of Bayonne, situated in the southwest of France in the Basque region of the Pyrenees, and famed as a producer of edged weapons. Bayonne was certainly one of the earliest producers of plug bayonets, although it is more likely that the neighboring Spanish Basques came up with the idea.

The plug bayonet itself was little more than a knife with a shaped grip that enabled it to be seated securely in the muzzle of the musket. When mated with the musket in this manner it could be used to fend off mounted troops or infantry at close quarters. The disadvantage of the plug bayonet was that once it was put in place the musket could no longer be loaded or fired, although the situations in which the bayonet would need to be mounted would undoubtedly have made loading impractical due to the proximity of the enemy.

The natural next stage in the evolution of the bayonet was the development of the socket bayonet. The socket was a simple metal tube that slid over the barrel so that the musket could easily be loaded and fired with the bayonet attached. The earliest socket bayonets had a split socket that relied on friction for fit; these were later enhanced by having a zigzag (stepped) slot cut into the socket. This slot, which mated with a stud on the barrel and helped retain the bayonet, was in use by the early 1700s. This attachment method did not absolutely guarantee that the bayonet would remain fixed, and it could be dislodged in combat with tragic results. Therefore, a variety of springs and screws were developed in the second half of the 18th century with the aim of retaining the bayonet securely on the musket.

Development continued in the early 19th century and the British **Land Pattern** bayonet used a spring over the slot, a

design also used by the East India Company on its bayonets. The idea was not wholly original, as the Danes had introduced the "Kyhl"-type spring in 1794.

The Austrians, French and Prussians used under-barrel spring catches during the late 18th and early 19th centuries. This idea was a natural development in bayonet technology, and was adopted by the British with the **1838** Pattern F (Hanoverian) and the **1844** Lovell's catch. Both systems relied on a spring catch mounted on the musket. The first bayonets secured by the use of a rotating collar, or ring, mounted on the bayonet socket appeared in 1769, compliments of the French. The French 1769 socket bayonet for the Mle. 1763 fusil used a basal locking ring that closed around the short slot thus preventing the bayonet becoming detached accidentally. The first standard-issue British bayonet utilizing a locking ring was the **1853** bayonet. This used a central locking ring, although a

ABOVE LEFT Reenactors portraying British Royal Marines from the Napoleonic era. The image gives an idea of the reach of the Brown Bess with bayonet fixed.

ABOVE British 1838 bayonet fitted to a musket, showing the socket detail and the way that the rudimentary foresight aided the fitting of the bayonet.

LEFT The plug bayonet was the first step in bayonet evolution; the grip was forced into the musket's muzzle to form a short pike-type weapon. Once inserted it was not possible to reload or discharge the musket.

OPPOSITE, TOP LEFT Early socket bayonets were prone to being dislodged from the musket. In an effort to remedy this a variety of catches were invented, most fitting on the musket and holding the bayonet more securely to the musket. Three bayonets produced to fit specific musket-mounted catches are shown: an Indian 1842 bayonet with a cut-out for East India Co. catch; a British 1839/44 with collar lug for Lovell's catch; and a British 1838 bayonet with prominent collar, which allowed the Pattern F (Hanoverian) catch to be fitted.

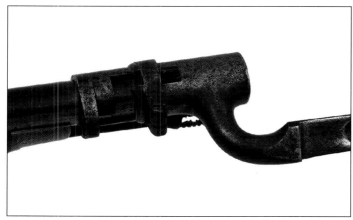

by the coiled spring introduced by Austria on their Werndl 1873 bayonet. Although this method was to form the most common method of attachment, and still remains in use, there are countless other methods of attaching bayonets to rifles, many illustrated within this work.

Socket bayonets provided the basis of infantry weapons until the mid-1870s, when the excessive weight of sword bayonets began to cause concern. France introduced the Gras **1874** with its slim but strong T-form blade, far lighter than the earlier 1866 but unsuited to anything other than thrusting. Germany, however, was to go against the accepted wisdom that considered reach as being of paramount importance in bayonet fighting. The short 250mm blade of the German S1871/84 bayonet provided the first true standard-issue knife bayonet, and was to form the basis of future knife bayonet development.

The use of knife bayonets was curtailed briefly during the early part of the 20th century when short rifles became popular. There had always been a recurring argument about the "handiness" of bayonets compared with their "reach." The British adopted the Short, Magazine, Lee Enfield (SMLE) rifle

basal ring had been used on the **1815** Baker bayonet and even earlier on the limited-issue Duke of Richmond musket of 1792. Many of the Duke of Richmond bayonets were later converted to fit Baker rifles. The original Baker bayonet was a long-bladed weapon, more a sword than a true bayonet. It utilized a flat spring and mortise attachment mechanism.

The most successful method of attaching the longer sword bayonets that evolved during the 1800s was the press catch and leaf spring. The sword bayonet was a restricted issue, popular with volunteers. In British service it was a badge of rank, only available to NCOs with other ranks using socket bayonets. France was the first nation to consider issuing the sword bayonet to all soldiers and NCOs. The 1840 was intended to be the first general-issue sword bayonet, but it was only issued in limited numbers. The 1840 was the first bayonet to have the double curved Turkish-style "yataghan" blade form that was to be copied by the British in 1852, and soon adopted worldwide. The leaf spring was a functional system of attachment, bettered

TOP *La garde*, on guard with a bayonet training rifle. This illustration comes from a commercial publication produced in France during the early part of World War I.

ABOVE LEFT The 1853 bayonet was the first British standard-issue bayonet to be provided with a locking ring. The median ring locked against the rifle sight, providing a positive fixing and preventing the loss of the bayonet.

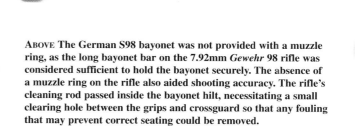

ABOVE The German S98 bayonet was not provided with a muzzle ring, as the long bayonet bar on the 7.92mm *Gewehr 98* rifle was considered sufficient to hold the bayonet securely. The absence of a muzzle ring on the rifle also aided shooting accuracy. The rifle's cleaning rod passed inside the bayonet hilt, necessitating a small clearing hole between the grips and crossguard so that any fouling that may prevent correct seating could be removed.

in 1903, replacing the older Long Lee Enfield and its short double-edged **1888** knife bayonet. The short **1903** bayonet first introduced with the SMLE provided a very short combination, especially when compared to the French Lebel and **1886** bayonet or the German G98 and **S98** bayonet combination. However, the longer **1907** bayonet soon replaced it, which was itself inspired by the Japanese **30th year** (1897), enabling the infantryman to regain some reach.

There were exceptions to international bayonet development. Russia clung resolutely to the **1891** socket bayonet through the two world wars. The U.S., somewhat reticent in its acceptance of the knife bayonet, adopted the Krag **1892** knife bayonet briefly before moving onto the useless **1903** rod bayonet and then the **1905** sword bayonet. The 1905 was shortened to knife form during World War II. Britain took a major step backward in bayonet evolution when it adopted the **No. 4** spike bayonet during World War II. The British soldier armed with the spike bayonet had little advantage over his counterpart in Wellington's army at the Battle of Waterloo. The adoption of the spike was linked to both economic factors and the minimum requirements for an efficient killing design.

However, by the end of World War II Britain had fallen into line with international thinking and adopted the **No. 5** bayonet and rifle, which, at the time, were intended for general issue. For the majority of British troops postwar economies saw the

spike bayonet continue in service until the adoption of the SLR rifle and bayonet in the late 1950s. The knife bayonet dominated postwar bayonet development, although Belgium, Switzerland and Great Britain were later to turn again to the socket bayonet principle, manufacturing tubular "socket" bayonets that fitted over the rifle muzzle (flash eliminator).

The later part of the 20th century saw a distinct move towards providing the infantryman with a more useful standard-issue bayonet, a process started with the introduction of the Soviet AKM bayonet with its integral wirecutter and sawback blade. Much emphasis was placed on the bayonet's usefulness as a knife, both for combat and general field use. Tool bayonets had been in use before with weapons such as trowel bayonets and the German S42 with integral combination tool. Many nations have now discarded bayonets entirely, some opting instead for a serviceable field knife.

POSITION OF READINESS—STANDING BEHIND COVER

EYES ON TARGET

MUZZLE AND BAYONET CLEAR OF COVER

SAFETY CATCH FORWARD

HOME GUARD

R HAND AT SMALL OF BUTT

L HAND NEAR NOSE CAP

SLING TO THE RIGHT

L KNEE PRESSING AGAINST COVER

LEFT An illustration from a British Home Guard training manual shows the position of readiness when behind cover with bayonet fixed. The bayonet is the M1917 attached to the .30-06in M1917 rifle, standard issue for the Home Guard.

Although principally designed as short-range killing weapons, bayonets also provided support for other implements, and amongst the more common attachments were wire breakers. The British **1888**, **1903** and **1907** bayonets could be fitted with simple attachment "Breaker, Wire" that slid over the blade and rested against the muzzle of the rifle when the bayonet was fixed. The first pattern was introduced in 1912. The Russians used a similar device on the 1891 bayonet, and France adopted an equally simple device that slipped over the blade of the mounted **1886** bayonet.

The wire breakers were easy to use. The bayonet blade was pushed below the wire to be broken and slid along the blade until it reached the muzzle of the rifle and the breaker attachment. The attachment had a notched guide that presented the wire to the muzzle of the rifle, thus a single round fired from the rifle would effectively break the wire. This was a quick and effective method of cutting a single strand of wire, but when confronted with multiple entanglements as used during World War I it was somewhat less practical and wasteful of ammunition. The British also designed more complicated lever-action cutting devices, all essentially similar in their operation. The cutter had a large forward-facing V-shaped jaw attached to the

The battle scenes from the film *Waterloo* (1970) look impressive, but closer inspection shows that many of the British and French troops are armed with Russian M1891 Nagant rifles and bayonets; hardly surprising when one learns that the extras were mainly Soviet conscripts. Even the movie epic *Zulu* (1964) has bolt-action rifles visible in the final scene.

Many regulation bayonets were altered to fit stage weapons. Socket bayonets had their sockets cut and wing nuts added to the locking ring enabling them to fit a variety of weapons. In the same vein genuine French **1866** and similar weapons had their hilts ground to fit other weapons.

Recent advances in the molding process have seen some splendid prop bayonets produced in rubber. The rubber prop bayonets used in films such as *Saving Private Ryan* (1998) and *The Four Feathers* (2002) look exceptionally convincing, even at close quarters, and could be considered collectable in their own right. Bapty & Co. have produced resin and aluminum Brown Bess models molded from originals, and many other patterns will be encountered by the collector. Aluminum prop bayonets are also relatively common.

front end of the rifle, and the bayonet, which fitted below it, was used as a guide to direct the wire into the jaw. As the soldier advanced into the wire, the cutter rotated up and back on itself closing the jaw quickly and easily cutting the wire. Highly effective against well-secured picketed wires, and quick and easy to use, the British device relied on there being some resistance from the wire to be cut in order to operate the jaws; it was therefore wholly ineffective against loose or coiled untensioned wire, which was merely pushed before it. The **No. 1 Mk. II** cutter was used with the **1907**, the No. 2 and 3 cutters were used with the Ross bayonet and the No. 4 with the **P13** bayonet. Other devices were available to be used in conjunction with the bayonet. A small pocket-sized trench mirror was retailed for use by British and American troops. The rectangular mirrors were attached to the end of the blades of the **1907**, **1913** or **M1917** bayonets and could then be held over the parapet in order to view the terrain without exposing the viewer to enemy fire.

The film industry has used bayonets in a number of epic war movies, and, historically, many of these were original pieces altered to fit available weaponry. Also, weapons that looked right, but were historically incorrect, were often used.

COLLECTING

As with all fields of militaria collecting, the value of bayonets has risen greatly over recent years, and many now see their collections as a sound investment. Prices of the rarer items are correspondingly high and outside the budget of many collectors, but for a minimal outlay a reasonable collection can still be readily acquired. It has long been the fashion that to be considered a serious collector one has to specialize in a particular sub-field, such as collecting the bayonets of a particular country or variants of a single type. Whilst this approach does have its merits the rarer pieces will command higher prices and the self-imposed restrictions can be somewhat limiting. The begin-

BELOW An early-production 1853 socket bayonet that has been converted for film work by having the socket split to allow it to fit a variety of prop weapons.

BELOW LEFT The socket of this film prop 1853 is split longitudinally, and the locking ring screw has been made adjustable by the addition of a winged extension to allow easy tightening. The ricasso is marked R & W.A. for the Birmingham company of Aston, who were contracted to produce 1,070 bayonets in 1853. Socket bayonets with a crudely stamped "MGM" have been noted.

BOTTOM Recent dramatic improvements in plastic molding techniques have allowed the manufacture of some very detailed plastic bayonets for the film industry. Looking convincingly good at even close viewing distances they appear 100 percent real in movies. Shown here are an Egyptian Remington 1869 and British 1856 both used in *The Four Feathers* (2002). A British 1907 from *The Lost Battalion*, and a French 1886/15 integrally molded with the scabbard.

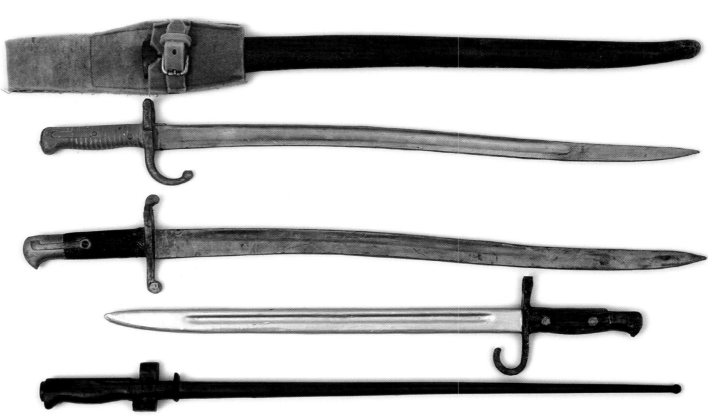

ner, or those on a limited budget, can readily purchase the more common bayonets based on cost alone. As an example, it would prove relatively easy to build a collection of all of the principal bayonet types in use with the major combatant nations of World War I or World War II. This would provide the beginner with an interesting collection for minimal outlay. It should be borne in mind that the cost of even the most common item reflects its condition, and if investment is a consideration only the best examples should be purchased. However, a particularly rare piece can have a value disproportionate to its condition. Ultimately, the decision as to what to collect, and how, lies with the individual and not his peers. Above all enjoy your hobby.

The days when bayonets could readily be found in any

junk or bric-a-brac shop have long since gone. Although the odd gem may still turn up in such places it is increasingly unlikely. Most collectors will have to content themselves with visits to militaria and arms fairs. Far from being a hardship, the collector will not only find bayonets at such venues, but will also meet other like-minded individuals and build up a rapport with dealers, to the benefit of both collector and dealer. For those so inclined, a search of eBay®, or similar internet auction sites, will turn up a plentiful supply of bayonets often at very reasonable prices. The more common items are readily available there as, occasionally, are some more spectacular rarities. Internet auctions should be approached with care, but they can provide excellent sources for bayonets and contacts. Always bid with sellers that have good feedback ratings. If in doubt, contact the vendor before bidding to enquire as to their shipping and handling fees. It is not unknown for some sellers to add extortionate handling fees, and once you have won a bid you are committed to purchasing. Always avoid those sellers that state "no returns," or have a low or excessively negative feedback. If there is a genuine reason for returning a bayonet to the seller, there should never be any reason not to do so. It is often quite possible to build up a rapport with internet auction dealers, especially when you provide repeat business, but it will never be the same as the face-to-face deal.

Collectors will notice that bayonets often enter the market in batches, and an item that was once scarce and hard to find can flood the market overnight. This generally only applies to modern bayonets, particularly when not previously released by

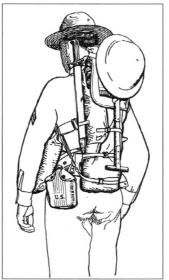

LEFT **U.S. field manual** *FM 21-15 1940, Equipment, Clothing, and Tent Pitching.* **This illustrates the 1928 pack with the bayonet fitted to the left side, an ideal arrangement for mounted or motorized troops.**

BELOW LEFT **Hilt detail of plastic film prop bayonets. The French 1886/15 (far left) has been molded as a single piece with the bayonet integral with the scabbard. The original upon which it was based had been placed in the scabbard at the wrong angle, being twisted 90 degrees so that the frog loop was on the same plane as the muzzle ring. This error has been duplicated in countless plastic copies. At this viewing distance the finish of the prop bayonets is obvious, on the big screen they appear quite real.**

the holding governments. Normally, only a very few bayonets currently in use with an army will find their way onto the collectors' market, and they will fetch correspondingly high prices. However, when the weapons become surplus the bayonets will often be released in large numbers and their prices will fall. Manufacturers are now wise to the collectors' market and will often make up bayonets specifically for commercial sale. Identical to issue items, these commercial bayonets are, however, often avoided by many collectors who prefer only military issue examples.

REPRODUCTIONS

At some stage every collector will come across a reproduction, or a fake. The only difference between the two is the method of marketing. A recently made copy of a German World War II police bayonet with horn grips is a reproduction only if sold as such. Once it is advertised as original, advertised ambiguously or sold as original it becomes a fake. Here there is no substitute for knowledge of one's field, and the friendship of other fellow collectors. Buying from a known and reputable dealer helps and their income may well rely on your continued patronage and that of your peers. An agreement to return the bayonet for a refund, if it later transpires to be dubious or other than the item it was believed to be, is easily agreed. Any dealer not wishing to offer such an undertaking is best avoided. Some of the common terms used to sell modern "copies" ambiguously in magazine advertisements are "pattern" and "type," with no indication that the item is a

recently manufactured reproduction. To make matters worse, some advertisements may also contain genuine period-made bayonets, or other items, listed as "pattern" and "type." If in doubt ask the vendor if the item advertised is a genuine item made during the era of the original and not a more recently made copy. The old adage *caveat emptor* (buyer beware) will always ring true.

There is a vast market in reproduction bayonets. Reenactors have long been supplied with Brown Bess bayonets, Charleville musket bayonets and the like. Other bayonets are reproduced to provide collectors with examples of exceptionally rare bayonets that they may otherwise never own. Personally I prefer genuine items. If a piece is too scarce to be in my collection I do without it. A reproduction bayonet is not a real one and it never will be!

Amongst the many reproduction bayonets that may be encountered are the Austrian flat-section ersatz bayonets; the Dahlgren Navy bayonet; Springfield 1873; 1873 trowel bayonet and scabbard, the scabbards also being available separately; Springfield 1905; 1941 Johnson; Finnish SKY short knife bayonet; World War II German police dress bayonet; EIC Sappers & Miners; the fantasy Vivian carbine bayonet; Elcho bayonet; 1871 Cutlass bayonet; Enfield 1853 and 1856 bayonets; Pritchard Greener bayonet; No. 4 Mk. I spike; and the ubiquitous Sten spike bayonet. The latter has been produced in vast numbers, but the original military bayonets are scarce. Prior to the flooding of the market with the reproductions the author knew of very few originals. Added to these reproductions are original bayonets that have been modified. No. 4 Mk. II bayonets with added fullering sold as No. 4 Mk. I bayonets; No. 5 bayonets with new grips and a single grip screw; and 1907 bayonets with added quillons, unlikely as most of the repros were manufactured after the official removal of the quillon.

ABOVE Relic condition bayonets, a German S98/05 and a British 1907. Whilst many bayonet collectors would never acquire such poor condition items other collectors specialize in such battlefield "dug" collectables. These were both found near the Belgian town of Ypres in an area once held by the 63rd (Royal Naval) Division. This gives them a historical interest that is difficult to attribute to most bayonets.

LEFT Miniature "bayonet" letter openers. A Spanish made S84/98, Swiss 1889 with national shield and a poor quality bayonet with a (crooked) World War II German police emblem on the grips. The S84/98 is quite detailed, including the ricasso maker's code and serial number, the 1889 is also well detailed but the police item is, at best, only a rudimentary representation of a bayonet.

LEFT An illustration from a British Home Guard training pamphlet showing the correct method of delivering a "point" from the "on guard."

BELOW Live rust has a rich orange-red color, it is an indication that moisture is present on the metal and that a chemical reaction is taking place, gradually turning your prized bayonet into red dust. Rust is best prevented by reducing contact with moisture and protecting the metal surface with a microcrystalline wax.

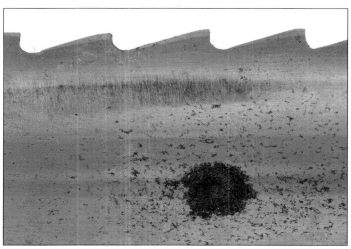

CARE AND PRESERVATION OF BAYONETS

The care of a collection is important if it is to be preserved for future generations, for in reality any collector is merely a temporary custodian. Bayonet blades are made of steel with hilts generally of brass or steel and grips of wood, plastic or leather. All require some care to preserve their condition and appearance. The debate over how to maintain bayonets and scabbards is never ending, and it is rare that any two collectors will entirely agree on the correct approach. The following are my views, and each collector must make up his or her mind on how they wish to approach this subject.

Steel rusts readily in moist environments, but leather scabbards will dry out in modern centrally heated homes. An environmental compromise is required if bayonets are to be kept in their best condition. The majority of items purchased from dealers will have received a minimal cleaning to realize their full selling potential. However, rust and verdigris will often still be present. Light surface rust can easily be removed with careful use of a fine 00 grade wire wool and penetrating oil, but for deeper pitting a stiff toothbrush is useful. If bluing or other finishes are present on metalwork, extreme care should be exercised to ensure that they are not removed by over-zealous cleaning. Once rust has been cleaned all traces of oil should be removed with a suitable solvent. The metalwork and grips should then be given a light coat of a quality microcrystalline wax or beeswax (an excellent preparation is retailed under the name of Renaissance Wax and is used by many museum collections). The wax serves to seal the surface, prevent build-up of rust and protect from any airborne contaminants. It can be used on any metalwork, wood, bone and even leather. Wax is vastly superior to oil. It is less messy, easily removed or re-applied and does not attract dust or dirt in the same way. It is also far friendlier to fabrics and furniture with which it may come into contact and will not stain leather or webbing in the same way that oil will. Neither will it wipe off with handling. If required, it can also be lightly buffed to provide an attractive finish to metal, woodwork and painted surfaces. Patina, beloved of many, is actually little more than the result of long-term deterioration of the metal surface due to

LEFT Typical "reproduction" bayonets, these examples dating from the 1980s. A British 1871 cutlass bayonet complete with scabbard; Elcho bayonet; and a fantasy piece sold as a "Vivian Carbine" bayonet. Although all are reasonably well made the cutlass lacks the refinement of the original and the Vivian bears modern-style numbering on the applied serial. Manufacturers and other markings are frequently also incorrect. All of these bayonets were available from a Birmingham dealership; none were listed as reproductions, caveat emptor.

aerial oxidants and chemicals, or contact with fingers. It should not be removed, but neither should it be encouraged on bright metalwork. Wax will preserve old patina as well as helping to prevent it from forming on well-preserved bright metal.

Although microcrystalline wax can be used on leather, it is best treated with a lanolin-based paste dressing that will maintain its suppleness and help prevent deterioration. Particularly dry leather can be given an application of an oil dressing that will soak in more easily. Although the oil will darken light-colored leather, it will not adversely affect the dark browns and blacks that form the base of most military leather finishes. The paste treatments have a less marked effect on the leather finish and, after an initial darkening, leather will normally return to a shade close to its original. I personally consider that it is better to have a slightly darkened item of leatherwork that will last for many years than the dry and brittle remains of something. To maintain the finish, the leather will require routine light applications of the dressing if it is not to dry out, shrink and become brittle. Dressings containing solvents such as white spirit should be avoided, and any dressing should use only the best quality natural products suitable for old leather. A fine dressing is retailed under the name Pecard.

Aerial pollutants are a threat to leather and metalwork. Sulfur dioxide, hydrogen sulfide and nitrogen dioxide result from the burning of fossil fuels and are present in the atmosphere of every home. They will add patina to unprotected metal and the results of absorption by leather can be catastrophic. Aerial pollutants, acids in particular, can cause "red rot" in leather. It is recognizable as a general drying out and breaking down of the surface of the leather, which acquires a distinct reddish-brown hue. Cut edges become fibrous, surfaces flake and, eventually, the item will disintegrate. Little can be done once red rot has taken hold, as the acids will already be in the leather and deterioration well under way. One professional remedy is to impregnate red rot-contaminated leather with resin. This will preserve it, but the drawback is that it will have a stiff and unnatural feel. The result is undoubtedly better than losing an item altogether. As well as possible damage from insects and rodents (hopefully unlikely in a domestically stored collection!), there is the likelihood of encountering verdigris.

Verdigris is a green wax-like deposit that often builds up on brass, copper or bronze, particularly where it is in contact with leather such as on scabbards or frogs. It should be removed as soon as it is spotted, as it is acidic and will damage both leather and metal. It is readily removed with a cocktail stick or toothbrush and should be checked for, along with rust, at regular intervals. It is particularly prevalent on the brass or copper

rivets used in the construction of bayonet frogs. Having taken the time to clean and preserve your bayonets, it makes sense to limit handling, particularly of polished metal. Fingers are covered in microscopic beads of dirt and moisture that will mark metalwork, often giving an excellent rust impression of one's fingerprints. Many collectors will not handle their valuable collection without first donning cotton gloves of the type used by photographers for negative handling; this is a wise precaution. However, for those still insisting on coating their bayonets with oil, a pair of rubber gloves may be more appropriate!

Any collection should be fully cataloged and insured. A computer database is ideal for producing a catalog, which can include any information the collector feels relevant. Some collectors merely list the designation. Others include date of acquisition, cost and other details. To keep track of the bayonets, it will be necessary to "tag" them in some way. Sticky numbers and inked-on numbers are simple methods, but labels can fall off and ink numbers can become worn or chipped. Copper tags and luggage labels are convenient, but, whichever method you use, make sure that the tags cannot become detached or otherwise removed.

COLLECTORS AND THE LAW

At this point, it is appropriate to consider the impact of national law codes upon bayonet collecting. In Great Britain, a bayonet is an offensive weapon under section 1 of the Prevention of Crime Act, 1953. The legal limit for a blade carried on the person is a folding pocketknife with a blade of less than 3.5in.

Therefore, in carrying home a bayonet from the dealer where it was purchased, you are in effect committing an offense. In reality, providing the bayonet is wrapped and concealed from public view, it could not be considered as being carried offensively, and the fact that it was a collector's item in transit may provide a reasonable excuse and therefore adequate "defense in law." Under no circumstances should any bayonet be made visible in public, the act of which would have no defense and could lead to confiscation and prosecution.

U.S. law is more complex than British law. State laws, which vary from state to state, supplement federal laws. U.S. readers are advised to make themselves familiar with their own state legislation regarding the transportation and carriage of edged weapons.

Under the U.S. 1994 Semi-Automatic gun ban, any semiautomatic (self-loading) firearm that has a detachable magazine and at least two of the following characteristics is illegal:

Conspicuous (pistol-type) grip
Bayonet mount
Flash suppressor
Folding or telescoping stock
Grenade launcher

The inclusion of the bayonet mount is interesting and would undoubtedly include permanently attached folding bayonets such as those encountered on the Chinese Type 56 rifle, which also has a detachable magazine, folding stock and pistol grip and would therefore be illegal. The SKS and Russian M1944 rifles would, however, be legal unless prohibited by state law.

NOMENCLATURE AND DESIGNATIONS

Every effort has been made to ensure that the bayonets illustrated in this work are correctly designated. However, the task is somewhat open to interpretation. Collectors often disagree over such detail, and designations can be difficult to determine exactly. Some bayonet patterns, although unaltered, had their official designations changed. A good example of this is the British 1907 bayonet, which was re-listed as the No. 1 Mk. 1 in 1926. Many nations merely cataloged bayonets as being for a particular weapon type. The generic South American Mauser bayonets were often used on successive weapons with no designation other than "bayonet," occasionally suffixed with the rifle designation. Many of these are subsequently hard to identify and the designations given in this work are for collecting purposes rather than to specify an official military title. Other bayonets have designations adopted by collectors. One such example is the Israeli Mk. 1A bayonet, universally referred to by collectors as the model 1949. In such cases as these, the official and the collectors' designations are provided in this work.

Details of the primary components of the bayonet and scabbard are given so that the reader may better understand the descriptions given in the text.

A. *Pommel.* The pommel is the section of the hilt farthest from the blade and next to the grips. It generally incorporates the *mortise* and *press catch*.

B. *Press catch.* The catch which, when operated, releases the bayonet from the rifle.

C. *Grip rivets (Bolts).* The means of fixing the *grips* to the *tang*.

D. *Grips.* A section of wood, plastic or bone that provides a grip for the hand.

E. *Quillon.* A curved extension of the *crossguard* that allows stacking of arms and acts as a "stop" for an opponent's bayonet.

F. *Crosspiece (Crossguard).* The section between the hilt and blade, generally encompassing the *muzzle ring* and *quillon*.

G. *Ricasso.* A flat, unfullered and unsharpened section of blade adjacent to the crossguard.

H. *Fuller.* The groove cut into the blade that serves to lighten it, yet retain it's strength. Often erroneously called the blood groove.

I. *Blade edge.* The sharpened section of the blade.

J. *Topmount (locket).* This is the metal top section attached to the leather *scabbard body*. It holds the *frog stud*.

K. *Frog stud.* This pronounced stud allows the scabbard to seat securely into the bayonet frog that is then suspended from a belt or other equipment.

L. *Scabbard body.* The main section of the scabbard that encloses the blade. It can be of steel or leather.

M. *Chape.* The lower metal section at the tip of the scabbard. This protects the scabbard and blade point, and also prevents injury to the wearer.

N. *Finial.* An ornate metal disc or ball at the end of the quillon or scabbard tip, and occasionally found mounted above the muzzle ring.

O. *Muzzle ring.* The muzzle ring fits over the rifle barrel, or a separate boss (as on the SMLE), to hold the bayonet steady on the rifle.

P. *Tang.* The *tang* is a flat extension of the blade that attaches to the *pommel* and to which the *grips* are fitted.

Q. *Mortise.* The *mortise* is a groove cut into the bayonet pommel, it fits the bayonet bar that was mounted on the rifle.

R. *Collar.* A ring of metal around the socket against which the locking ring rotates. On some socket bayonets, small studs served the same purpose.

S. *Locking ring.* This ring rotates to close off the *mortise*, locking against the weapon's foresight or bayonet stud to retain the bayonet.

T. *Bore.* The bore is the internal measurement of the socket, equivalent to the muzzle ring on knife or sword bayonets.

U. *Elbow (or shank).* The section between the blade *shoulder* and socket that joins the two.

V. *Shoulder.* The join of the blade to the *elbow*. Normally angular, on later socket bayonets the shoulder is streamlined and almost a continuation of the *elbow*.

W. *Mortise slot.* A straight or zigzag slot cut into the socket through which the bayonet stud or foresight passes when fixing the bayonet to the weapon.

X. *Bridge.* A raised reinforcement at the start of the *mortise slot*, it prevents the open end of the slot from being damaged and thus prevents fixing or removal of the bayonet. The bridge often forms a collar around the entire base of the socket.

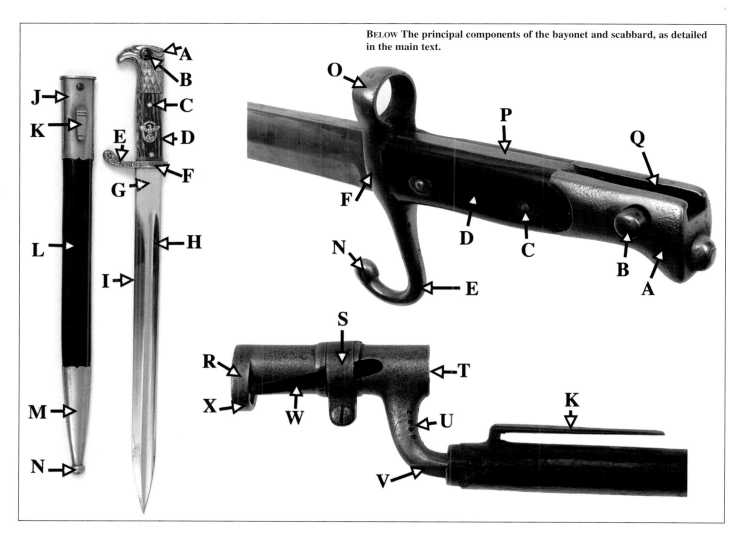

BELOW **The principal components of the bayonet and scabbard, as detailed in the main text.**

Argentina

	Overall length	Blade length	Muzzle ring
1879	590mm	465mm	18.5mm
1891 and 1909	520mm	400mm	15.5mm
Type A (1953)	322mm	202mm	15mm
Type C	292mm	162mm	22mm

Spain ruled Argentina until the Republic was formed in 1816. Understandably, Spanish weapons predominated in the immediate post-independence period. The popular Remington rolling-block rifle was adopted in 1867, along with the *Remington Modelo 1867/71, Corta*, a standard short-shank Remington export bayonet. A brass-hilted saber bayonet with yataghan blade form based on the French **Mle. 1866** was also used on the Remington. The German-made **1879** bayonet was also used by other South American nations, but these lack any Argentine "RA" markings. The Remington was soon seen to be lacking compared to the Mauser rifle that was progressively being adopted by many nations, and, in 1891, Argentina adopted a new German-supplied 7.65mm Mauser rifle, similar

to the G98. The **1891** bayonets had ribbed grips of brass or white metal, a forward-facing quillon and steel scabbards. An identical bayonet, but with wooden grips, was adopted a few years later as the **1909**. At this time, Argentine bayonets had the national coat of arms on the ricasso, but most of the bayonets encountered by collectors will have had this marking ground off when the bayonets were declared obsolete and sold on from military stores. The pommel often bears the marking "RA" within an oval, standing for *Republica Argentina*.

The stocks of older-style Mauser rifles were later supplemented with Belgian M24 rifles in 7mm caliber, supplied with the *Bayoneta Mauser Modelo 1935*. Belgium continued to be the principal supplier of arms, and, in the 1950s, Fabrique National provided the self-loading SAFN M1949 rifle, which was accompanied by the **M1949** knife bayonet. This bayonet had the same wooden-gripped hilt as the earlier 1935 bayonet, but had a double-edged blade. The *Bayoneta M1 Modelo 1943 (Garand)* was issued during the early 1950s. It was the standard U.S. **M1**.

In keeping with an almost universal trend amongst non-Warsaw Pact nations, Argentina adopted the FN FAL in 1955, using the standard 7.62mm caliber. The first weapons were delivered from Belgium in 1958. These were later made under license. The FALs were used with the **Type A (1953)** bayonet with integral flash eliminator and plastic grips. From 1961 the **Type C** socket bayonet and the folding-stock FAL rifle were in use. The **Type C** bayonets manufactured under license in Argentina have a distinct socket finish, giving the appearance of concentric rings along the full length. The FAL rifles are currently still in service but are being replaced by the Steyr AUG rifle and *Bayoneta Steyr AUG Modelo 1978*.

BELOW The brass hilt of the German-made 1879 bayonet resembled that of the 1869 Remington bayonet, which itself was based on the French 1866 bayonet. The left ricasso bears the "RA" marking within an oval, signifying *Republica Argentina*, the right ricasso is marked "W.R.KIRSCHBAUM, SOLINGEN."

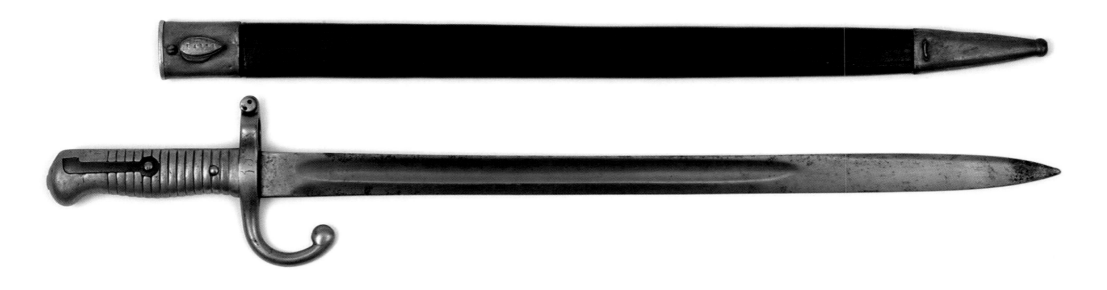

LEFT Bayonets for the 1891
Mauser rifle. Top, brass-gripped
1891 in steel scabbard with brown
leather frog, below, 1891 bayonet
with grips made from white metal.
Weyersberg and Kirschbaum made
both of these.

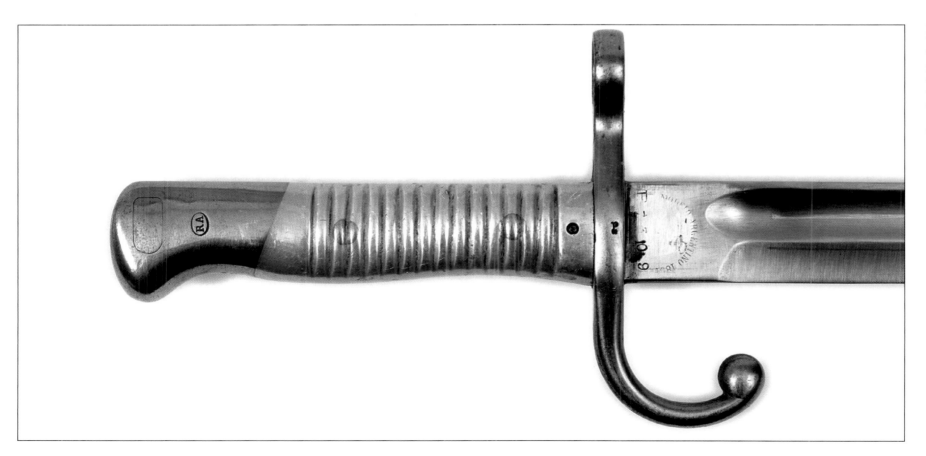

LEFT Detail of the hilt of the 1891
bayonet with white-metal grips.
The ricasso bears the Argentine
property mark of "RA" within an
oval. The ricasso originally bore
the Argentine crest and the designation "MODELLO ARGENTINO
1891," the crest has been ground
off prior to disposal.

ABOVE The 1909 bayonet was issued with the German-made 1909 rifle, a copy of the G98. It was similar to the earlier 1891 bayonet but had wood grips and the press catch was located on the right side of the pommel.

RIGHT The ricasso of the 1909 bayonet is marked "MODELO ARGENTINO 1909," it retains the Argentine crest, which was normally ground off when the government sold off obsolete weapons. Below the crest is the weapon serial number "F9655."

BELOW Plastic gripped FN FAL Type A (1953) bayonet. This is the standard Belgian-pattern bayonet as adopted by Argentina in 1955. It has a green leather frog with hilt retaining strap. This example was recovered from Goose Green, Falkland Islands, in 1982.

LEFT Hilt detail, left side. The prongs, integral with the muzzle ring, acted as a flash disruptor. The pommel bears the unusual vertical release latch unique to the Type A bayonet series.

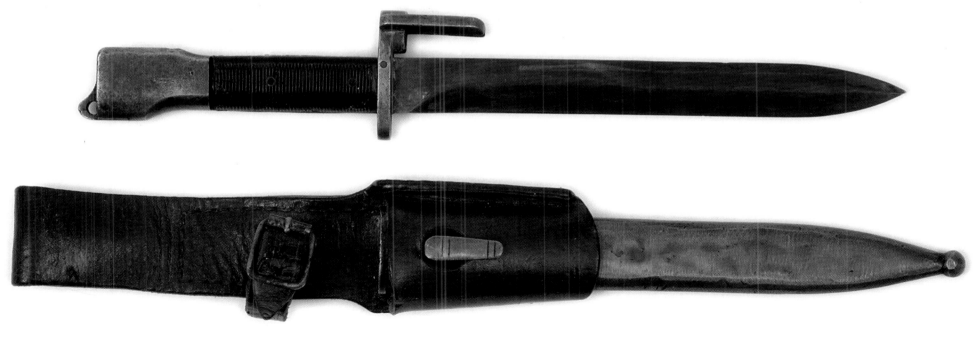

ABOVE Argentine Type C bayonets and scabbards. Top is the lower face of the Type C bayonet with ridged release catch and an early steel scabbard with integral webbing belt loop. Below is the upper face of the Type C bayonet with release catch "ears," bearing the serial "01-79111." The prefix identifies the branch of service, "01"—army, "02"—marines, "03"—air force. Below this is the plastic-bodied scabbard with steel frog stud. It is fitted with a nylon "Tempex" frog attached using a wire key and strap with press fastener. These bayonets were taken during the Falklands War.

RIGHT Hilt detail of the Argentine-made FN Type C tubular bayonet. The cut-outs in the socket align with the vents in the rifle flash eliminator.

Australia

	Overall length	Blade length	Muzzle ring
1907	556mm	435mm	16.5mm
Owen Mk. 1	381mm	254mm	16.6mm
L1A2	300mm	198mm	15mm

From its discovery until the 19th century, British troops provided the military garrisons of Australia. Locally recruited volunteer units raised in each of the Australian states, New South Wales, South Australia, Queensland, Western Australia, Victoria and Tasmania, also bolstered these forces. These colonial troops mainly employed standard British arms, but a number of other weapons were used, including Albini-Braendlin rifles. In 1901, the six states were federated as the Commonwealth of Australia, and weapons procurement came under the control of the Commonwealth's Ministry of Defence.

In 1912 Australia's first national arms factory was established at Lithgow, New South Wales. The earliest Australian weapons to be produced came off the production line in 1913. They were the SMLE rifle and **1907** bayonet, and both were suitably stamped "LITHGOW." The scabbard was a copy of the standard British **No. 1 Mk. II**. However, the Australian

1907 continued to be produced with a quillon long after it was deleted on the British version. From 1915, there was no quillon on newly produced bayonets, and it was retrospectively removed from older bayonets. From 1922 a clearing hole was added to the pommel.

During the 1920s the British **No. 2 Mk. I** scabbard was made for a short period. It was distinctive in having a double section of body leather, with a raised seam at the front as well as the rear, which required a specially shaped chape. A variation of the **No. 1 Mk. II** scabbard was also produced from the 1920s. It had a small round frog stud replacing the earlier teardrop pattern. Following the British lead, the Australian **P07** was reclassified as the **No. 1 Mk. I** in 1926. The following year, all Australian bayonet production ceased and did not start again until 1940. Initially, Lithgow produced their own scabbards, but from 1941 production was shifted to Sydney where Mangrovite Belting took on production. Mangrovite Belting scabbards are generally marked "MANGROVITE" on the reverse, adjacent to the seam. In 1942 a second arms factory was opened at Orange, with weapons manufactured there being marked "O.A." for Orange Arsenal.

The 9mm Owen was an Australian-designed SMG produced to meet the requirements of troops serving in the jungle,

ABOVE The Lithgow factory logo of an "A" within a star, over a shield bearing the pattern date 1907. Below this is stamped "LITHGOW" over "6'20" for June 1920.

LEFT An Australian 1907 bayonet made in 1920. It has a plain pommel with no clearing hole, a modification that had been introduced to British-production models in 1916. The unusual No. 2 Mk. I scabbard has a double seam, made up of two sections of leather rather than one as was usual.

following experience gained in New Guinea. Initially, shortened **No. 1 Mk. I** bayonets were used with the Owen, but production of the short-bladed **Owen Mk. 1** bayonet was soon underway. The purpose-made Owen bayonet had a blade length of 254mm, and was easily differentiated from the cutdown version by its short fullers, which terminated some 85mm from the point. On cut-down blades, they ran through to the end of the blade point. The grips of the **1907** and **Owen Mk. 1** bayonets are often stamped "SLAZ" followed by a date; this indicates manufacture by the Australian firm of Slazenger.

A most unusual variant of the No. 1 Mk. I bayonet was made in Australia in 1944, combining the hilt of the No. 1 Mk. I with a machete blade. The 1944 "Parachutist" bayonet was only made in very limited quantities, but countless copies have been produced and, unlike the original bayonets, are frequently

encountered. The web and canvas scabbards were the same pattern as used on the standard late-war Australian machete.

The No. 4 rifle was not adopted by Australia, although some examples were used by Australian troops. The SMLE rifle continued to serve Aussie soldiers until the introduction of the NATO 7.62mm round when Australia adopted its own version of the L1A1 SLR rifle, manufactured at Lithgow. The bayonet used by Australians was based on the British L1A2. The Australian **L1A2** can be differentiated from similar British- and Canadian-produced bayonets in that they are void of any markings. The **L1A2** was also used on the 9mm F1 submachine gun. Numbers of U.S. M16 rifles are in use with Australian forces, but the current weapon is the Steyr F88 rifle. It is equipped with the American M7 bayonet with camouflaged M10 scabbard, or the M9 bayonet.

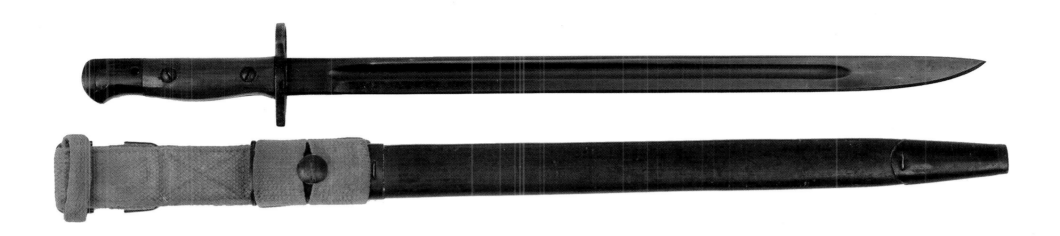

ABOVE A World War II production No. 1 Mk. I (1907) bayonet. It has the pommel clearing hole introduced with the WorldWar II made bayonets. The 1943-dated scabbard has a brown finish, and the late-war P37 bayonet frog, approved in April 1945, for use with the modified P37 web equipment for jungle use.

BELOW LEFT The manufacturers marking impressed into the leather, just below the topmount, it reads "MANGROVITE 43," indicating manufacture in 1943.

BELOW RIGHT The rear of the late-war Aussie P37 frog has twin belt hooks, these attached to the P37 belt and prevented lateral movement of the frog on the belt.

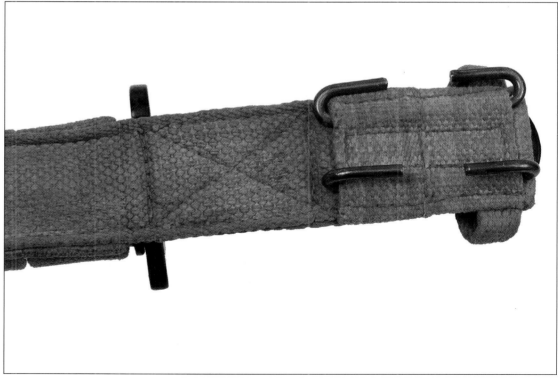

ABOVE Hilt of a bayonet made in World War II. The ricasso is marked "MA 1907" with "2 43" for February 1943. The bayonet was refurbished after World War II with new grips being added. The grips are marked "SLAZ 56" showing that Slazenger made them in 1956.

ABOVE RIGHT The hilt of this Australian No. 1 Mk. I bayonet, made in January 1942, was originally painted green for camouflage. The paint now only remains on the wooden grips.

BELOW Owen Mk. I bayonet. This is basically a No. 1 Mk I bayonet with a new 254mm blade. It was issued with the 9mm Owen SMG.

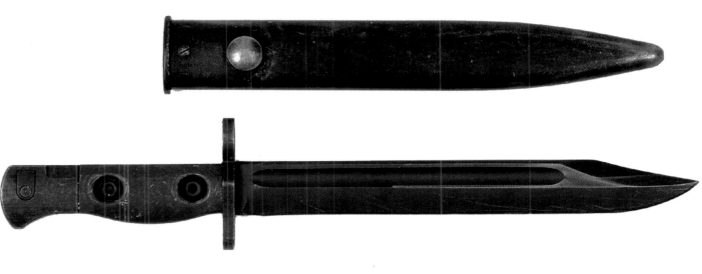

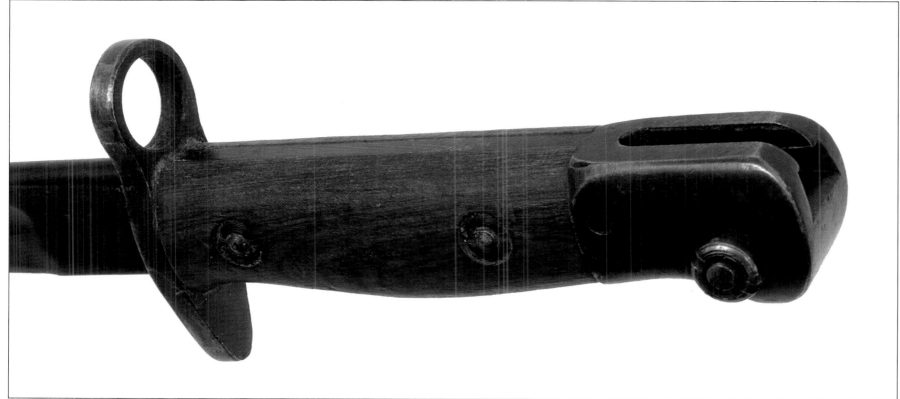

ABOVE LEFT The scabbard chape of the Owen bayonet has the "OA" marking for Orange Arsenal.

ABOVE The Australian L1A2 bayonet was issued with the L1A1 rifle. Like the Canadian C1 it had a protruding press catch. The L1A2 was the only pattern of the L1 series to be made in Australia. Unlike British and Canadian bayonets, it is void of any markings.

LEFT Owen Mk. 1 bayonet hilt, identical to that of the No. 1 Mk 1 bayonet. The grips are lightly impressed with "SLAZ 43."

Austria

	Overall length	Blade length	Muzzle ring
1838	556mm	465mm	22.5mm
1854 sword	710mm	594mm	23mm
1854 socket	559mm	486mm	22mm
1870	701mm	572mm	18.2mm
1888	375mm	248mm	16.3mm
1895	356mm	247mm	15.5mm
Ersatz 1895	403mm	248mm	15.5mm
1904 export	375mm	250mm	14mm
M77	285mm	165mm	N/A

Since the early 1800s, Austria had been a powerful European nation, but by 1867 the empire's declining supremacy led it to form a federation with Hungary. Austria-Hungary was created, with each country still run by its own government. The rather uneasy alliance controlled a large swathe of central Europe. During this period Austrian-designed arms predominated, but the alliance was to crumble following defeat at the end of World War I. The fall of the Austro-Hungarian Empire brought with it the emergence of a number of new nations including Czechoslovakia, Romania and the Kingdom of Serbs, Croats and Slovenes which was later to become Yugoslavia. In 1938 Austria was incorporated into the greater German Reich and ceased to exist. After the defeat of the Nazi's Austria was occu-

pied by Allied forces, not regaining sovereignty until 1955.

A long sword bayonet was produced for the Model 1838 carbine, and a bayonet with a similar socket style was used on the 1838 rifle. The standard **1838** had a cruciform blade section, but both bayonets used the "Laukart" spring fixing. In 1854 the Lorenz system was adopted by Austria, with a standard rifle and carbine being issued. The **1854** sword socket bayonet for the Lorenz Jäger carbine had a blade similar to the old 1838 sword socket, but had a new socket with a basal locking ring and long helical slot. The short **1854** socket bayonet issued with the Lorenz rifle had a similar socket, but with a central locking ring and a cruciform section blade like that used on the **1838**. The 1854 bayonets were later used on early 13.7mm Wanzl 1854/67 rifles and carbines, breechloading conversions of the Lorenz. This conversion was soon replaced by the 11.4mm (later 11.15mm) Werndl 1867 rifle. The **1870** Werndl bayonet was similar to the 1867 that preceded it, but was somewhat lighter than the original bayonet. In Austrian service it was known as the *Leichtere Gattung* (lightened version). It was followed by the 1873 pattern that had a press catch with coiled spring instead of the leaf spring, as well as a shorter blade. The old 1867 and **1870** patterns were also shortened to conform to the new blade length.

In 1886 Austria adopted a new 11mm Mannlicher rifle, and, in keeping with current international ideas, the short 1886 knife bayonet. This was the first knife bayonet in Austrian

service. Somewhat short lived, the 1886 rifle was replaced by an 8mm version in 1888. The **1888** bayonet was identical to the earlier 1886 pattern, but had a slightly smaller muzzle ring to accommodate the reduced caliber barrel. Only seven years later another Mannlicher rifle was adopted as standard. The **1895** bayonet issued with the new rifle was similar to the preceding knife types, but was noteworthy in that the blade was reversed with the edge being uppermost when fixed to the rifle. The short *Stutzen* version of the 1895 rifle was issued with a special **S1895** bayonet, which had a sight attached to the top of muzzle ring in order to compensate for the rise in bullet trajectory when the carbine was fired with the bayonet attached.

It was common practice for Austrian NCOs to wear a knot attached to their bayonets, and to accommodate this knot, bayonets for NCOs were provided with a loop at the pommel. The 1886, **1888** and **1895** NCO bayonets also had a hooked quillon on the guard. Some other ranks' bayonets were modified with the addition of just a pommel loop or a pommel loop and quillon; some simply had the pommel loop added with a second knot loop added at the crossguard. Bayonets made during this period can be found marked with the Austrian "OEWG" stamp for Oesterreichische Waffenfabrik Gesellschaft, or "FGGY" showing manufacture in Hungary by Femaru Fegyver es Gepgyar.

Austria produced its own variations of the German "ersatz" bayonet. The standard design used a flat blade that also formed a rudimentary hilt, often with a twist through 90 degrees. A

FAR LEFT Muster 1838 socket bayonet with Laukart fixing. This bayonet has a long, typically Austrian cruciform blade. This bayonet has also been designated as the 1836/44.

LEFT Right socket detail of the 1838 bayonet. It has a straight slot with a high bridge, a spring on the rifle engages under the bridge to hold the bayonet secure on the weapon.

brazed or riveted muzzle ring was attached between the blade and hilt, and a flat spring was used to secure the bayonet on the rifle bayonet bar. The ersatz-type bayonets were made for both captured and Austrian weapons. The **Ersatz 1895** is typical of the type.

The 1895 bayonet was the principal Austro-Hungarian arm of World War I and it remained standard between the wars until the annexation of Austria by the Nazis. During World War II Austrian military units were absorbed into the Wehrmacht and used German weaponry. After the war it was some years before the military forces were allowed to re-arm. The Austrian army adopted the Belgian FAL rifle as the STG 57 in 1957

During the 1970s the Austrian company of Ludwig Zeitler produced the experimental **M77** bayonet as a commercial venture. "Zeitler 77" was engraved on the heavily blackened clip-point blade. It had a gray-green plastic hilt but no obvious method of attachment, although it did have a hollow socket to the rear of the hilt. The bayonet bar was mounted on the rifle barrel and inserted into the hilt recess, using its own fixing mechanism, to secure the bayonet in place. This type of fixing device was adaptable and could be secured to any suitable weapon barrel. The bayonet's short crossguard had a small lug that served as a bottle opener. The blade was housed in a plastic scabbard that had a steel belt hook and webbing hilt strap. It was intended that the **M77** bayonet would be used on the Steyr AUG rifle, but it was only produced in limited numbers for trial purposes and never adopted. Eventually, and without the bayonet fixing recess in the hilt, the Austrian Army used it as a combat knife. Eickhorn later produced a close copy of this bayonet, the FM80. This was again offered with adaptors to fit various weapons, or, with a plug in the pommel recess, it could be issued as a combat knife.

LEFT Left side view of the 1854 sword bayonet socket detail, showing the heavy collar, bridge and basal locking ring. Just visible on the shank is the star mark of the Vienna State Arsenal, found on many Austrian bayonets of the time.

BELOW LEFT The standard infantry socket bayonet model 1854 was used on the Lorenz rifle. It has the same helical slot as found on the sword bayonet, but has a median locking ring. The leather-covered wooden scabbard has an internal steel chape and locket, and a long frog stud.

ABOVE The *haubajonet* 1854 for the Lorenz Jäger carbine has a long helical-type slot with basal locking ring. The slot uses the foresight and a supplementary guide stud to secure the bayonet. These bayonets were later used on the 1867 breechloading conversion of the Lorenz.

BELOW Austrian soldiers pose for a studio portrait, very popular during World War I. The soldier at right is armed with an 1873 bayonet.

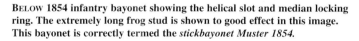

BELOW 1854 infantry bayonet showing the helical slot and median locking ring. The extremely long frog stud is shown to good effect in this image. This bayonet is correctly termed the *stickbayonet Muster 1854*.

ABOVE The 1870 yataghan bayonet replaced the earlier and heavier 1867 pattern. Both were for the 11.4mm 1867 Werndl rifle and differed mainly in that the 1870 had an adjustment screw on the muzzle ring, whilst the 1867 had a decorative finial.

BELOW The 1870 bayonet has regimental marks on the quillon, "72 R 3 B 11 104," showing issue to the 3rd Battalion 72nd Regiment.

BELOW The left ricasso of the 1870 bayonet has a faint "OEWG" marking as well as the crowned double-headed Austrian eagle device.

CENTER RIGHT A standard 1895 bayonet made by OEWG (Oesterreischische Waffenfabrik Gesellschaft). The scabbard is of World War I manufacture with a riveted, rather than brazed, frog stud.

BELOW 1870 hilt showing the split upper face to the muzzle ring, which allowed for adjustment. The grips are heavily crosshatched to provide a firm hold.

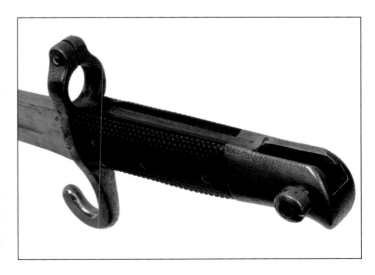

TOP LEFT An adjustment screw on the muzzle ring of the 1888 bayonet allowed for deficiencies in the manufacturing process, enabling fine-tuning to fit any individual rifle. Like all Austrian bayonets made up to World War I, the blade edge is uppermost.

LEFT The short cavalry carbine bayonet S1895 (*Stutzen* 1895) was provided with a compensatory sight on the muzzle ring. This corrected for the marked effect that a fitted bayonet had on the path of the bullet, the fitted bayonet causing the bullet's trajectory arc to be considerably higher than normal.

ABOVE An 1888-pattern bayonet is worn at the side of this Austrian soldier of World War I. His brass belt buckle displays the Austrian splayed eagle.

ABOVE Austria exported a number of bayonet types, this pattern, the 1904 or "Irish Mannlicher," was one such variant. It resembles the German S71/84 bayonet but was made by Oesterreischische Waffenfabrik Gesellschaft in Steyr. Austrian- and German-made bayonets were exported to the Irish Republican Army, who imported 10,000 Austrian bayonets that were used in the various incidents culminating in the Easter Rising of 1916.

ABOVE RIGHT Right side view of the hilt of the 1904 bayonet. This view shows the contoured hilt back and shaped grips. The crossguard is marked "7096."

BELOW A standard NCO-issue 1895 bayonet with pommel loop and hooked quillon. The bayonet knot was threaded through the pommel loop and looped around the quillon.

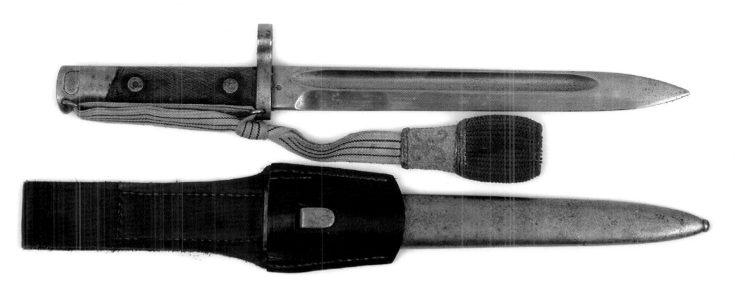

LEFT The adjustment screw is absent on this 1888 bayonet that has been modified for use by an NCO. The grips have been finely hatched and a loop has been added to both the pommel and short crossguard, allowing use of the bayonet knot. The ricasso bears the Austrian double-headed eagle mark.

RIGHT Austria made a number of very simple "ersatz" bayonets to fit various domestic and captured weapons. This rather crude example of an ersatz bayonet was made for the 1895 rifle. It was recovered from the Caporetto region, the site of a major 1917 Austro-Hungarian victory.

LEFT Many weapons were captured on the Italian front. This Italian M1891 TS has been paired with a newly manufactured Austrian-made scabbard and frog prior to being re-issued to Austrian troops.

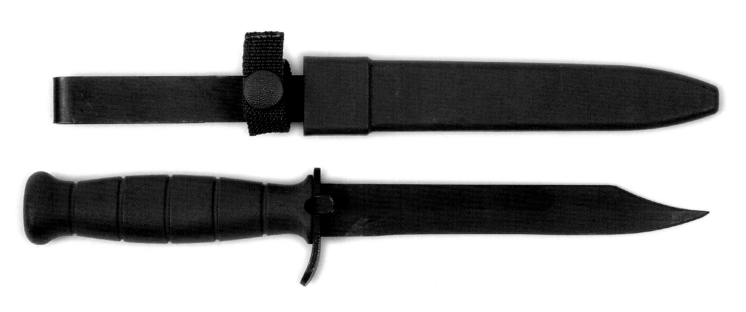

ABOVE The Zeitler M77 bayonet was a commercial venture manufactured for the Steyr AUG trials rifle. An adaptor that fitted the rifle barrel and a recess in the hilt enabled it to fit the AUG or a number of other weapon types, providing great flexibility.

BELOW The blade marking "ZEITLER 77" on the Austrian M77 bayonet.

ABOVE The pommel recess on the M77 took an adapter that enabled the bayonet to be fitted to a variety of weapons in addition to the Steyr AUG. The German KCB77M1-type bayonet was also offered as an alternative to the Zeitler M77 for use with the AUG rifle.

BELOW M77 scabbard reverse showing the spring steel belt hook secured to the plastic scabbard by four screws.

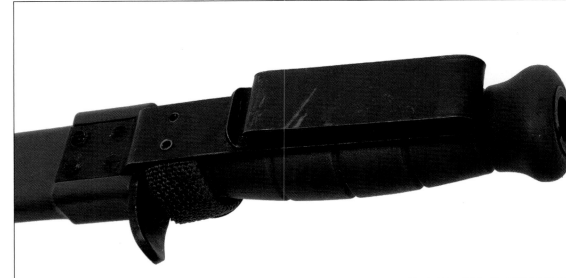

Belgium

	Overall length	Blade length	Muzzle ring
1867/41	534mm	448mm	17.5mm
1867	562mm	489mm	17.5mm
1916	570mm	449mm	17.5mm
1924 long	514mm	384mm	15mm
FAL Type C	292mm	162mm	22.3mm

The "Republic of the United Belgian Provinces" broke away from the Austro-Hungarian empire in 1790. France absorbed the area as nine administrative departments in 1795. The French retained control until 1815 when, under the Congress of Vienna of 1815, Belgium and the Netherlands were combined.

In 1830 a revolt allowed the Belgians to break away from the Netherlands and form their own independent monarchy. This was not ratified until the Treaty of London in 1839. Dutch and British weaponry predominated during the nation's early years, but Belgium was soon to become a world leader in weapons design and export.

Bayonets inspired by French designs predominated for many years during the 19th century. The *Fusil d'infanterie Mle.1841* was first true Belgian arm. This was replaced by the Mle. 1853. In 1867 the earlier models were converted to the Albini-Braendlin system. The original weapon designation was retained but suffixed 1867, so the 1853 musket became the 1853/67. The new weapons were in the smaller 11mm caliber, requiring the sockets of the older bayonets to be reduced.

The Belgian Mle. 1868 bayonet was a close copy of the French **1866** bayonet. Used on the Tersen rifle, it differed only in minor detail from the original French bayonet. During the 1860s, the Albini-Braendlin rifle was adopted. The first bayonets used with the rifle were converted 1841-pattern socket bayonets whose sockets had been cut to reduce the bore. The **1867/41** socket has a distinctive off-center bridge and noticeable join line where the socket was cut. **1867** bayonets that were newly made for the rifle are similar to the conversions but do not have the offset bridge. Belgian 1867 scabbards are distinctive. The first pattern illustrated was worn with a leather

bayonet frog to which it buckled using a short buff leather strap integral to the throat of the scabbard. A second pattern attached to a sword using two leather loops that slipped over the sword scabbard, the sword hangers retaining it in place. French influence was also apparent in the 1882 bayonet for the 11mm lever-action breechloading Comblain rifle; its "T"-section blade was essentially that of the French **1874**, although it had a different hilt. In 1889 Belgium succumbed to international trend, introducing a series of Mauser-action rifles. Each rifle type was issued with its own specific pattern of 1889-type bayonet, differing in detail so as to serve best the arms of service for which they were destined. All the bayonets shared a common hilt design, first used on the 1882 bayonet, but differed in blade patterns.

During World War I, Belgium produced the **1916** bayonet. It was made with two different muzzle ring sizes, initially

Two Belgian bayonets and scabbards. Above is the socket bayonet model 1841 converted to fit the Albini-Braendlin rifle. The converted 1867 bayonet socket has a distinct short section to the second step of the socket, and an off-center bridge where the socket has been cut and reduced in diameter. It has the regulation-pattern Belgian socket bayonet scabbard. The standard 1867 bayonet is illustrated below, it has the scarce pattern scabbard designed to be carried fitted over the saber scabbard.

17.5mm and later 15mm. The former fitted the old 1889-series rifles and carbines, and the latter was made for the model 1916, and, later, the 1935 and 1936 rifles. The **1916** bayonets have a hilt similar to the 1889 ones, though without a quillon, and a long cruciform-section blade.

The Belgians took a large chunk of the international arms trade following World War I, and resumed their exports after World War II. The best-known exports of this period were the Fabrique National model 1924 and 1930 rifles, along with the accompanying bayonets. The M1924 rifle was manufactured in 7mm, 7.65mm and 7.9mm, and the M1930 rifle was generally 7.9mm, although .30in caliber and 7.62mm NATO versions were also produced. The **1924** export bayonet was provided in two blade lengths, the long 384mm, generally provided with the 1930 short rifle, and the shorter 292mm pattern (see Yugoslavian section). Both were exported in some quantity.

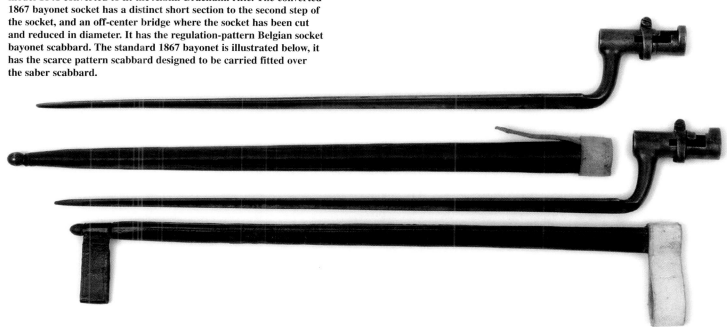

prior to and again after World War II. Yugoslavia alone purchased 90,000 M24 rifles and bayonets during the 1920s, and FN bolt-action rifles and bayonets were also exported to Argentina, Belgian Congo, Bolivia, Brazil, Chile, China, Colombia, Costa Rica, Ecuador, Ethiopia, France, Greece, Haiti, Indonesia, Persia, Israel, Liberia, Lithuania, Luxembourg, Mexico, Morocco, Netherlands, Paraguay, Peru, Saudi Arabia, Siam, Uruguay, Venezuela and Yemen.

The first self-loading rifle produced in any quantity by Belgium was Fabrique National's SAFN M1949 rifle. The rifle and double-edged **1949** bayonet were sold to Argentina, Egypt, Belgian Congo, Brazil, Columbia, Indonesia, Luxembourg and Venezuela. Contrary to popular belief, they were also used by Belgian troops. The bayonet combined a standard **1924** export-type hilt with a double-edged blade, the blade had the form of the **1924** cruciform pattern but was considerably shorter.

Belgium continued to lead the world arms trade during the 1950s. The limited success of the SAFN 1949 was to be overshadowed by the worldwide acceptance of FN's second generation of self-loading weapons, the 7.62mm FN FAL. The prowess of the Belgian arms industry in the 1950s is aptly illustrated by the worldwide sales of the FAL rifle. In addition to arming Belgian troops it was supplied to, or made under license, by a number of nations including Argentina,

Australia (L1A1), Austria (Stg 57), Bangladesh, Barbados, Brazil, Burundi, Cambodia, Canada (C1), Chile, Congo, Cuba, Dominican Republic, Dubai, Ecuador, Gambia, Great Britain (L1A1), Greece, Guyana, India (IASL) Indonesia, Ireland, Israel, Jamaica, Jordan, Kenya, Kuwait, Lebanon, Liberia, Libya, Luxembourg, Malawi, Malaysia, Mexico, Morocco, Mozambique, Muscat, Nepal, Netherlands, New Zealand (L1A1), Oman, Panama, Paraguay, Peru, Portugal, Qatar, Ras al Kahima, Rhodesia, Rwanda, Singapore, Santo Domingo, South Africa (R1), Syria, Thailand, West Germany (G1) and Venezuela. The original bayonet for the FN FAL was the Type A, or 1953 pattern. It was distinctive in that it had two prongs fitted to the muzzle ring that acted as a flash disruptor when the bayonet was fitted to the rifle. Some nations, such as Great Britain, made their own licensed variants of the FN FAL rifle and adopted their own national bayonet design. The FAL Type B bayonet was similar to the **FAL Type A** but did not have the prongs. It also had a shorter blade and slightly larger muzzle ring. The FAL Type B was only produced in limited quantity.

From 1961 the FAL rifles were fitted with the NATO flash eliminator. This required a new bayonet, the **FAL Type C**, which was of the tube/socket type with a plain unfullered blade. The new socket bayonet was used on a variety of weapons including the 5.56mm FN CAL and FNC rifles.

BELOW 1916-pattern bayonet hilt and frog. The frog has a strap and buckle arrangement to secure the scabbard. The hilt loop is greatly oversized and would only have provided a limited reduction in the free movement of the hilt.

BOTTOM A trio of Belgian infantrymen armed with 1889 rifles and 1916 bayonets.

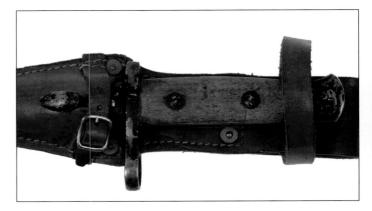

BELOW The blade of the 1916 bayonet is unusual; it appears cruciform in section, but it is perhaps better described as double-edged with a broad central ridge. It is, nonetheless, of little use as anything other than a thrusting weapon. Its adoption was hardly a step forward in bayonet evolution.

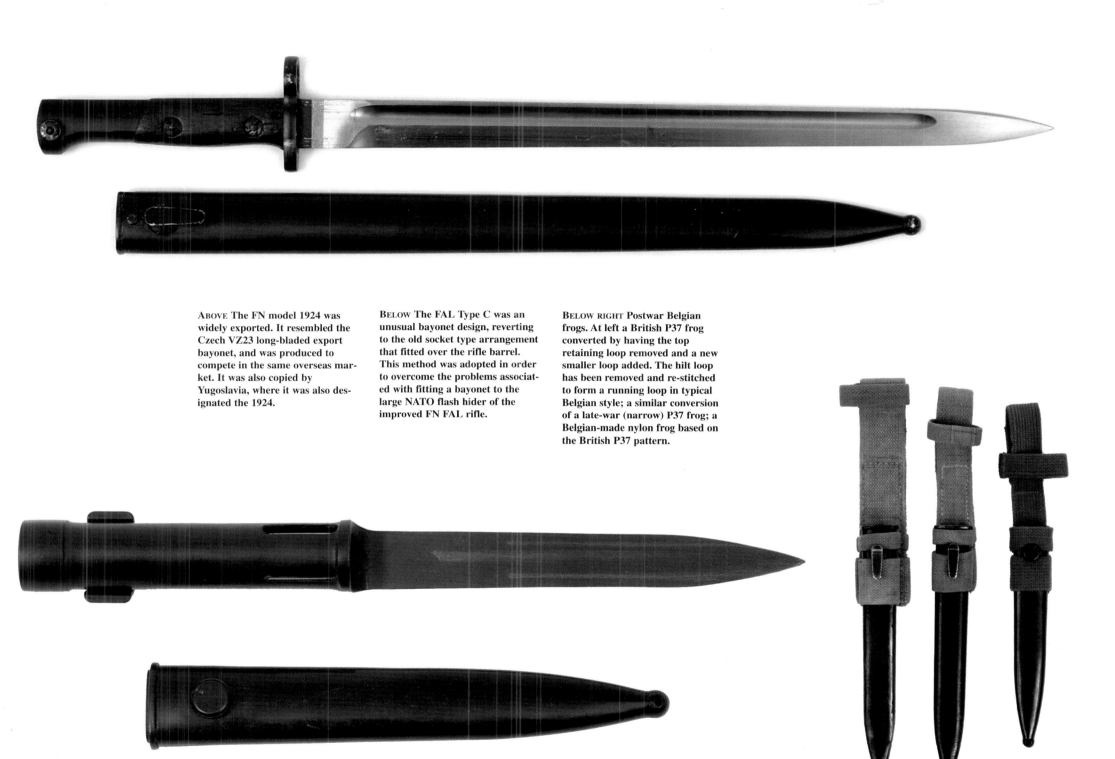

ABOVE The FN model 1924 was widely exported. It resembled the Czech VZ23 long-bladed export bayonet, and was produced to compete in the same overseas market. It was also copied by Yugoslavia, where it was also designated the 1924.

BELOW The FAL Type C was an unusual bayonet design, reverting to the old socket type arrangement that fitted over the rifle barrel. This method was adopted in order to overcome the problems associated with fitting a bayonet to the large NATO flash hider of the improved FN FAL rifle.

BELOW RIGHT Postwar Belgian frogs. At left a British P37 frog converted by having the top retaining loop removed and a new smaller loop added. The hilt loop has been removed and re-stitched to form a running loop in typical Belgian style; a similar conversion of a late-war (narrow) P37 frog; a Belgian-made nylon frog based on the British P37 pattern.

Brazil

	Overall length	Blade length	Muzzle ring
1908	432mm	299mm	15.5mm
1934	518mm	384mm	15.5mm

Unlike most of continental South America, Brazil had been under Portuguese rule, not Spanish, since the 1500s. The 19th century saw Brazil at war with Argentina and Paraguay, the latter conflict almost totally destroying Paraguay as a nation. Brazil joined the allies during both World War I and World War II. The Americans equipped Brazilian troops serving in Italy during World War II with Garand rifles and **M1** bayonets.

During the 19th century, Brazil used a number of weapons of foreign design, including the 11mm 1874 Comblain rifle. A design based on the French Chassepot **Mle. 1866** bayonet was

issued with the Comblain as the 1880 bayonet. In 1892, a copy of the German 1888 Mauser rifle was adopted. This was replaced only two years later by the model 1894, basically a Spanish 1893 Mauser rifle. In 1904, Brazil adopted a 7mm Mauser Vergueiro-action rifle. The accompanying sword bayonet with its distinctive "yataghan" blade was probably the last bayonet to be produced with this type of blade that had seen its heyday during the mid-19th century. A short-bladed bayonet, similar to the Portuguese 1904, was also used on this rifle. A new 7mm rifle and short rifle were adopted in 1908. These weapons had an attractive knife bayonet with hook quillon and a brass-mounted leather scabbard. The **1908** bayonet can also be found with a plain steel-mounted leather scabbard, but it is believed that this may have been used by other South American nations. In keeping with worldwide military thinking, a shortened .30-06in caliber carbine version of the 1908

rifle was adopted in 1934 as the 1908/34. Made in Czechoslovakia the **1934** bayonet was similar to the **1908**, but had a longer blade to make up for the shorter length of the M1934 rifle. Like the **1908** pattern, it had a black leather scabbard, but was found only with heavily blued steel mounts. A modernized version of the 1908/34 carbine was also later produced as the 1954 short rifle.

During the 1950s, numbers of Danish export M1947 rifles and bayonets were used by Brazil, as were the FN 1949 rifles with their double-edged blade bayonets. The current Brazilian rifle is the Belgian FAL, made by the Brazilian state arsenal, IMBEL, as the LAR. It is supplemented by the 5.56mm MD-2 and MD-3 rifles, which utilize a copy of the Belgian FAL Type C bayonet. A large number of the 1908 bayonets and re-barreled 7.62mm 1908 Mauser rifles are retained for ceremonial and parade use.

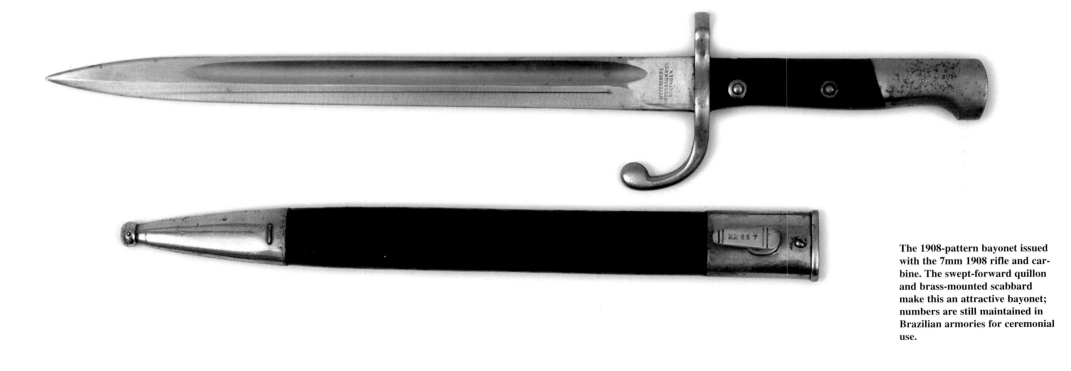

The 1908-pattern bayonet issued with the 7mm 1908 rifle and carbine. The swept-forward quillon and brass-mounted scabbard make this an attractive bayonet; numbers are still maintained in Brazilian armories for ceremonial use.

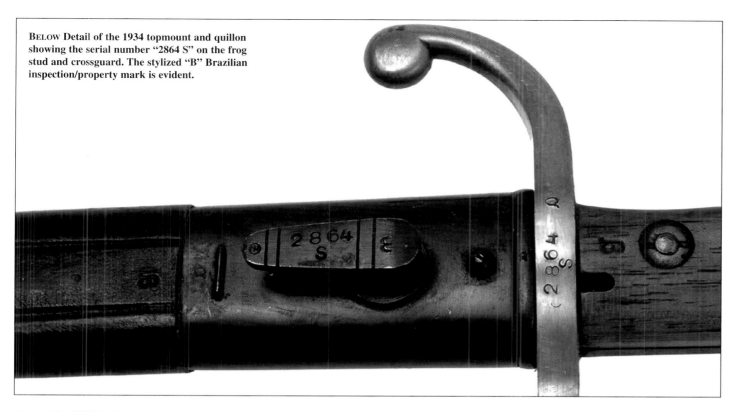

BELOW Detail of the 1934 topmount and quillon showing the serial number "2864 S" on the frog stud and crossguard. The stylized "B" Brazilian inspection/property mark is evident.

ABOVE A Brazilian armorer works on a U.S. .50in HMG. Behind him is a rack of 1908-pattern bayonets in their brass-mounted leather scabbards, still used for ceremonial occasions. (*Exercito Brasileiro*)

BELOW The 1908/34 rifle was made in Brazil, but the accompanying bayonet was produced in Czechoslovakia. Similar to the 1908 bayonet, it differed in having a longer blade and grips retained by screwbolts rather than the rivets used previously. The scabbard mounts were heavily blackened.

Canada

	Overall length	Blade length	Muzzle ring
1899	352mm	230mm	15.5mm
Ross Mk. II	371mm	254mm	16mm
No. 4 Mk. II	254mm	203mm	15mm
C1	302mm	199mm	15mm
C7	302mm	171mm	22mm

Canada gained Confederation in 1867. Prior to this time, Britain had provided the Canadian military with the majority of its weapons. A small number also came from the U.S. Post federation, but Canada continued to acquire British arms, primarily the 1853 and 1856 rifles. In 1878, all the modern Canadian provinces (except Newfoundland, which was added in 1949) were brought together under one dominion. Arms continued to be imported, but in 1893 Canada introduced its first national bayonet design. The 1893 Martini Metford bayonet had the blade of the British **1888** and a wood-gripped hilt similar to that of the **1887 Mk. III**. Only around 1,000 were manufactured before it was decided to adopt the Lee Metford and **1888** bayonet. The SMLE and 1903 bayonet were issued for a short period whilst Canada was awaiting delivery of its native Ross rifle and bayonet. The new bayonet was approved in 1909 and is generally referred to as the Ross Mk. I. The muzzle ring had a small rearward extension and an internal annular spring to improve bayonet to rifle fit. These features were deleted on the **Ross Mk. II** introduced in 1912. During World War I, the blade of the Ross Mk. II bayonet was modified, giving it a sharper and more aggressive point and replacing the previous rounded style. The modification was authorized in 1915. The Mk. I and II scabbards had a leather body and belt loop with internal chape. The Mk. I fitted the Oliver equipment belt and the Mk. II differed in having a loop that allowed it to fit the wider belt of the 1915 equipment set. The Mk. I and Mk. II are often called the 1905 (or 1908) and 1910 respectively. Although a fine rifle, the Ross failed to stand up to the rigors of trench warfare, and, in 1916, Canadian troops on active service in Europe were re-armed with the SMLE and **1907** bayonet.

Just prior to World War I, the Montreal Home Guard purchased a quantity of .303in Savage 1899 lever-action rifles and

ABOVE The Ross bayonet had a particularly short blade when compared to bayonets such as the British 1907 and German S98. Above is the Ross Mk. II, introduced into service in 1912. Below is the post-1915 modification of the Mk. II, with a modified blade point that provided better penetration.

RIGHT Ross Mk. II pommel, right side, showing the markings "ROSS RIFLE CO. QUEBEC. PATENTED 1907."

bayonets. It is believed that no more than 600 of the **1899** bayonets were ever produced. The ricasso of the conventional blade bore the Savage Arms trademark of an Indian head. The hilt had wooden grips secured by a single screw, aluminum pommel and an unusual locking mechanism pivoting on a pin in the pommel. The simple leather scabbard was of the type used with commercial sheath knives and would not have stood up well to heavy military use. The Quebec Home Guard had purchased surplus Mauser 1871/84 rifles from the Hudson Bay Company. These were fitted with a cut-down P.1853 bayonet.

During World War II, No. 4 rifles and bayonets were manufactured in Canada at the Long Branch plant. Long Branch produced around 910,000 bayonets, nearly one-third of which were supplied to Britain, the remainder being used by Canada. **No. 4 Mk. II** bayonets are identifiable as Canadian by the plant mark of an "L" imposed over a "B" and the government stamp of an arrow within a "C." The Canadian Government acceptance stamp was changed from an arrow within a "C" to an "A" within a "C," for Canadian Arsenals, in 1946.

In the mid-1950s, Canada undertook trials of the FN FAL rifle and FAL Type 1 bayonet, designated the X2E1. The trials resulted in the adoption of the 7.62mm C1 rifle and **C1** bayonet in 1955. The bayonet was based on the British L1A2 with riveted pommel and protruding press catch, but differed in having a less pronounced clipped point to the blade. With the introduction of the 5.56mm round by NATO, the Canadians adopted the U.S. M16A2 rifle as the C7 and the **C7** bayonet, based on the U.S. **M7**. Nella Cutlery made the C7, the designation "C7" and "NELLA" were stamped on the crossguard. The C7 rifle has been exported to a number of countries, including Denmark and the Netherlands. The Canadian Government is currently considering a new "utility" bayonet type to replace the aging **C7** pattern.

FAR RIGHT Canadian soldiers armed with SMLE rifles and bayonets. In this image from early in the war, the Canuck's are still wearing 1908 web equipment, which for many was not replaced until they arrived in England.

ABOVE RIGHT The Savage M1899 bayonet was a commercial item sold in limited quantity to the Montreal Home Guard during World War I. It had an unusual construction and locking mechanism.

RIGHT French Canadians from the 22nd Regiment parade before the King and Queen, *c*.1940. All are armed with the .303in SMLE rifle with No. 1 Mk. I bayonets fixed.

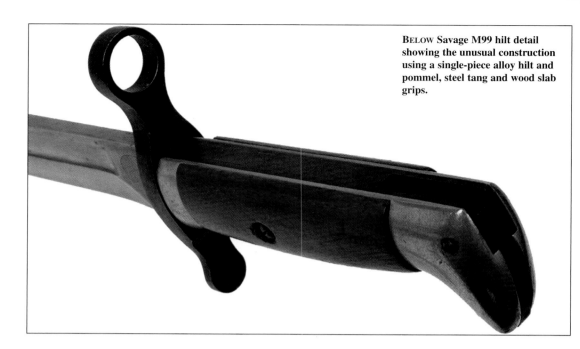

BELOW Savage M99 hilt detail showing the unusual construction using a single-piece alloy hilt and pommel, steel tang and wood slab grips.

ABOVE The Savage Arms Company's makers mark, "Savage Quality," showing an Indian chief with a Savage lever-action rifle. The U.S. company used this logo after supplying weapons to Cheyenne Indians in 1901. In return, the Indians undertook promotional work for the company, demonstrating the guns at western shows throughout the U.S.

RIGHT Canada produced the No. 4 rifle and the Mk. II spike bayonet at the Long Branch arsenal. The Canadian Mk. II spikes were well made. The scabbard is fitted with the unique Canadian frog introduced in 1944.

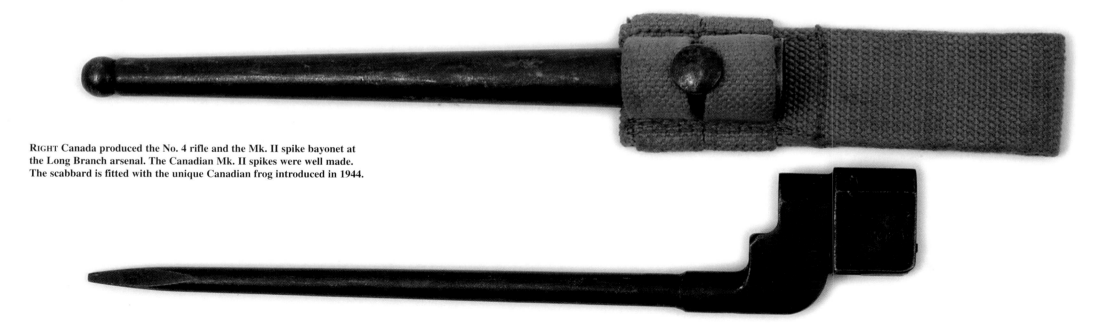

ABOVE A Canadian-made No. 4 Mk. II showing the socket marking "No 4 MK II." The entwined "LB" showing manufacture at Long Branch, and the Canadian Government marking of an "↑" within a "C."

BELOW The C1 bayonet was the Canadian-production version of the British L1A2. It was used on C1, C1A1 and C2 rifles.

ABOVE The ricasso of the C1 bayonet is marked with the "CA" marking of Canadian Arsenals Ltd., which superseded the old C arrow mark in 1946. Alongside this is the year of production, in this instance 1957.

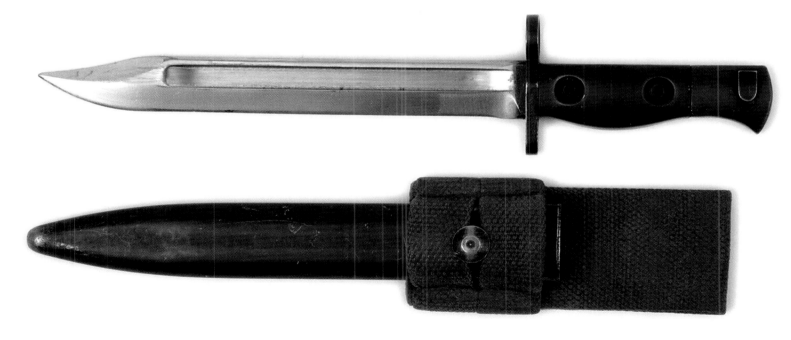

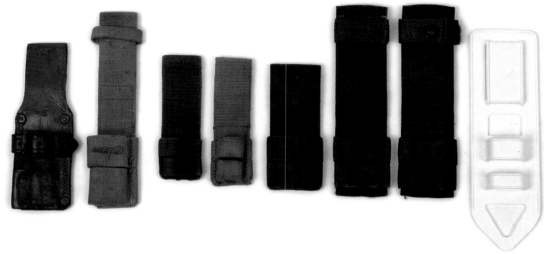

ABOVE Typical Canadian-issue bayonet frogs. Canadian-pattern 1915 leather equipment frog for use with the 1907 bayonet; P37 frog with additional stitched button hole for the No. 4 bayonet; two frogs introduced for use with the No. 4 Mk. II spike bayonet in 1944; pattern-1964 frog for the C1 bayonet; two patterns of pattern-1982 nylon frog for issue with the C7; and a white plastic ceremonial frog for use with the C1 and C7.

ABOVE LEFT The press catch of the C1 bayonet protrudes, unlike the catch on standard British L1A3 and L1A4 bayonets. The C1 was of the L1A2 pattern that was not adopted by the British, as it was felt that the catch could be accidentally activated in action, leading to the loss of the bayonet. It would appear that the Canadians did not consider this a problem.

LEFT C7 bayonet. A direct copy of the U.S. M7, the Canadian bayonet differs in its markings and scabbard. The underside of the cross-guard is marked "NELLA" and "C7" in typical U.S. M7 fashion. The scabbard is plastic and has a frog stud for use with a bayonet frog rather than an integral belt loop.

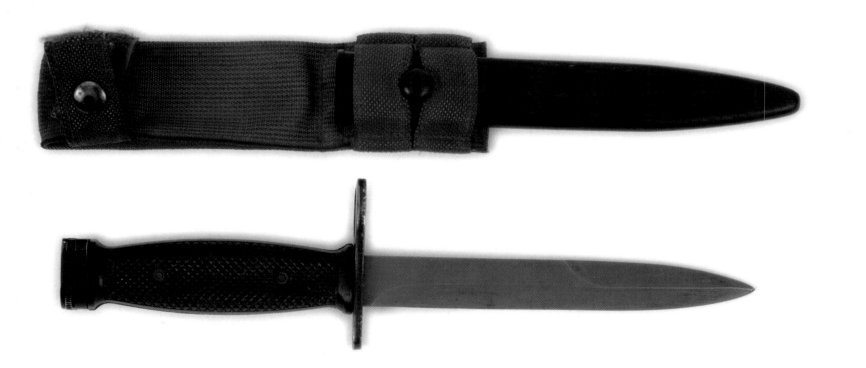

BELOW Photographed during the Bosnian conflict, WO Ed Storey wears the Canadian-issue load-carrying vest. Of note is the carriage of the C7 bayonet inverted on the left front of the vest. (Courtesy Ed Storey)

RIGHT A Canadian C7 bayonet with plastic scabbard shown carried in its nylon frog on the pattern-1982 equipment belt. The C7 was the Canadian version of the American M7 bayonet.

Chile

	Overall length	Blade length	Muzzle ring
1895	374mm	252mm	15mm
1910	403mm	294mm	18mm
1912	385mm	250mm	15.5mm

As with most of South America, Chile was under Spanish rule for nearly 400 years, latterly as a part of Peru, until finally gaining independence in 1817, after seven years of bloody conflict. Between 1879 and 1883, Chile was at war with neighboring Bolivia and Peru, emerging triumphant. Shortly after this conflict the 8mm Mannlicher 1888 was adopted, later to be replaced by the 7mm Chilean Mauser M1895 rifles and carbines, which were made in Germany. The **1895** Mauser bayonet bears the German manufacturer's marking on one side of the ricasso and the Chilean crest on the other. The crest is a horizontally bisected shield with a five pointed star imposed. A number of the **1895** bayonets were made in Austria by Steyr. The 1912 rifle, also in 7mm, had a typical Mauser-style bayo-

net. The blade and scabbard of the **1895** and **1912** bayonets were identical, but the hilts differed in detail. The **1895** bayonet was fixed using a bar on the barrel band, which required a long crossguard, whilst the **1912** bayonet had a shorter crossguard, placing the muzzle ring closer to the hilt in typical Mauser style. Steyr made the 1912 rifle and bayonets in Austria, and they bear the national shield on the right ricasso and "OEWG" on the left.

In 1910, the Chilean police were provided with an ornate sidearm that had a brass hilt bearing the Chilean coat of arms, and a brass-mounted steel scabbard. Not a bayonet per se, the **1910** police side arms were nonetheless made up using the crossguard and part of the blade from French **1874** bayonets. Czech VZ24 rifles were imported in a small quantity, along with **VZ24** bayonets. In 1935, the M1935 rifle, a standard Mauser-type carbine similar to the German K98, supplemented the 1912 rifles. The old 1912 bayonet fitted the standard Mauser bayonet bar and was therefore retained. In 1941, the Chilean Government purchased 1,000 Johnson M1941 rifles

from the USA. It is assumed that a similar number of **1941** bayonets were also acquired.

In the late 1940s, Danish Madsen rifles and **1947** bayonets were imported. The later decades of the 20th century saw the Belgian 7.62mm FN FAL and Swiss Stg 57, with Swiss-style bayonet, in service with Chilean troops. This was replaced by the SIG 510, followed in 1986 by the SIG 540 and the SIG **540/542** bayonet. The M35 rifles were re-barreled to 7.62mm after the adoption of the NATO round. Along with the 1912 bayonet, many were retained for ceremonial and parade use and can still be seen in service.

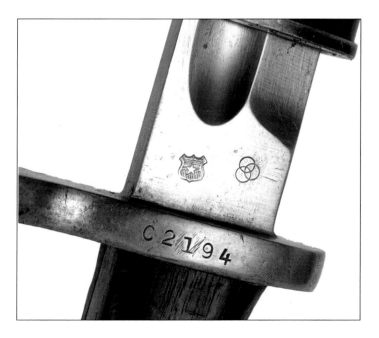

FAR LEFT Right ricasso of the 1895 bayonet showing the Chilean national marking of a star on a horizontally bisected shield. The crossguard bears a letter-prefixed serial number "C2194."

LEFT 1895 left ricasso showing the makers marking, "WEYERSBERG KIRSCHBAUM & Cie, SOLINGEN."

ABOVE The Mauser 1895 rifle was supplied with a knife bayonet. It had a single-edged blade and wood grips. Weyersberg Kirschbaum in Germany made the majority; however, some were made in Austria and are marked "OEWG." Below the 1895 bayonet is the 1912; although it has the same blade and scabbard, it is immediately distinguishable by the Mauser hilt and the muzzle ring positioned closer to the hilt back.

LEFT The hilt bears the Chilean coat of arms. The central shield and star motive can be found on the ricasso of Chilean bayonets.

ABOVE The M1910 police sidearm used a section of the blade and the crossguard of the French Gras 1874 bayonet. This was mated to a solid brass hilt bearing the Chilean coat of arms.

China

	Overall length	Blade length	Muzzle ring
1935	570mm	435mm	15.5mm
Type 56 carbine (SKS)	298mm	241mm	14mm
Type 56 carbine short	283mm	205mm	14mm
Type 56 carbine long	381mm	309mm	14mm
AKS	270mm	146mm	17.5mm

As an ancient culture credited with the invention of gunpowder, China surprisingly undertook little in the development of firearms and artillery. When confronted by modern weaponry, China was rapid to accept the power of the breechloading firearms, and countless numbers of weapons were purchased for the Chinese military during the 19th century. The principal provider was Mauser, with China using most patterns of Mauser weapons including the German-made G1871 and G1888 rifles. China also acquired Belgian FN 24 and 30 rifles, as well as the Czech VZ24. Besides the imported rifles, China also made copies of the various types of weapons in use and also produced bayonets to suit. The M35 "Chiang Kai Shek" rifle was a copy of the German Mauser short rifle. It was pro-

LEFT The M35 "Chiang Kai Shek" bayonet had a typical Mauser-type hilt with a blade similar to that used on the Japanese 30th year bayonet. The simple leather scabbard had an integral belt loop and retaining strap with press-stud. After the Civil War, the M35 rifle was retained by the Communist regime but was renamed the Type 79.

ABOVE The M35 was not finished particularly well, with much of the work evidently being done by hand, as shown by the poorly fitting reverse to the press catch.

duced in great numbers along with the **1935** bayonet. The rifle and bayonet were retained after the revolution when the People's Republic of China called them the Type 79.

The Russian Type 1944 Nagant carbine had an integral folding bayonet, the **M1944**. An exact copy of this bolt-action carbine and bayonet were adopted by China as the Type 53 rifle. The Chinese 7.62mm Type 56 carbine was again a copy of a Russian weapon, this one being based on the SKS, and, again, included its folding-blade type bayonet. However, later versions of the Type 56 carbine used a bayonet that differed from that used on the SKS in that it had a 305mm chisel-point triangular-section blade. The second-pattern **Type 56** carbine bayonet had a much better finish than the original. China also produced its own version of the AK series rifles. The bayonet

for the Type 56 rifle (as opposed to the Type 56 carbine) was again a folding spike, but only 222mm long, and is often erroneously referred to as the "para" version. Unlike the **Type 56** rifle bayonet, the carbine bayonet does not have a muzzle ring but rather a small lug that engages with a bracket on the fore sight mount. Later versions of the Type 56-1 rifle with the folding stock used the double-ring **AK47** type of bayonet. Based on the Russian **AK47** bayonet, early patterns had wooden grips that were later replaced with plastic. The Type 68 bayonet was similar to the Type 56 rifle bayonet, but had a 300mm blade. It fitted the Type 68 rifle, which was a hybrid of the Type 56 rifle and the Type 56 carbine, embodying the best features of both weapons.

More recent development has seen Chinese troops issued

with the **AKS 75** bayonet, which was similar to the Russian second-pattern **AKM** but with no provision for a wire-cutter. This made the accompanying scabbard seem rather short by comparison to its Soviet counterparts. In the early 1980s, the Chinese had a major re-think on bayonet design. Whilst the hilt of the **AKS 75** was retained, it was mated with a much narrower double-edged blade. Longer than the preceding bayonets types, unusually it featured double fullers. The AKM 81 had a new type of scabbard with a narrow composite body and standard suspension loop. The leather hilt strap had a press catch bearing a communist star emblem. Very few of this pattern of bayonet have reached private collectors.

The first Chinese Type 56 carbine bayonet was a copy of the Russian SKS bayonet. A triangular-section bayonet (bottom), using the same locking mechanism, replaced it. A similar bayonet, but with a shortened blade (center), has been marketed as a "para" bayonet. On inspection, these are merely standard Type 56 carbine triangular bayonets with crudely shortened blades. The Type 56 rifle bayonet was similar to the Type 56 carbine bayonet, but did not have a muzzle ring, using instead a lug that engaged the rifle's foresight bracket.

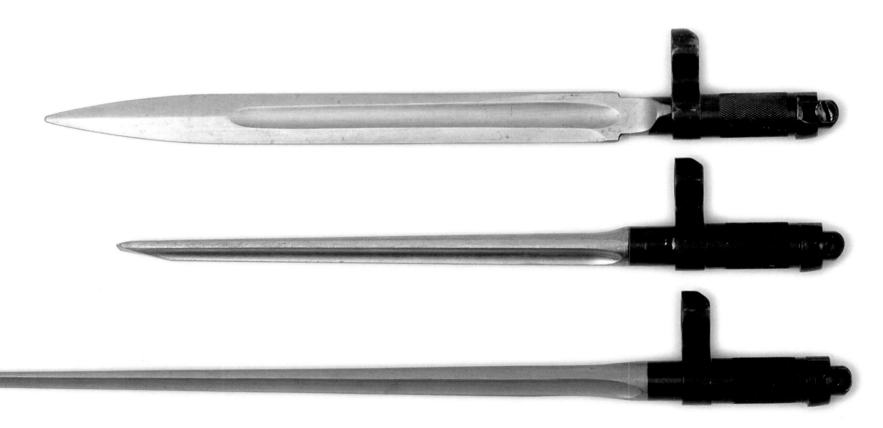

ABOVE Early Type 56 rifles used a triangular bayonet; however, the later 56-1 patterns were provided with AK47 bayonet fittings. Here a standard AK47 bayonet is shown attached to the muzzle of a Chinese Type 56-1 rifle.

RIGHT The Chinese AKS 75 bayonet was based on the Soviet AKM II. The hilt was a direct copy. The blade, whilst retaining the original blade style, did not have a saw-back or the recess for the scabbard wirecutter attachment. The scabbard was based on that of the AKM II but without the steel wire-cutter section on the tip.

Czechoslovakia

	Overall length	Blade length	Muzzle ring
1895	356mm	247mm	15.5mm
VZ23 long	540mm	401mm	14.9mm
VZ23 short	385mm	250mm	15.5mm
VZ24	432mm	298mm	14.9mm
VZ33	356mm	229mm	14.9mm
VZ52	282mm	175mm	N/A
VZ58	285mm	175mm	N/A

The end of World War I saw the Austro-Hungarian Empire divided. Czechoslovakia was a product of this post-war reorganization, a new nation born from the old Hapsburg Empire. Initially, the Czechs were armed with Austrian weaponry, including the **1895** bayonet, but the emerging nation rapidly proved its prowess in arms manufacture. The old state arms factories at Brno and Pilsen continued to produce the Austrian-pattern **1895** *bodak* (bayonet), but with the Czech "CSZ" mark (standing for *Ceskoslovenska Statni Zbrojovky*—Czech state manufacture) on the left ricasso and the Czech rampant lion within a shield on the right ricasso. Often listed as Czechoslovakian-made bayonets produced for the Austro-Hungarian Empire, they are actually true Czech bayonets made by, and for, the new nation. As part of their war reparations, the Czechs received German G98 machinery. The first new products of the Czech arms industry were a Mauser-action rifle and carbine. The accompanying **VZ23** (VZ was the Czech abbreviation for model) pattern bayonet was made in both a long sword type and as a shorter knife bayonet. Those made prior to 1926 have hilts 2mm shorter than those in later production. All had an identical hilt style. The long sword bayonet had a blade length of 400mm. It was supplied in two patterns, one of typically Austrian influence with the blade edge uppermost, and an alternative with a downward-facing blade. Persia imported this type of **VZ23** long bayonet for use on the 98/29 short rifle. This can be identified as Persian as it has the standard frog stud replaced by a frog loop. By comparison, the shorter knife bayonet had a blade of 250mm. In 1924, the Czech Army adopted the 1924-pattern rifle as standard. Like

its Austrian predecessors and the **VZ23** bayonet, the new **VZ24** bayonet had a reversed blade with the edge orientated uppermost when mounted on the rifle. It was very similar to the **VZ23** pattern but had a 298mm blade length. A number of countries received imports of the **VZ23** and **VZ24** bayonets. Among them were Brazil, Bolivia, China, Colombia, Ecuador, Estonia, Guatemala, Persia, Japan, Latvia, Lithuania, Mexico, Nicaragua, Peru, Romania, Salvador, Siam, Spain, Turkey, Uruguay, Venezuela and Yugoslavia. Around 1,290,300 model 23 and 24 bayonets and rifles were exported by the Czech arms industry. In the immediate postwar years many **VZ24** were refurbished and sold to Israel.

Gendarmes and Financial Guards were issued the model VZ33 short rifle. The accompanying bayonet **VZ33** was a smaller version of the **VZ24** with a reduced hilt and blade length. Only 30,000 of these weapons were produced. In March 1939, the German Army marched into Czechoslovakia, having already taken control of the Sudetenland in 1938, and absorbed the fledgling Czech nation into the greater German Reich. Arms production continued under the Germans with

both **VZ24** and **VZ33** bayonets being issued to German troops. In line with German ballistic thinking, the muzzle rings of the bayonets were removed to improve weapon accuracy when the bayonet was fitted to the rifle.

The defeat of the Axis returned Czechoslovakia once more to nationhood, but under the yoke of the Soviet regime. In line with Russia's adoption of the Simonov SKS automatic rifle, the Czechs developed a similar weapon and, in 1952, introduced the VZ52 rifle. The accompanying **VZ52** bayonet was a permanently attached blade-type bayonet that folded against the right side of the forend when not in use. It had two blade lengths, the standard 287mm and the rarely encountered 357mm. Soviet domination soon saw the demise of the VZ52. However, unlike the majority of Warsaw Pact nations, Czechoslovakia continued to use their own weapon and bayonet designs, though based on Russian patterns. The Czech VZ58 rifle used the standard Warsaw Pact 7.62mm caliber and 30-round magazine, and was based on the Russian AK47. The **VZ58** bayonet was of a simple design. Its fixing catch was behind the short crossguard and the bayonet was attached to the rifle by sliding it forward onto the

A Czechoslovakian-made 1895 bayonet, a direct copy of the Austrian 1895. This was made after World War I in the old Austrian arsenals and was one of the first weapons produced by the new nation.

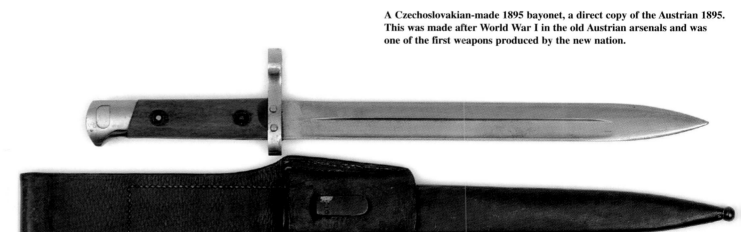

Czech VZ23 short-bladed bayonet. This type of bayonet was exported widely. It, and its accompanying rifle, proved the building block of the Czech arms industry that was to prosper during the interwar years. The frog stud is marked with a "23," for the year of production, "CSZ," and the Czech lion within a circle.

BELOW The Czech 1895 bayonet carries the "CSZ" logo on the left ricasso and the national Bohemian rampant lion in a shield marking on the right ricasso. Note the very prominent crossguard rivets. The accompanying brown leather Czech frog, again a direct copy of the Austrian pattern, is marked with the rampant lion and a "5."

ABOVE A long-bladed VZ23 export bayonet with the sharpened edge on the lower side of the blade, an alternative version of the long-bladed VZ23 had a reversed blade. This particular example is for export to Persia, and it has an Arabic serial on the pommel end and the distinctive bayonet frog loop rather than frog stud. This frog loop was a modification carried out in Persia, rather crudely as shown by the poor brazing. The hilt is typically Czech.

bayonet bar rather than back, as was normal practice, and there was therefore no muzzle ring. This could be considered a weakness, as any thrust by this fixed bayonet would have taken the whole impact on the locking bolt, but the problem was undoubtedly considered by the Czechs and deemed acceptable. On the original version of the bayonet, the grips were of the wood slab type, but in 1962, a new pattern of grips was introduced, made of resin and woodchip.

Early versions of the **VZ58** had no crossguard, but a slightly protruding type was later added to the specification to prevent the fingers slipping onto the blade when the bayonet was used as a knife. In 1968, a further modified **VZ58** bayonet was introduced. Similar to the preceding patterns it had an exten-

sion of the tang at the pommel end. The tang had previously finished short of the pommel leaving the grips liable to damage. Unlike the majority of bayonets, which are drop forged, the **VZ58** was cast using the lost wax process. The simplicity of the bayonet extended to its scabbard design, which was a plain leather sheath of the type encountered on hunting knives. The bayonet could be cleaned following any nuclear, biological or chemical contamination, but the leather sheath was absorbent. This problem was overcome by the issue of a disposable rubber bayonet sheath as a part of the Czech soldiers' NBC outfit. It was easily decontaminated or discarded at little cost. The leather scabbard could be safely stored away during any periods of nuclear, chemical or biological threat.

BELOW LEFT The Czech VZ24 was little more than a longer version of the VZ23; its blade length was 298mm as compared to 250mm for the VZ23.

BOTTOM LEFT The rather small VZ33 bayonet was issued to the Gendarmerie and Financial Guard. It resembled the VZ24 but had a shorter blade and hilt; it retained the typically excellent quality of Czech-made bayonets. This example was made in 1935.

BELOW VZ24 ricasso mark and frog stud markings. This bayonet has the standard "CSZ" marking on the ricasso and frog stud, with "E3 lion 37" on the frog stud showing that it was made in 1937. "CSZ" is the state arsenal marking.

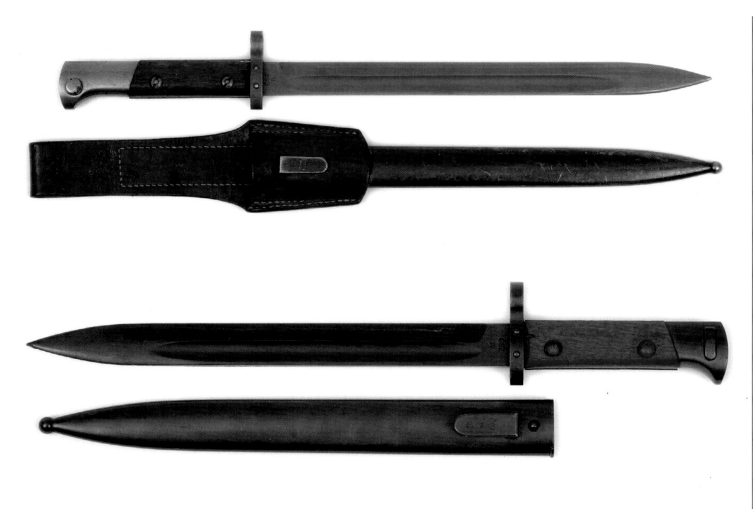

BELOW The pommel of the VZ33 bears a serial number, "8605," and the "CETN" mark of the Czech gendarmerie. Note the standard Mauser-style mortise slot with oval section for the rifle's cleaning rod.

BOTTOM In the immediate post-war era, the Czechs continued their efforts in arms design. The first product of which was the self-loading VZ52 rifle. This had a double-edged knife-type bayonet, which folded back against the right side of the wooden fore stock when not in use.

ABOVE Soviet domination of Eastern Europe led to the Czechs adopting their own version of the Russian AK47 rifle, the VZ58. The accompanying bayonet was of a simple design and resembled a hunting knife. From left to right: the standard leather scabbard issued with all VZ58 series bayonets; an early-production VZ58 without crossguard extension, right side; second pattern with rudimentary crossguard extension; final model with pommel extension to the tang; green plastic scabbard for use in nuclear, biological, or chemical warfare environments.

LEFT The tang of early-production VZ58 bayonets extended just beyond the attachment slot. This left the end of the pommel prone to damage. The problem was rectified by extending the tang beyond the pommel on later production bayonets (top). The mortise slot was at the front face of the hilt, the bayonet being pushed forward to fix, rather than drawn back as was standard practice.

ABOVE Typical Czech markings on VZ58 scabbards, the ordnance crossed swords, and a date. Above is a plastic NBC scabbard made in July 1977 and marked on the front of the belt loop. Below this, the standard leather scabbard made in 1976 and marked on the reverse of the reinforced tip.

Denmark

	Overall length	Blade length	Muzzle ring
1854	572mm	503mm	21.5mm
1889	353mm	232mm	N/A
1947	312mm	209mm	15.3mm
1950	349mm	248mm	16mm
M62	289mm	169mm	N/A

Until 1814, Denmark had been a part of Norway. After independence, the Danes imported arms that best suited their own national requirements. In 1848, Slesvig Holstein rebelled against Danish rule, and, aided by Germany, took up arms against Denmark. The rebels were issued with a number of weapon types including the *Dornbüchse M/1849*. This was used with a socket bayonet bearing the "Khyl" spring catch, designed in 1794. The rebellion was defeated in 1851, and the rebels' weapons were taken into Danish service. The 1849 rifles were rebored to 16.9mm caliber, and reissued as the Suhler Tapriffel model 1854. The bayonet was the pattern **1854.**

In 1889, the Danes introduced the Krag-Jorgensen rifle in 8mm. It was accompanied by the *knivbajonet* **1889.** The blade and hilt were forged together, it had leather grips and no muzzle ring. In 1892, the leather grips were replaced by wood on all new-production bayonets, although stocks of leather grips

were used up. The scabbard was steel-mounted leather, the topmount having a spring-catch to keep the blade secure in the scabbard. A long sword bayonet was issued to bring the reach of Danish weapons in line with that of Germany. The 1915 bayonet had a long 455mm "T" back blade, muzzle ring and wood grips. The scabbard was a longer version of that used with the **1889.**

During World War II, the "Danish Brigade" was trained as a "police" force in neutral Sweden. They were armed with Swedish 1896 rifles and bayonets, which accompanied them when they returned to Denmark at the end of the war. Danish occupation troops in Germany were issued the No. 4 rifle and bayonet.

After World War II, Denmark attempted to gain a foothold in the international arms market at a time when the world was awash with surplus weapons. The Madsen model of 1947 was a 7mm bolt-action rifle. It was manufactured in Denmark but was only intended for export. The rifle and its **M47** bayonet was purchased by several nations including Brazil, Chile, Columbia, Guatemala, Indonesia and Thailand. The die-struck scabbard has distinct edge seams, which is undoubtedly the most interesting point about this otherwise basic bayonet pattern. In the aftermath of World War II, Denmark was supplied with both British and U.S. weaponry. The .30-06in U.S. M1 Garand rifle (GM 50 in Danish service) was issued in some quantity along with the **M1** bayonet, and later the **M5**, as well

as U.S.-surplus **M1** bayonets, called the **M1950** by the Danes. The native **M1950** bayonet's ricasso was impressed with the Danish crown and "FKF" (*Forsvarets Krigsmaterial Forvalning*, for Defence War Material Administration) and the date of manufacture. The throat of the Danish **M7**-type scabbard can be found stamped with a crown over "FKF" and the year of manufacture, and also a crown over "HTK" (HTK standing for *Haerens Tekniske Korps*, Army Technical Corps) in place of the flaming bomb normally found on the U.S. topmount. HTK was later replaced with "HMAK" (*Haerens Material Kommando*, Army Material Command). The scabbard body had the distinct woodgrain effect found on American-type scabbards produced in Germany.

The Danes were equipped with both British 37-pattern webbing and new-production web based on the British issue. There was no provision for the attachment of the U.S.-style equipment hook found on American scabbards, and a web "carrier" was therefore issued. The short section of webbing was fitted with twin 37-pattern belt hooks to the rear for attachment to the web belt, and two small double loops to the front for the attachment of the U.S. scabbards.

The Danes used a copy of the U.S. M4 bayonet. Issued as the M57, it was intended for use as a trench knife and was not issued in accompaniment with the U.S. M1 carbine. Another U.S. bayonet issued as a trench knife was the **M5A1.** This was also newly made for the Danish Army and was identical to the

BELOW **Khyl spring catch bayonet. Taken up by the Danish as the 1854 bayonet for the Suhler Tapriffel model 1854 following the defeat of the Slesvig rebellion in 1851.**

FAR RIGHT **Khyl catch bayonet. Unit markings show that this bayonet was taken into Danish service in 1855. The Khyl catch was an efficient system that provided a firm and secure fixing on the rifle.**

U.S. issue. It was designated the HTK **M62**. It was supplied in a U.S. **M8A1**-style scabbard, but with British 37-pattern belt hooks added to the rear of the integral webbing belt loop section. The pommel was stamped with a crown over "HTK" above "M/62." At the throat, the scabbards bore the Danish crown stamp over either HTK or "M8A1" and "Made in West Germany" in two lines. Some scabbards were unmarked, but all are identifiable as Danish rather than American by the double belt hook attachment. They can be found with the body in woodgrain or plain plastic finish, with green webbing and gray parkerized metal fittings. Both the M57 and M62 bayonets were issued as knives regardless of the rifle or other weapon type carried.

The Garand was replaced with the ubiquitous 7.62mm G3 rifle and M75 bayonet, a copy of the German **G3**. This in turn was replaced with the current Danish rifle, the C7FT, made in Canada by Diemaco and based on the Canadian C7 rifle. The Danish armed forces no longer issue bayonets. Their use is restricted to ceremonial purposes by the Royal Lifeguard, who use an American **M7**-type bayonet on the C7FT. The Royal Lifeguard **M7** bayonet is made in Solingen.

BELOW The 1889 bayonet was a simple design that was easy to manufacture, the blade crossguard tang and pommel all being a single forging requiring no brazing of components, merely machining to shape. The steel-mounted leather scabbard had a frog loop on the topmount, which also incorporated a locking stud to keep the bayonet secure in the scabbard.

BELOW A long mortise slot negated the need for a muzzle ring, the bayonet bar seating sufficiently well to provide support. Upward pressure operated the simple pivoting release catch, it was retained by a pommel screw. The pommel is marked with the unit, "31B," and the weapon number, "472." This identifies the bayonet as having been issued to the Danish Army's 31st battalion, which was disbanded in 1932.

RIGHT This 1889 bayonet was made in Solingen, Germany, by Alex Coppel. Their trademark of scales appears on the ricasso along with the company name. The crossguard bears a Danish inspection stamp for 1893. The bayonet-retaining spring on the scabbard topmount was pressure activated, a sharp pull on the bayonet releasing it from the scabbard.

ABOVE The 1947 bayonet for the Madsen rifle was not used by Danish forces. It was an attempt by Denmark to gain a foothold on the international arms market. However, the weapon was not a success and did not sell in great numbers.

BELOW The scabbard of the M47 bayonet had a broad edge seam that was spot-welded, the method of construction being shown here. This is the most identifiable feature on what is otherwise an uninspiring bayonet.

BELOW RIGHT A short mounting slot of the Mauser type was machined into the pommel of the Madsen bayonet, with a standard crossguard and muzzle ring mounting the rifle barrel.

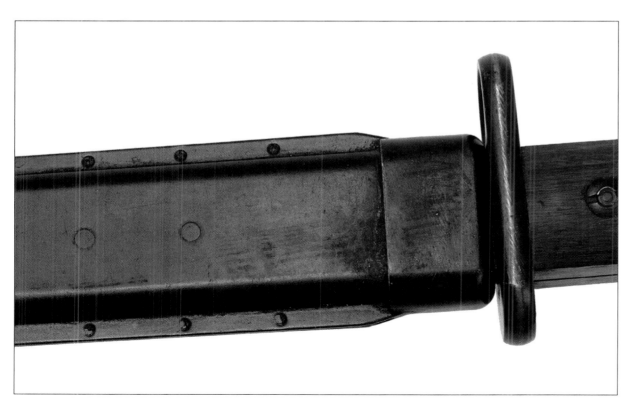

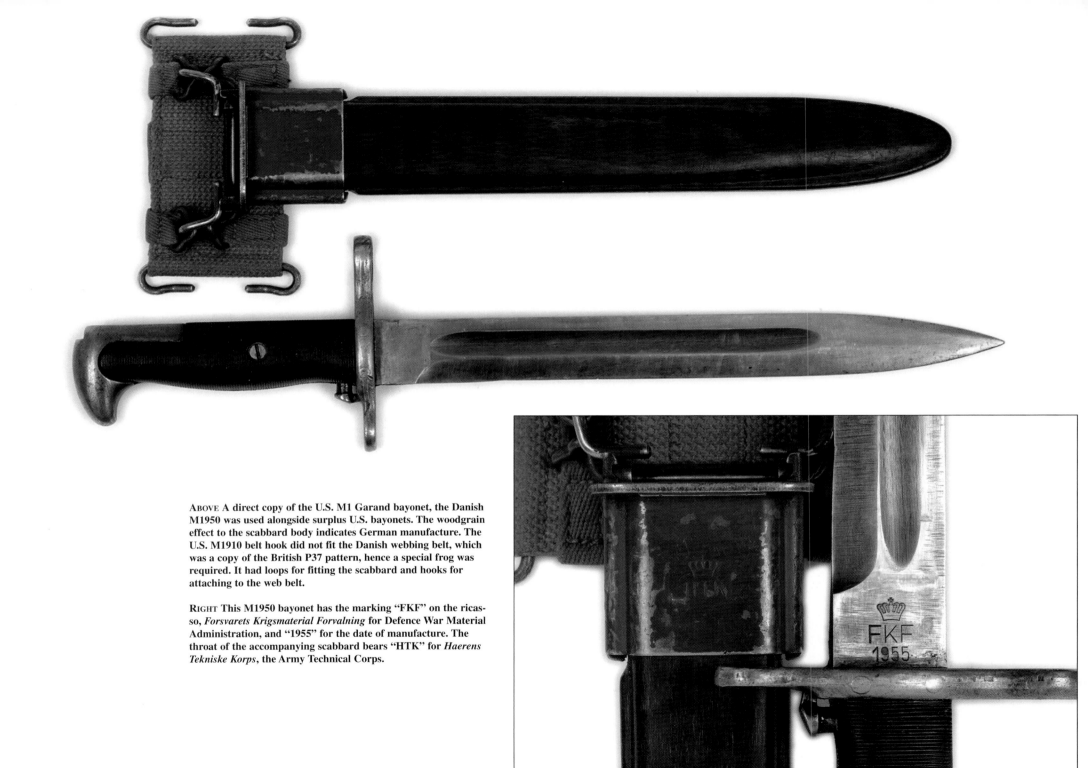

ABOVE A direct copy of the U.S. M1 Garand bayonet, the Danish M1950 was used alongside surplus U.S. bayonets. The woodgrain effect to the scabbard body indicates German manufacture. The U.S. M1910 belt hook did not fit the Danish webbing belt, which was a copy of the British P37 pattern, hence a special frog was required. It had loops for fitting the scabbard and hooks for attaching to the web belt.

RIGHT This M1950 bayonet has the marking "FKF" on the ricasso, *Forsvarets Krigsmaterial Forvalning* for Defence War Material Administration, and "1955" for the date of manufacture. The throat of the accompanying scabbard bears "HTK" for *Haerens Tekniske Korps*, the Army Technical Corps.

LEFT The U.S. M5A1 was produced under license for Denmark. It was made in Germany. In Danish service the bayonet was cataloged as the M62. It was an exact copy of the American original. The U.S. M8A1-style scabbard was modified by having British P37-style belt hooks added to the rear of the belt loop, allowing it to be fixed in place on the web belt.

BELOW LEFT Although the U.S. M5A1 was marked on the crossguard, the Danish M62 was marked at the pommel end: "HTK" over "M/62" surmounted by a crown.

BELOW An ordnance-sealed M62 bayonet showing the Danish designation and year of packing: "KNIVBAJONET M/62 - 1 EA-PAKKET JAN. 1994"

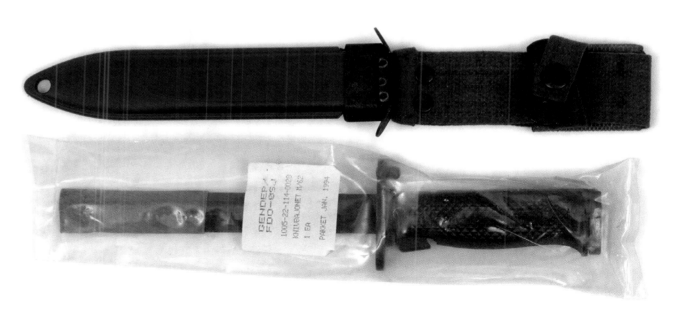

Egypt

	Overall length	Blade length	Muzzle ring
1853 quadrangular	544mm	460mm	20mm
1869	695mm	570mm	18mm
1876 Snider	695mm	570mm	21.5mm
1914	685mm	560mm	17mm
1949	362mm	230mm	18mm
Hakim 49	334mm	212mm	15.4mm

An ancient nation, Egypt had been a part of the Ottoman Empire for many decades. However, during the 19th century, the weapons employed by Egypt were influenced directly by Great Britain and France, who both vied for economic domination of Egypt, with Britain eventually winning the day and taking control of Egyptian finances. Egypt again became an independent nation in 1922, but Britain retained interests and a military presence, due to the Suez Canal, that were to last until after the Second World War and bring the two nations into conflict during the Suez Crisis of 1956.

During the 19th century, the Remington rolling-block rifle had proved popular amongst many emerging nations. The

Egyptians purchased a number direct from the Remington Arms Company in America. The rifles were equipped with the **1869** bayonet; a direct copy of the French **1866** yataghan but with an un-chamfered mortise slot. Many British weapons were also in use with the Egyptians. Snider Enfield rifles were provided with bayonets not dissimilar to the **1869**, from which they were possibly converted. With fine German-made blades, the hilt of the Snider Enfield **1876** was poorly constructed with two-piece brass slab-type grips riveted in place.

A number of **1869** bayonets were later converted for use on the Martini Enfield rifle, the new crossguards frequently being stamped "M.H.", presumably for Martini Henry. The Egyptians did not differentiate between the .577in Martini Henry and the re-barrelled modification, the .303in Martini Enfield. These

converted **1869** bayonets, with new crossguards and muzzle rings, were issued to the police as the **1914** bayonet. The standard bayonet used by the Egyptians with the Martini Enfield was the **1895**. Converted from the British **1876** socket bayonet it had a blade orientated under the barrel. The conversion was done by cutting off the socket behind the locking ring, rotating

BELOW This crudely made quad-rangular-bladed bayonet fits the 1853 rifle. It bears numerous machining marks and is poorly tempered. Little else is known about this bayonet that originated in Egypt and was undoubtedly of local manufacture.

BOTTOM Based on the French 1866, the M1869 Remington bayonet was virtually identical. It differed in not having the chamfered edge to the mortise slot and in not having a cut-out in the muzzle ring (see comparison in the French section). The bayonet was used on the Remington rolling-block rifle.

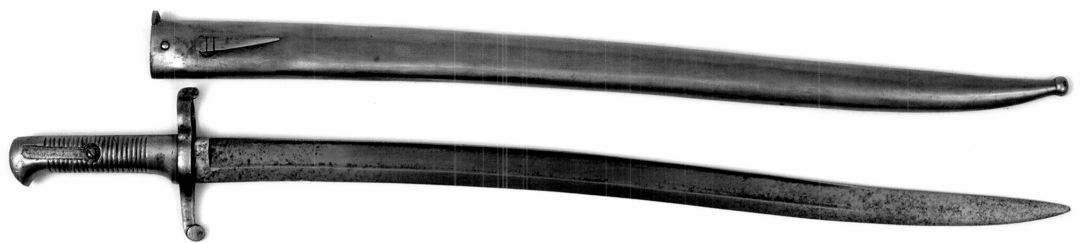

it through 90 degrees and re-fixing it. A new mortise was cut forward of the locking ring, to align with the rotated section, and the old mortise was filled. A less complicated conversion was the **1876/95**, which had a cut in the bridge and a new locking ring to accept the higher sight of the Martini Enfield, but fitted to the right of the barrel. The Egyptians made quadrangular-bladed bayonets. They fitted the Martini Enfield and Remington rifles but were of noticeably poorer quality than the British Ordnance bayonets.

British Long Lee and SMLE rifles and bayonets provided the bulk of Egyptian weaponry for the first half of the 20th century. During the early 1950s, Egypt also used the Belgian FN ABL export rifle and **1949** bayonet. A copy of the Swedish AG 42 Ljungman rifle was adopted in 7.92mm caliber as the Hakim 49. The **Hakim 49** bayonet owes much to the Swedish **1896**. The Egyptian bayonet retains the blade, scabbard and release mechanism of the **1896**, but has a new hilt with wooden grips. The Hakim rifle was later upgraded to the Soviet 7.62mm cartridge and renamed the Rashid. With its leanings toward the Soviets during the Cold War, Egypt was to adopt the AK47 and later a version of the AKM. The AKM bayonet was the same as the Soviet AKM II but with brown grips.

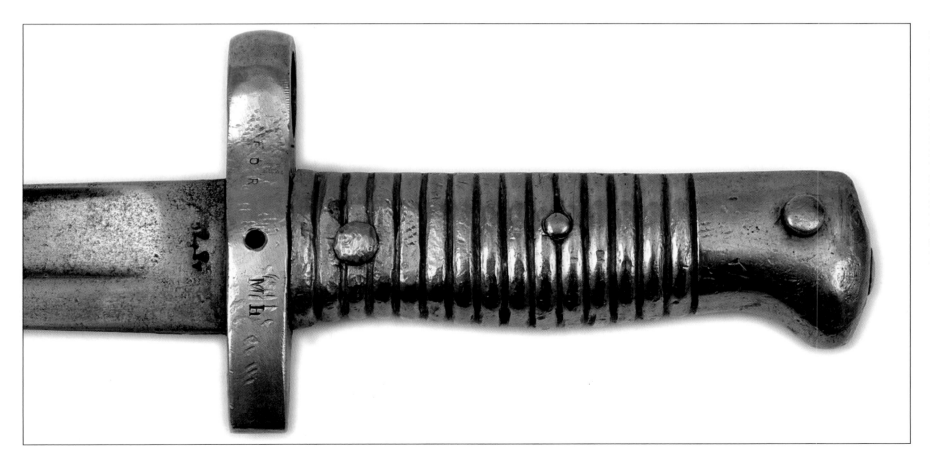

ABOVE **Martini Enfield M1914 bayonet. This bayonet was converted from a Remington 1869; it retains the unmodified scabbard as only the crossguard was altered.**

LEFT **The crossguard of this M1914 bayonet is marked "FOR MH," meaning that it fitted the Martini Henry. This was an erroneous stamping as it actually fits the .303in Martini Enfield rifle. It is assumed that the Egyptians did not differentiate between the original Martini Henry .577in rifle and the modified version with .303in barrel, the Martini Enfield. The scales logo on the ricasso shows that the blade was originally made by Alan Coppel of Solingen.**

ABOVE An Egyptian-made quad-rangular socket bayonet for the Remington rifle. The Remington was a breechloader and as such the bayonet only required a short elbow between the socket and blade. The bayonet blade was still orientated to the right side of the rifle to give access to the under barrel cleaning rod.

BELOW The Belgian SAFN M1949 was exported to several countries including Argentina, Egypt, Belgian Congo, Brazil, Columbia, Indonesia, Luxembourg and Venezuela. This example is an ex-Egyptian bayonet bearing an Arabic serial number. The M1949 rifle and bayonet were not used by the Belgian armed forces. (ABL)

RIGHT Hilt detail of the left side of a Belgian-made M1949 bayonet. The Arabic numerals on the pommel translate as "25212." The mortise slot has a typical Mauser-style "T-O" configuration.

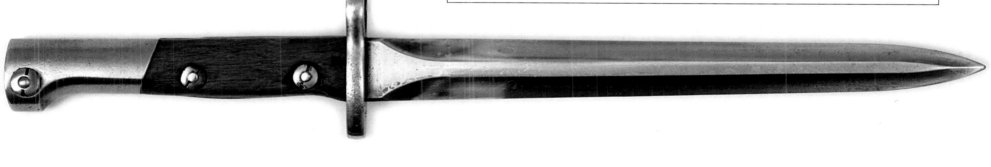

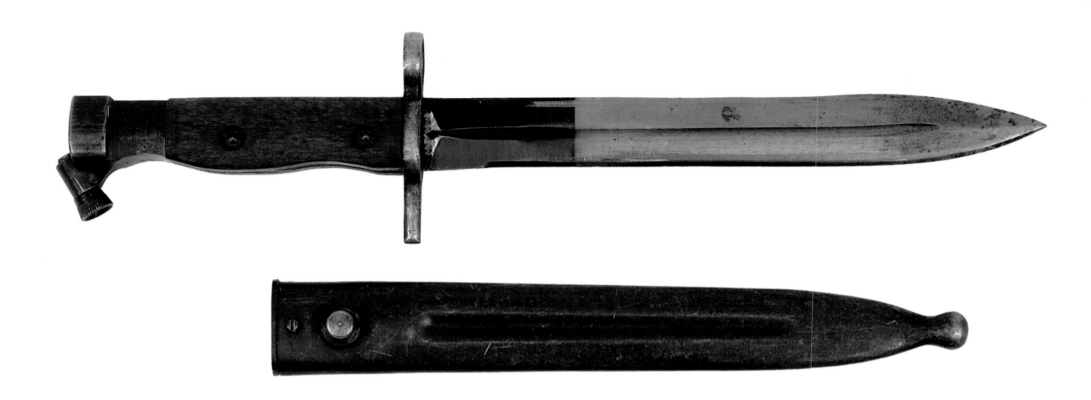

ABOVE The Egyptian 7.92mm Hakim M1949 rifle was a copy of the Swedish AG 42 Ljungman rifle. The bayonet of the Hakim 49 is more than similar to the Swedish 1896, having the same scabbard, blade and attachment mechanism, but with wood grips.

LEFT This view of the pommel of the Hakim bayonet shows the bayonet release catch, an unusual, yet nonetheless effective, Swedish design. However, it was undoubtedly easier to manipulate in the Egyptian climate than it would have been in a Swedish winter using gloved hands.

Finland

	Overall length	Blade length	Muzzle ring
1927	411mm	298mm	16mm
M62	265mm	159mm	N/A
Training bayonet	292mm	190mm	19.5mm

Finland was originally a part of Sweden but the Swedes' territorial claim had long been disputed by Russia. Finland was eventually ceded to Russia in 1809, becoming an autonomous Duchy within Russia. Following the Russian Revolution, Finland became an independent republic, but not without a civil war that saw a Soviet defeat. Despite land losses and defeat by the Russians in World War II, Finland retained her independence in the postwar period.

Whilst Swedish weapons had armed the Finns in the 18th century, Russian weapons were predominant after 1809. Following the Revolution and Finnish independence, the Russian Mosin Nagant and **1891** *pistin* (bayonet) were the principal infantry arms, the bayonet being issued with a leather scabbard in Finnish service. The Finns were to modify the Mosin Nagant action to produce their own series of rifles. These included the M91 carbine, M27, M28, M28/30, M30 and M39 rifles., the bayonets for these rifles, were generally similar, with the exception of the bayonet for the M39 rifle, differing only in minor detail. The illustrated bayonet model **1927** is typical of the Finnish bayonets of the interwar years. The exceptionally scarce 1939 bayonet had a much shorter blade and was provided with a leather sheath rather than a steel scabbard. It has been widely reproduced for the collectors' market.

After World War II Finland developed her own self-loading rifle, the 7.62mm Valmet M60, with a modified version issued in 1962. The M60 resembled the Russian AK47, and operates in the same manner. A 5.56mm version was later produced as the M71. The very rare bayonet for the M60 was similar to the Italian folding SMG bayonets of the late 1930s. It had wooden grips and a leather sheath. The standard **M62** bayonet for the M62 and M71 rifles was based upon hunting knife design, and this reflected its principal use. It was a simple and efficient design. Not unlike the Czech VZ58, it had a green leather scabbard that enclosed the blade and most of the ribbed plastic grips. The grips were embossed with the manufacturer's name,

The 1927 bayonet had an extended, quillon-like and round crossguard, but was otherwise of regular pattern. Only the press catch and scabbard were blued, other metalwork was polished white metal. This example was made by "HACKMAN & Co."

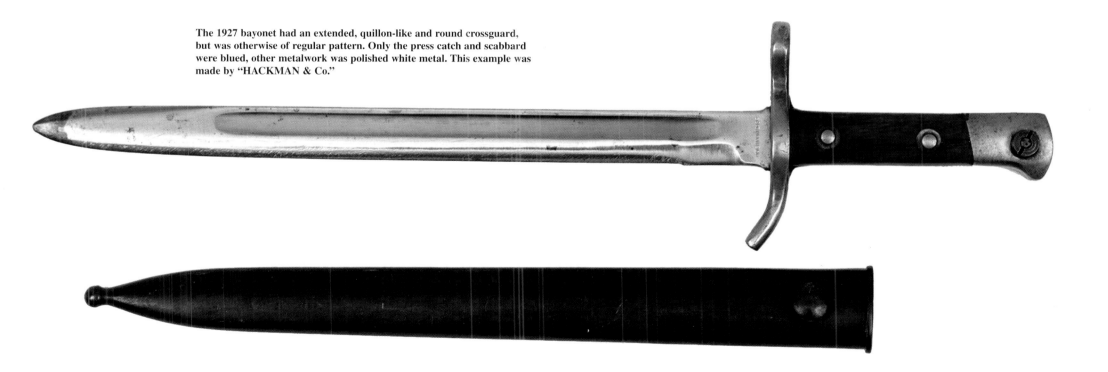

Fiskars. The blade was of high-quality steel. Heavily parkerized, it had a finely sharpened edge not usually found on bayonets, which made it an excellent general-purpose knife. The **M62** is still used on the current Valmet M62/76 rifle.

The Finns introduced a special (fencing) training bayonet in the 1960s. Made entirely of rubber, it was a safe but effective training device that fitted the old and obsolete M39 rifle. This is one of only a very few specially made training bayonets, and the only pattern made of rubber.

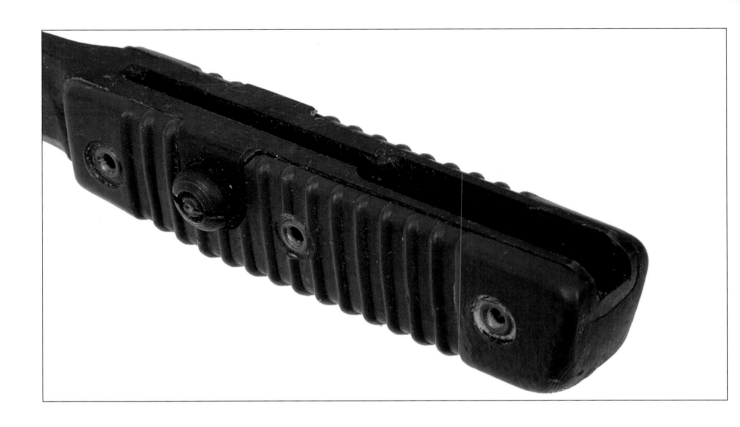

BELOW Finnish M62 bayonet used on the Valmet M62 and 62/76 rifles. Fiskars, whose name is embossed into the right grip, made the bayonet. The blade is exceptionally sharp and holds a keen edge, making this bayonet a useful general-purpose knife when operating in the field. The design of the bayonet and scabbard owes more to typical Finnish hunting knife design than that of a bayonet.

RIGHT An exceptionally long attachment groove negated the need for a muzzle ring. The release catch was positioned well forward on the grip making it far easier to operate than the standard pommel fitted catch, particularly with cold or gloved fingers.

LEFT The Finns adopted a rubber training bayonet in the early 1960s. It was designed to fit obsolete bolt-action weapons such as the Mosin Nagant-based M39 rifle. It was attached using a muzzle ring and an aperture in the rear of the bayonet hilt into which the rifle-cleaning rod was fitted, the bayonet being adequately retained by its tight fit. The right side of the bayonet is embossed "6550," just below the muzzle ring. The muzzle ring was frequently torn in use; many examples of the training bayonet have been repaired.

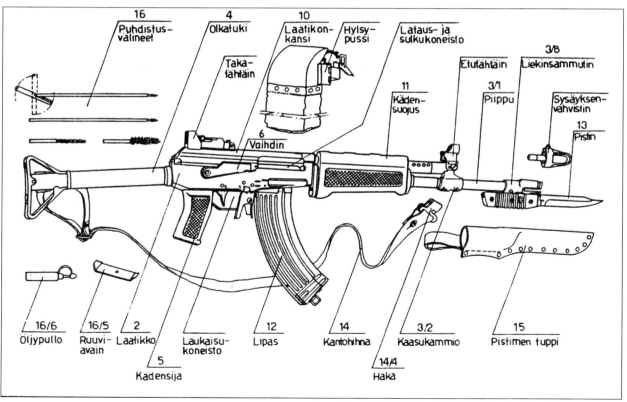

16	4	10	
Puhdistus-välineet	Olkatuki	Laatikon-kansi	Hylsy-pussi

Lataus- ja sulkukoneisto

Taka-tähtäin

6
Vaihdin

3/8
Liekinsammutin

Etutähtäin

11
Käden-suojus

3/1
Piippu

Sysäyksen-vähvistin

13
Pistin

16/6
Öljypullo

16/5
Ruuvi-avain

2
Laatikko

Laukaisu-koneisto

12
Lipas

14
Kantohihna

3/2
Kaasukammio

15
Pistimen tuppi

5
Kadensija

14/A
Haka

LEFT Extract from a Finnish Army manual showing the Valmet rifle with the M62 bayonet fitted. (Finnish Army)

France

	Overall length	Blade length	Muzzle ring
1866	694mm	571mm	22.6mm
1874	643mm	522mm	17.6mm
1886	639mm	521mm	15mm
1886/35	459mm	340mm	15mm
1892	514mm	392mm	13mm
1914	521mm	405mm	15mm
M36	430mm	N/A	N/A
M36/39	384mm	N/A	N/A
MAS 56	340mm	216mm	22mm
FAMAS	340mm	216mm	22mm

France was possibly the birthplace of the bayonet, and it was the French who invented the locking ring, both basal and median, and who from 1688 were the originators of many designs. In 1840, France was to introduce a novel blade type that was to be copied worldwide, the re-curving "yataghan" blade. The Mle. 1840 *Baionnette* had a ribbed brass hilt and crossguard. The all-steel scabbard had a frog loop through which the frog strap was buckled. This was the standard method of attaching the frog to French bayonet scabbards. The 1840 bayonet design was short lived, as the Mle. 1842, which was similar to the preceding design but had a blade some 50mm longer and a stronger iron crossguard, replaced it only two years after its

BELOW Yataghan-bladed 1866 bayonet. The king's-head mark on the ricasso shows that Gebrüder Weyersberg made this bayonet in Solingen, Germany. The black leather frog, missing a section of the attachment strap, was originally patent leather.

RIGHT A British landing party return to their ship following operations against the Vichy French in Madagascar. One of the Marines has a French 1866 bayonet tucked into his 1908 web belt, a trophy taken from the French garrison.

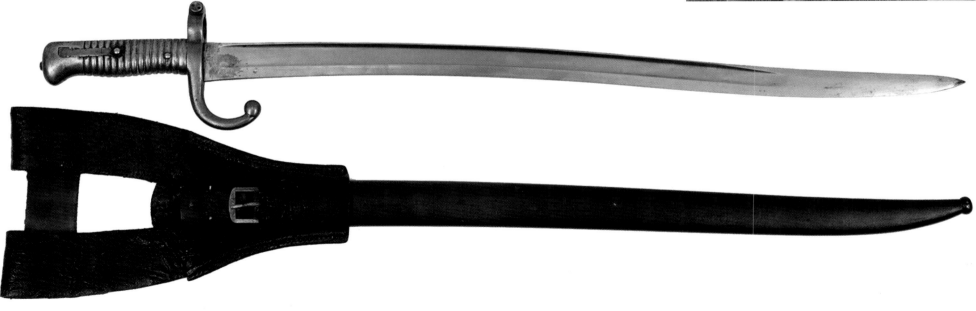

introduction; both patterns had a short rear-swept quillon and were used on the 18mm 1840 and 1840/2 rifles respectively. The year 1859 saw the leaf spring of the Mle. 1842 bayonet replaced with an internal coil spring on all newly manufactured bayonets. The resulting modified bayonet is generally referred to as the Mle. 1842/59. The well-known **Mle. 1866** bayonet soon superseded it. Similar to the earlier yataghan bayonets it had a lighter blade and reverted to the simple leaf-spring catch release. The crossguard terminated in a long forward-swept quillon with finial, whilst the muzzle ring incorporated a small adjustment screw to allow for manufacturing tolerances when fitted to the rifle. The 11mm 1866 Chassepot rifle was an improved version of the German Dreyse needle-fire system. It was used against the Prussians during the Franco-Prussian War of 1870–71.

The Chassepot rifle was soon modernized and upgraded to take a metallic cartridge, and the result was the Gras 1874 rifle. The bayonet developed for the new rifle provided a departure from the long yataghan blades previously employed by the French. The **Mle. 1874** bayonet had a "T"-section blade married to a wood-gripped hilt with brass pommel. It was the first standard-issue French bayonet to have wooden grips. Although the blade was much lighter than those of the preceding yataghan bayonets it was a strong design, but could only be used as a thrusting weapon. In keeping with current thinking, the crossguard extended to form a quillon that was riveted to the blade tang. The **Mle. 1874** Gras was the last French bayonet to be routinely engraved with the manufacturer's details and date of manufacture on the blade back, close to the hilt. Although a few very early-production **Mle. 1892** bayonets can also be found engraved, the majority are unmarked**.**

The 1886 Lebel rifle was issued with the cruciform-bladed **Mle. 1886** bayonet with a 520mm long blade that was later to epitomise the image of the World War I "*Poilu*," although stocks of the old **Mle. 1866** and **Mle. 1874** bayonets remained on issue to second-line troops throughout the war. The **Mle. 1886** was an inherently fragile design. Adopted at a time when most nations were looking at introducing knife bayonets, it went against international thinking and natural bayonet development. The decision to adopt this form of bayonet was, at best, uninspired. The bayonet's white-metal hilt, which was later made in brass or steel, had a swept-forward quillon and a novel attachment mechanism. A standard muzzle ring fitted over the rifle barrel with the release catch immediately behind the crossguard. There was no mortise cut into the hilt but

BELOW "*La Pousée*," pushing away an opponent with the rifle prior to delivering a thrust. An illustration from *Les Principes du Combat à la Baionnette*.

BELOW An attempt at reducing the excessive weight of the yataghan bayonets carried by French troops resulted in the narrow "T"-form blade of the 1874 bayonet. Having wood grips reduced the amount of metal used in the hilt, although brass was retained for the pommel. The two dark circles on the pommel are the pins used to secure the pommel to the tang.

instead a raised circular section on the end of the pommel fitted into a recess on the rifle's forend. The bayonet underwent some modification. Firstly, in 1893, a simpler model replaced the earlier type of round press catch. The most visible modification produced the **Mle. 1886/15** bayonet. This change occurred during World War I with the deletion of the quillon on all bayonets produced from 1915. A number of earlier bayonets were retrospectively modified, but it would seem that the vast majority retained their quillon. In 1935 a number of **1886** bayonets were further modified by having their long blades shortened to 335mm, the resulting **1886/35** bayonet conformed to the international move towards shorter bayonets, also remedied the bayonet's propensity for breaking. All of the earlier variants can be found modified to the shorter length **1886/35**, and many bayonets had previously had their points reground when the tips broke leaving them slightly shorter than the prescribed length. The **1886** bayonet and its variants also fitted the Mannlicher Berthier 1916 rifle, which should not be confused with the earlier Mannlicher Berthier 1892 carbine.

The **Mle. 1892** bayonet was introduced for use on the Mannlicher Berthier artillery carbine. Early examples had black horn or composition grips held by small steel rivets. These were found to be somewhat weak, and were replaced with wooden grips and larger rivets. A forward-curving quillon was standard on French bayonets, but many examples had the quillon partially removed during 1915 when they were declared obsolete. The quillon was shortened on the **Mle. 1892** bayonets but not completely removed as the weapon serial number was

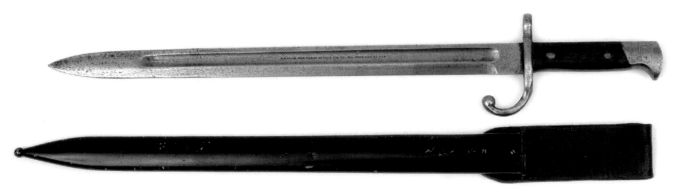

LEFT French bayonets of the later 19th century, from the 1840 pattern, have the manufacturer's marking engraved on the back of the blade. This 1874 bayonet has a typical period marking showing the bayonet was made in "PARIS – OUDRY – 1880." It was not possible to mark the 1886 bayonets in this way. Although the early-production 1892 bayonets had a manufacturer's engraving applied, the practice soon died out and the majority of 1892 bayonets are unmarked.

BOTTOM LEFT In 1914 France purchased a number of M1902 Remington rifles chambered for the 8mm Lebel cartridge. They were issued with the US made Mlle. 1914 bayonet. The accompanying steel scabbard had a typically American integral leather belt loop.

ABOVE 1874 bayonet fitted to a Gras rifle. The bayonet was fixed to the right side of the barrel. Of note is the long tenon (extension of the bayonet bar) that ran the length of the bayonet hilt back and engaged with the cut-out in the lower edge of the muzzle ring. A short tenon bar was fitted on the opposite side of the barrel and mated with the cut-out in the upper part of the muzzle ring (see also the comparison with the 1866 and 1869 bayonet hilts).

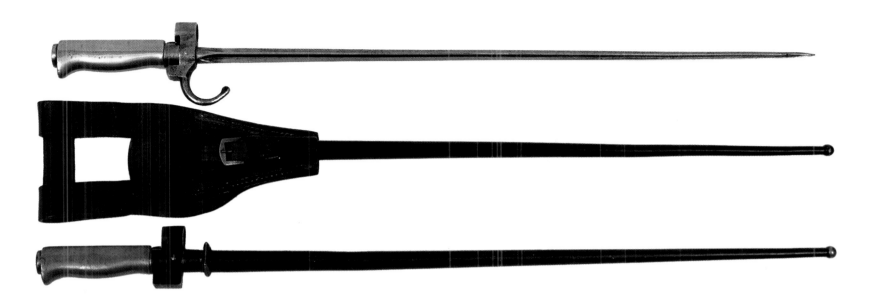

generally stamped on it, close to the crossguard. The blade was notched either side, near to the ricasso. The notches engaged with springs in the steel scabbard to hold the blade firmly in place. Interestingly, the back of the blade of the **1892** is fullered near to the point. The pommel had no mortise slot but a hole at the end that mated with an extension bracket on the rifle.

Like all of the combatant nations, France found herself unacceptably short of modern weapons at the outbreak of World War I. To help overcome this shortfall a number of M1902 Remington rifles were purchased from the United States. They were chambered for the 8mm Lebel cartridge and were supplied with the **Mle. 1914** bayonet, a long 405mm-blade version of the standard short-blade export bayonet as supplied to Mexico. The left fuller of the blade was marked "REMINGTON ARMS-UNION METALIC CTG. CO., REM-WORKS, ILLION, N.Y. USA."

Despite France's important input into the early development of the bayonet, the 20th century was to see little progress of any note. In 1936 France adopted a new 7.5mm rifle, the MAS 36, produced by Manufacture d'Armes de St. Etienne. The rifle had a simple spike bayonet with a short cruciform-section blade similar to the **1896**. It was stored reversed in a socket beneath the fore-end of the stock, reversing to fix in its extended position, and therefore requiring no scabbard. A shorter version of the **M36** bayonet was used with the folding-stock MAS 36/39 rifle. Apart from the reduced length, the **M36/39** bayonet was identical to the **M36**. In the postwar

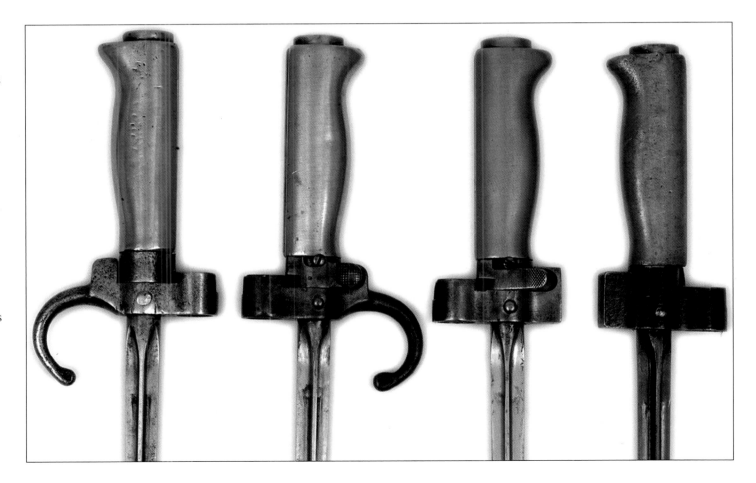

ABOVE French 1886 bayonet fitted to the 1886 Lebel rifle. This was a long combination that led to the Germans adopting the S98 bayonet on their G98 rifle in order to counter the reach of the *Poilu* in any possible future combat.

ABOVE In 1935 a number of the 1886 and 1886/15 bayonets were cut down. The short blade of the 1886/35 bayonet was considerably stronger than its predecessors, which were prone to breakage. This 1896/35 was cut down from an 1886/15, the scabbard being shortened to match the new blade length.

ABOVE A *Poilu* of the 53rd Infantry Regiment armed with a Mannlicher Berthier 1916 rifle and the 1886/93/16 bayonet, which was also used on the 1886 (Lebel) rifle.

ABOVE RIGHT 1892 bayonet for the Mannlicher Berthier artillery carbine. This is the second pattern with wood grips. The small notch in the lower blade edge, just forward of the crossguard, engaged with the scabbard spring retaining the bayonet in the scabbard.

years, the MAS 36 continued in service seeing limited use in Indo-China and Algeria. As with the **1886** bayonet, the **M36** was only of use as a stabbing weapon and served no other practical purpose, but unlike the **1886** it could not easily be used as a handheld weapon as it had no grip. Germany copied the design of the **M36** bayonet for use on the *Fallschirmjäger Gewehr* 42, at first using cut-down French bayonets but later producing their own bayonet that differed in having a much narrower ridge to the center of the hilt tube.

A double muzzle ring was an unusual feature of the **MAS 56** bayonet issued with the 7.5mm MAS 49/56 rifle. It had a standard crossguard ring and a second ring at the pommel end. Despite the double ring arrangement the length of the hilt meant that it was not uncomfortable when used as a handheld weapon, the rearmost muzzle ring did not interfere with the grip, unlike the one on the Russian **AK47** bayonet. This

almost unique method of attachment was necessary as the 49/56 rifle was fitted with a permanently attached grenade launcher. The release method was similar to that used on the Norwegian Krag **1894**. Pivoting internally a small stud protruded from the grip back and engaged the rifle's flash eliminator. The bayonet had a small extension stud on the upper edge of the ricasso, adjoining the muzzle ring into which it extended slightly. This engaged a recess in the scabbard throat and helped secure the bayonet firmly. The close-fitting steel scabbard was contoured to fit the blade, which came in two different styles. It had a leather belt loop and hilt strap that also incorporated a U.S.-style belt hook. Interestingly, the **MAS 56** was the first true knife bayonet to be adopted by the French, many years after it had become standard in most other armies.

In the early 1980s, the MAS 49/56 rifle was replaced by the 5.56mm bullpup FAMAS rifle. The new weapon retained the

MAS **56**-style bayonet with the second-pattern blade. The **FAMAS** bayonet had a new plastic scabbard with a webbing belt loop and hilt strap. The bayonet's ricasso extension stud engaged with a short spring on the scabbard throat, helping to retain the bayonet in the scabbard. Apart from the scabbard, the bayonet issued with the FAMAS was identical to that issued with the MAS 49/56, and, like the German **G3** bayonet, the **FAMAS** fitted above the rifle barrel.

During the period that France was rearming with the FAMAS rifle, the Swiss Stg 540 was issued in some numbers. Made under license by Manurhin, the accompanying **540/542** bayonet (see Switzerland) had a tubular hilt with a plastic outer sleeve forming the grips. It was similar to the Belgian **FAL Type C** bayonet. The all-plastic scabbard had a nylon belt loop with hilt fastener. The French license-built version of the 540 rifle and the 7.62mm Stg 542 variant were exported to a number of countries: Chile, Bolivia, Ecuador, Indonesia, Jordan, Lebanon, Nicaragua, Oman, Paraguay and the Seychelles, as well as a number of African nations.

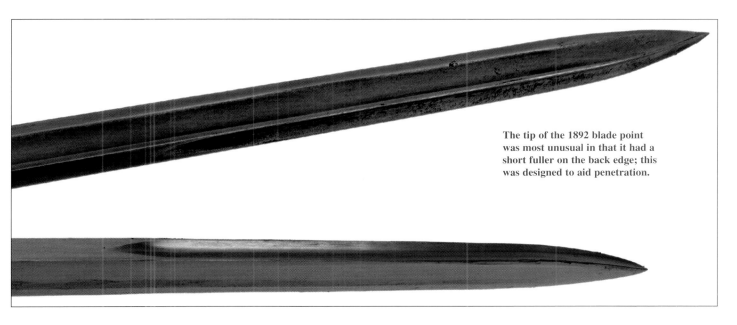

The tip of the 1892 blade point was most unusual in that it had a short fuller on the back edge; this was designed to aid penetration.

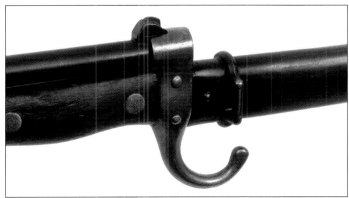

ABOVE The 1892 bayonet fitted to a Mannlicher Berthier artillery carbine. The recess in the top of the muzzle ring engages the foresight.

LEFT 1892 hilts. At left, the right side of a second-pattern bayonet with wood grips and, at right, the left side of a first-pattern with black composition grips. The bayonet frog was originally issued with the 1886 bayonet, it has been modified to fit the 1892 by cutting slits in the leather alongside the frog strap loop and a large vertical slit in the reverse bottom edge.

RIGHT A French Army messenger dog and handler photographed during the early stages of the blitzkrieg. The handler carries a Mannlicher Berthier carbine and an 1892 bayonet. The bayonet has the shortened quillon, a modification carried out in 1916.

BELOW Detail of the MAS 36 hilt showing the fixing mechanism. When one end of the double-ended fixing was used to secure the bayonet, the other provided the release catch. It was pivoted in the center, and pushing down the exposed end depressed the opposite "locked" end.

ABOVE LEFT Colonial French troops from the 1st Regiment of Moroccan Spahis. Both are armed with Lebel rifles and the 1886/93 bayonet.

BOTTOM The M36 bayonet was made in two lengths. Above is the original long version for the MAS 36 rifle, and below the shorter version used with the MAS 36 CR 39 "paratroop" rifle.

ABOVE Legionnaires of the French Foreign Legion parade with MAS 36 rifles. The bayonets are reversed in the rifles' fore-ends, but the hilts remain visible. England, July 1940.

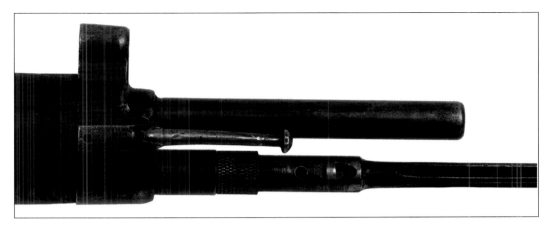

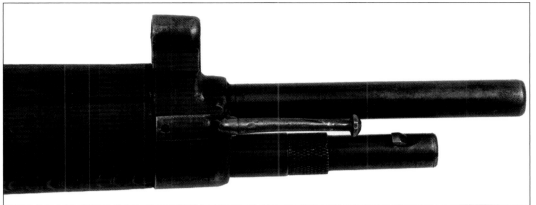

ABOVE LEFT The MAS 36 bayonet was stored in a recess beneath the barrel of the rifle; it was removed from the fixed position, reversed and re-inserted, in the fixed position. This method removed the need for a scabbard.

ABOVE When stored, the blade of the MAS 36 bayonet passed into the recess beneath the barrel of the MAS 36 rifle. The rod-like extension between the barrel and bayonet is a stacking hook.

LEFT Officers of the Cadets de la France Libre parade their colors past the statue of Marshal Foch, London 1941. They are armed with P14 rifles and No. 3 Mk. I (P13) bayonets.

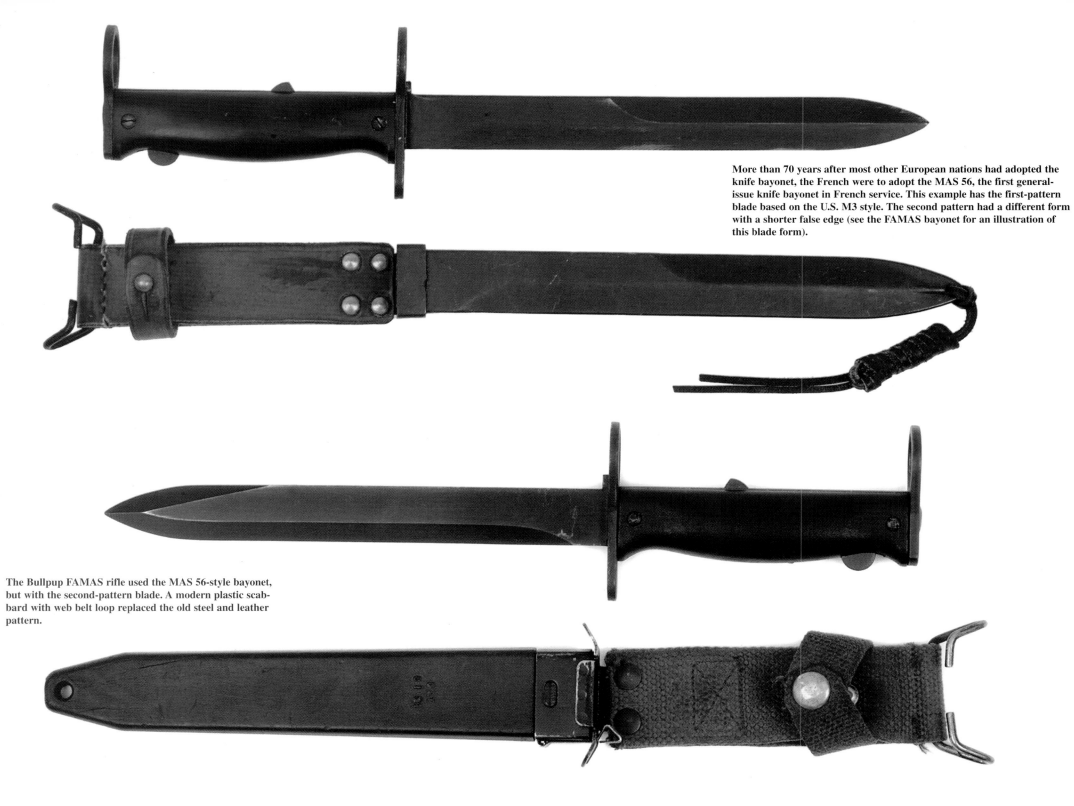

More than 70 years after most other European nations had adopted the knife bayonet, the French were to adopt the MAS 56, the first general-issue knife bayonet in French service. This example has the first-pattern blade based on the U.S. M3 style. The second pattern had a different form with a shorter false edge (see the FAMAS bayonet for an illustration of this blade form).

The Bullpup FAMAS rifle used the MAS 56-style bayonet, but with the second-pattern blade. A modern plastic scabbard with web belt loop replaced the old steel and leather pattern.

ABOVE LEFT Typical FAMAS bayonet markings include the maker and date of manufacture. The scabbard shows "DLT 01 81" for January 1981; the bayonet is marked "DLT 03 81" for March 1981.

LEFT Hilt of the FAMAS bayonet showing the unusual double muzzle ring arrangement. This design was carried over from the MAS 49/56 rifle, which had an integral grenade launcher that required this unusual feature. The locking mechanism is a modified Krag type.

ABOVE The tang extension stud on the FAMAS (visible on the lower edge of the muzzle ring) engaged with a simple spring clip on the scabbard to hold the blade securely.

Germany

	Overall length	Blade length	Muzzle ring
1829/30	485mm	400mm	23mm
1854	512mm	435mm	23mm
1871	608mm	465mm	17.3mm
S98	654mm	521mm	N/A
S98/05	502mm	370mm	N/A
S84/98	384mm	251mm	N/A
S98/14	441mm	308mm	N/A
Typical ersatz	441mm	310mm	*
S98/05 ersatz	480mm	360mm	*
German police	445mm	329mm	N/A
VZ24	432mm	298mm	N/A
G3	305mm	165mm	22mm
Rohrbajonett R1	292mm	162mm	22mm

* Ersatz bayonets have a double aperture to the open top muzzle ring. This allowed fitting to the G98 and G88.

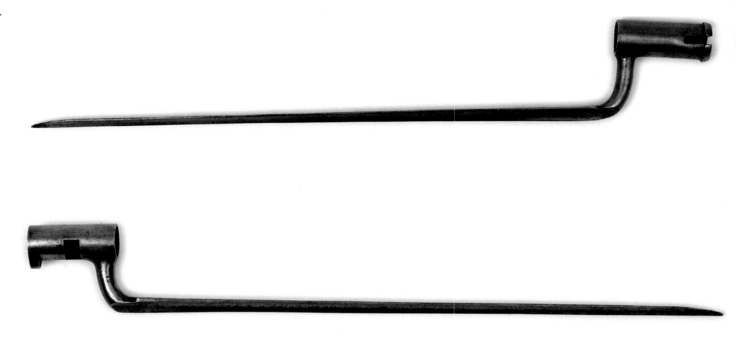

Germany existed for many years as a number of self-governing states. They were brought together under Prussian influence to form a German Empire only in the mid-19th century. Two representative bayonets from the pre-unification era are illustrated in this work, the **1829/30**, issued to troops in Wurttemberg, and the Hanoverian **1854**. In 1871 Germany triumphed in the Franco-Prussian War. Following the victory, Bismarck united the Germanic states and the Prussian King became the new Kaiser of the greater Germany. The first new standard-issue "German" bayonet was the *Seitengewehr* **1871**; a fine brass-handled weapon with a re-curving "S" quillon. This weapon accompanied the bolt-action 11mm Mauser *Infanterie Gewehr* 1871. The next major firearm issued to the German soldier was the Mauser 71/84. Again in 11mm the new rifle had a six-round tubular magazine. The S71/84 bayonet was the first true standard-issue knife bayonet. It had a short 255mm blade and a wooden-gripped hilt with a distinctive-shaped tang. The Mauser bolt-action rifle was to be the dominant infantry weapon worldwide, and was to shape future rifle design well into the 20th century. In various models, it almost entirely equipped the armies of South American nations as well as being the principal infantry firearm in the Middle East, Far East and Europe.

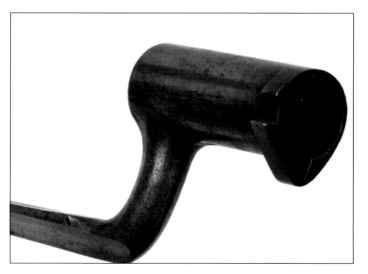

TOP 1829/30 socket bayonet used by Wurttemberg. It has a very short straight slot and originally had a basal locking ring, now missing.

ABOVE Hanoverian *Pickelgewehre "neuen Modell" von 1854*. It has a standard triangular-form blade and a heavy socket with an "L"-shaped slot. The elbow is marked with the number "12."

LEFT Left rear view of the 1854 bayonet's socket showing the narrow bridge allowing for passage of the foresight. The collar has a lip for a spring-catch fixing similar to that used on British bayonets.

OPPOSITE RIGHT German *Landsturm* reservists were generally armed with obsolete weapons, with the newer models going to the front. These reservists are armed with the Mauser 1871 and its brass-hilted *Seitengewehr* 1871 bayonet.

In 1898, the German Army adopted a new rifle, the *Gewehr* 98. The bayonet for this and subsequent German rifles was to have no muzzle ring. Many factors affect accuracy of shooting, but ideally the barrel of a rifle should be "free-floating"—not in contact with any fixture or fitting other than where it is attached to the breech. In military weapons, this is impractical. Undue wear or obstructions at the muzzle are particularly relevant to loss of accuracy; the muzzle ring of a bayonet did much to affect the movement of the rifle barrel as a fired bullet passed straight through it. It was considered that a long bayonet bar on the rifle was sufficient to securely hold the bayonet without the use of a muzzle ring. The muzzle ring required extremely tight manufacturing tolerances. Removing it from the design reduced labor and costs, without adversely affecting the security of the fixed bayonet. A further benefit was the enhanced accuracy of the weapon. The long bayonet accompanying the new 7.92mm *Gewehr* 98 was adopted as the *Seitengewehr* 98. The **S98** had a long thin blade with a "pipe-back" to the point, grooved wooden grips and a small swept-back quillon. Early bayonets manufactured prior to 1902 had a fragile one-piece "wrap-around" grip. Later examples (*nA, neuer Art*—new pattern) have the universal two-piece wooden grips. A copy of the **S98** bayonet was exported to Peru where it entered service as the **1909** pattern. A short saw-back bladed bayonet with a bird's-head pommel was introduced for specialist troops, initially machine gunners and, later, airship units. The ornate KS98 design was later used as the basis for walking-out bayonets, the pattern still being used for this purpose at the start of World War II.

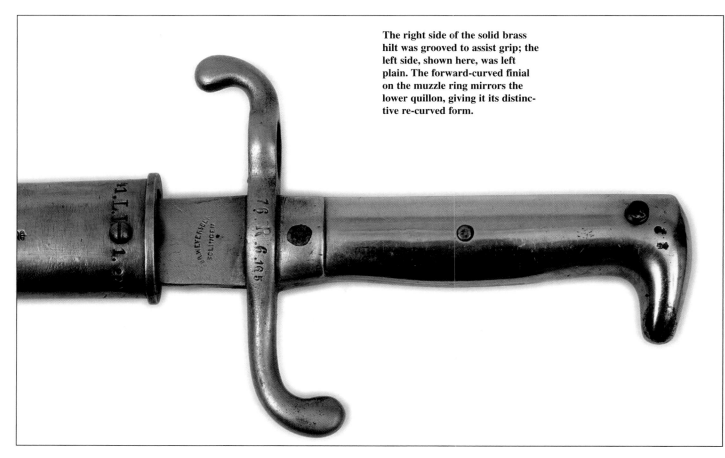

The right side of the solid brass hilt was grooved to assist grip; the left side, shown here, was left plain. The forward-curved finial on the muzzle ring mirrors the lower quillon, giving it its distinctive re-curved form.

RIGHT The S1871 was an attractive bayonet with a brass hilt and re-curving quillon. It was the standard bayonet for use with the Mauser 1871.

The year 1905 saw the introduction of the **S98/05** bayonet. With a hilt similar to the **S98,** it had a longer quillon and a distinctive bulbous point to the blade, earning it the nickname of the "butcher bayonet." The introduction of the *Karbiner* 98AZ in 1908 led to the modification of the **S98/05** hilt. The carbine only had a short section of barrel protruding at the fore-end, with the bayonet bar immediately below it. This meant that, when mounted, the bayonet grips were actually forward of the muzzle. Muzzle flash from the short rifle scorched the bayonet grips, and thus a flashguard was added to the back of the hilt from 1915. This new type was called the **S98/05** *nA* and the old the *aA* (*alter Art*—old pattern). Both types were issued with plain blades for infantry units and saw-back for pioneers. The saw-back was found to be wholly useless as a cutting tool and was later deleted from production, with many pioneer bayonets having the saw-back ground off. During World War I, Britain made much propaganda of the Germans' use of saw-backed blades and the injuries they could cause, the British themselves chose to ignore their own previous use of saw-back blades. The first bayonets to receive the designation S84/98 appeared around 1905. They were old stocks of S71/84 bayonets modified for use with the G98 by the removal of the muzzle ring and the fitting of a new pommel of the type used on the **S98** bayonet, the latter requiring new "shaped" grips. In 1915 the designation was revived on newly produced bayonets. The new **S84/98** bayonets were a wartime expedient: shorter, less expensive and much simpler to produce than the **S98** or **S98/05**. They were also produced with saw-back blades, which,

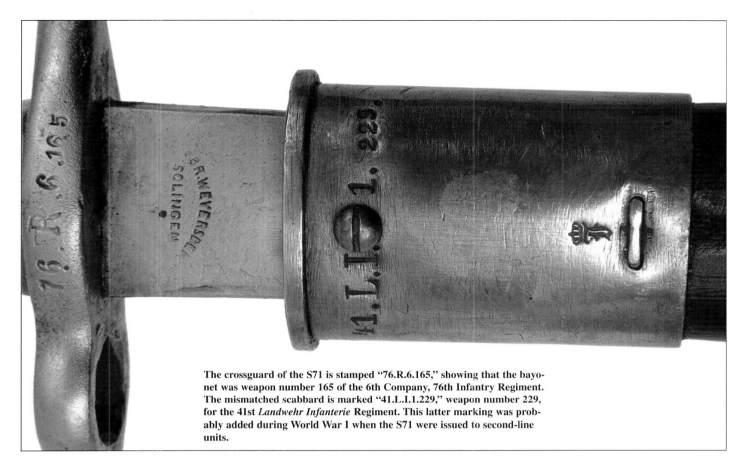

The crossguard of the S71 is stamped "76.R.6.165," showing that the bayonet was weapon number 165 of the 6th Company, 76th Infantry Regiment. The mismatched scabbard is marked "41.L.I.1.229," weapon number 229, for the 41st *Landwehr Infanterie* Regiment. This latter marking was probably added during World War I when the S71 were issued to second-line units.

BELOW **S98.** *aA* bayonet with two-piece grips. This example has no flashguard, although one was added to S98 bayonets manufactured later. The long blade gave good reach and was much stronger than the French 1886 bayonet, against which it was compared when commissioned for service.

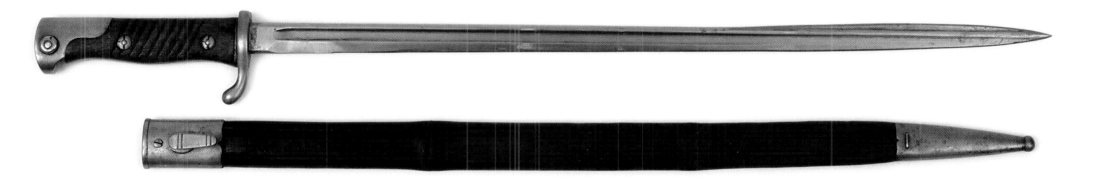

in keeping with general practice, were frequently ground off. The **S84/98** was to be the standard German bayonet from its introduction in 1915 until 1945.

The outbreak of World War I saw Germany facing a shortage of rifles and bayonets, and thus it was decided that export items would be taken up from the trade. The **S98/14** bayonet was one such example used in some quantity by German forces. Examples of the **S98/14** exist without a flashguard for use on the G98 and with a flashguard for the K98. Even after taking up bayonets from the trade, the German Army was still short of weapons. The quality and finish of the prewar bayonets was, of necessity, dispensed with and in 1915 the "ersatz" bayonet was issued. The ersatz bayonet did away with the refinements of shaped hilts and wooden grips. It became a mass-produced, simple and poorly finished shadow of the previously fine German blades. Many minor variants existed. Almost all had plain steel hilts with integral pommel and grips, and fullered or plain blades. A variant was based on the S98/05, and others were produced with brass hilts. During the war, all were issued with a field-gray painted overall finish.

The end of World War I saw Germany defeated and suffering greatly under the humiliating Treaty of Versailles that was to follow, which was to sow the seeds of resentment that would lead to a second worldwide conflict. In the 1930s, Germany rapidly rebuilt its armed forces under Hitler and the Nazi Party. In an effort to regain territories lost under the Treaty of Versailles, Hitler instigated policies of expansion and annexation. This greatly upset the political balance in Europe, and the eventual German and Russian invasion and partition of Poland provided the catalyst that started World War II. The **S84/98** remained the standard bayonet during World War II with production recommencing in 1935. The new bayonets differed slightly from World War I bayonets; World War I examples have full tang flashguards, the sides being visible in the underside of the grips. On the Third Reich examples, the sides of the flashguard are shorter and are not visible on the underside of the grips. Originally made of wood, grips were also manufactured from Bakelite from 1937 until 1944, when wood once again became an alternative due to the diminishing supply of Bakelite. **S84/98** scabbards of World War I and World War II also differ. A screw holds the internal blade-retention spring of the scabbard on both, but on World War I examples the screw head is on the front face of the scabbard above the frog stud, and on post-1935 scabbards it is on the right side. Although most World War I bayonets bore a maker's mark, only a few of those produced after 1935 did so. The majority were marked with a three digit number code with an "S" prefix, often called the "s-code," occasionally suffixed by a letter

BELOW S98 unit mark and inspection stamps. The reverse of the scabbard's topmount is marked with "139.R.12.212." This indicates the bayonet was weapon number 212, 12th Company, 139th Infantry Regiment. The pommel and topmount both bear small crowned inspection letters.

RIGHT A World War I seaman from the German *Matrosen Division II*, he is armed with the G98 rifle and S98 bayonet.

BOTTOM World War I walking-out bayonet. It has the hilt of the S98, which has a shaped pommel, accommodating contoured and grooved wooden grips, and the blade style of the S84/98.

ABOVE **The back of Imperial German bayonets carry an inspection mark and issue date. This S98/05 *aA* has a crowned "W" over "06." The "W" stands for the Prussian Kaiser Wilhelm II and the "06" for 1906. The crowned gothic letter is an inspection marking. Just visible on the cross-guard is "19. P4. 129" showing that the 4th Pioneer Regiment used this bayonet.**

indicating the year of manufacture. A serial number was also applied to the blade and scabbard. In 1940, the old "s-code" was discontinued and a new letter code was introduced, each manufacturer having a unique three-letter code.

During the Weimar period, the German police were issued a beautifully ornate service bayonet with eagle head pommel, horn grips and a clamshell guard. The long-bladed bayonet was later shortened under the Nazis and the clamshell was removed. The original Weimar grip device was also replaced by the Nazi police eagle. A small number of bayonets were later made with short blades and without the clamshell, but the majority of police bayonets encountered by collectors will show signs of having had the blade shortened and the guard ground off. The police bayonets can be found with scabbard bodies of either black or brown leather. The black scabbard was for municipal police, the brown being used by the rural police, the colors matching the uniform facings.

In the interwar years, many European nations were producing Mauser 98-type rifles made on German machinery, obtained as war reparations after the Treaty of Versailles. As

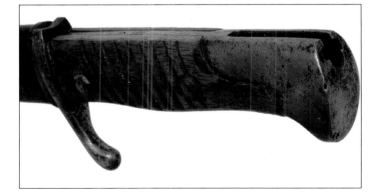

LEFT **Although the walking-out bayonet has a pommel mortise, it has no locking bar. The press catch, although present, does not work. Although this bayonet was never intended to be actually fitted to a rifle, the mortise slot does allow it to be fixed, but not locked in place.**

ABOVE **Variants of the S98/05 bayonet. From left to right: *aA* with no flashguard, extended muzzle ring "ears," and saw-back blade; steel-mounted leather-bodied scabbard; S98/05 *nA* with flashguard and saw-back blade; standard-pattern steel scabbard with leather belt frog; S98/05 *nA* with original saw-back blade removed; steel scabbard; S98/05 *nA* with flashguard made with a plain blade. (*aA* is *alter Art*—old pattern, with *nA, neuer art*—new pattern).**

LEFT In full pack and equipment, this World War I German soldier carries the S98/05 "butcher" bayonet attached to his *Gewehr* 98.

BELOW LEFT 1915. A German infantryman poses with G98 Rifle and S84/98 bayonet, one of the shortest bayonets issued during World War I.

RIGHT World War I S84/98 with original saw-back removed, made by Bontgen & Sabin; Standard World War I scabbard with leather frog; World War I S84/98 with plain blade form, manufactured by J.A. Henckels. The blade back is dated 1917. World War II scabbard marked "42 agv," made in 1942 by Berg and Co. Fitted with "cavalry" frog with hilt strap; World War II S84/98 with wood grips, ricasso marked "S/175g;" World War II scabbard marked "42 cof," indicating 1942 manufacture by Carl Eickhorn. This scabbard is fitted with a webbing bayonet frog as used by the Afrika Korps and later manufactured as an "ersatz" supplement to the leather frogs; World War II S84/98 with grooved bakelite grips. The blade is marked "F.W. Holler 1938."

Germany absorbed much of Europe into the "Greater Reich," the machinery and weapons once again became available to German forces. Amongst other material, Polish and Czech rifle and bayonet stocks were readily assimilated into the German armory, with some of the captured machinery being turned to producing newly made weapons for the Reich. In Czechoslovakia, the state factory at Brno became "Waffenfabrik Brunn AG" under German occupation. It produced rifles and **VZ24** bayonets modified to German specifications. The German-issue **VZ24** differed from the original Czech model in having no muzzle ring and being heavily blued overall. German inspection stamps were applied along with the standard "dot" three-letter code for Waffenfabrik Brunn AG. The Germans also adapted captured Czech bayonet frogs, dyeing them black and adding a hilt strap before issuing them with the modified Czech bayonets. In 1945, the combined might of the allied forces defeated Germany, and the short-lived fatherland of the Reich was subsequently divided between the Russians in the east and the British, French and Americans in the west. The western nations eventually allowed West Germany its freedom, forming the Federal Republic of Germany. Russia retained its powerful hold over East Germany, which became the German Democratic Republic under its Soviet rulers. West Germany was to become a bastion for NATO forces, with West Germany's membership in the organization affecting German development of rifles based on the 7.62mm and, later, the 5.56mm round. The West German contribution to NATO firepower was the G3 rifle. Introduced in 1959, it was based on the Spanish CETME rifle. The **G3** bayonet had ribbed plastic grips and a blade similar to the American **M3** knife blade. It fitted above the rifle barrel in an inverted position. The fixing method was unique to the **G3** and

BELOW LEFT S98/14 ricasso showing the "BK" within an oval frequently found on this type of bayonet.

ABOVE Typical World War I manufacturer's markings as found on S84/98 bayonets. At left, a standard blade bayonet made by J.A. Henckels, Zwillingswerk. At right, an S84/98 that has had the sawback removed. Bontgen & Sabin, Solingen, made this example.

BELOW S98/14 bayonet. The "pattern" for this type of bayonet apparently started out as part of an export order that, due to Germany's requirement for weapons, was taken up into German service, possibly having had the quillon and muzzle ring removed. However, it is believed that the true S98/14 was made from new. This example was for use with the G98. There are also known examples with flashguards, for use with the *Karabiner* 98.

ABOVE The most noticeable difference between World War I and World War II S84/98 bayonets is in the form of the flash guard. On the World War I example at left, the sides of the flashguard (which wraps around the tang) are just visible on the lower side of the hilt between the grips and the tang. On World War II bayonets, the flashguard does not extend to the lower edge of the hilt, instead the grips meet the tang directly.

consisted of a stud on the rear of the pommel, which fixed into the gas port of the rifle. The scabbard was based on the U.S. **M8**. The body had a distinct woodgrain finish that was unique to German-made scabbard bodies. The G3 was exported in large numbers to some 60 nations, as well as being made under license by Greece, Mexico, Norway, Pakistan, Portugal, Saudi Arabia and Turkey.

With the memory of World War II fading and the threat from the Warsaw Pact ever present, West Germany was soon free to undertake business ventures in the armaments industry, commercially producing rifles and bayonets for export. The Eickhorn Company made a number of bayonet variants that fitted popular weapon types. One of the earliest was the FN FAL Type 1, known in Germany as the *Rohrbajonett* **R1**. Similar to the standard FAL Type C bayonets, the German example has a distinctive edge seam caused by drop forging. Other commercial Eickhorn bayonets included the G3-type bayonets in standard **AG3** and long **G3L** blade lengths, the short having a black plastic scabbard and the long a woodgrain scabbard. The **EW77SS** was produced with the attachment mechanism used on the Swiss Stg 57, the design later forming the basis of the Stg 90 bayonet. Several bayonet types were manufactured for the M16 rifle and derivatives. The **KCB77**

M1 fitted the M16 or AR18 rifles. It was very different to the **M7** bayonet and it had a chunky square-form grip and a heavy clip-point saw-back blade, which formed a wirecutter attachment when fitted to the scabbard. A 1984 Eickhorn catalog listed the **KCB77 M1** bayonet at DM 55.98. wholesale, with a retail price of DM 93.30. A slightly modified version of the **KCB77M1** is currently issued in Spain as the KCB77M1/KH-JS. The **M7/S KH** offered a standard M7-style bayonet but with a wirecutter. The scabbard tip incorporated the wirecutter (in combination with the blade), a bottle-opener, wire-stripper/nail-puller and screwdriver. The KH in any Eickhorn designation indicated a detachable belt loop, an option on many bayonet types. This enabled the scabbard body to be taken off the belt without removing the hook attachments. For belts without belt-hook attachments, the scabbard was secured using a belt loop threaded over the equipment belt. The use of the detachable belt loop meant that other equipment could remain on the belt while removing the scabbard (such as on the **KCB77M1**). A modified copy of the standard U.S. **M7**, the **M7/S KH** bayonet fitted the M16 or AR18 rifles. Eickhorn also offered adaptors that allowed various combinations of bayonet and weapon types, such as fitting the M7 bayonet to the G3 rifle and so on.

BELOW The right hilt of the ersatz S98/05 bayonet. The sheet steel hilt is riveted to the tang. The open top muzzle ring has a double aperture, one slightly larger upper opening imposed over a smaller lower one, the small variation is just visible in this view. Common to most ersatz bayonets, this allowed the bayonet to fit the G98 and earlier weapons, including the G88 on which it fitted laterally, to the right side of the barrel jacket.

BELOW Ersatz bayonet based on the S98/05 bayonet. It has a ridged grip, swept-forward quillon and a blade similar to that of the S98/05, but with a less pronounced tip form. As with the S98/05, the ersatz version can be found with a saw-back blade and with the saw-back ground off. The scabbard tooling resembles the tooling found on the leather scabbard bodies, a superfluous addition on an ersatz bayonet.

LEFT Ersatz bayonets. These examples are typical of the many variants that can be encountered; all are made of steel and have open-topped muzzle rings. From left to right: an example with its original frog and *trodell*, the *trodell* colors signifying 10th Company; pattern with stepped back muzzle ring, scabbard made by FAG (Friedrich August Gobel); riveted sheet steel hilt, FAG scabbard (rear); unfullered blade, FAG scabbard; similar type with fullered blade and beaked pommel, ornate ridged scabbard; bulbous hilt type; variant with distinctive hilt.

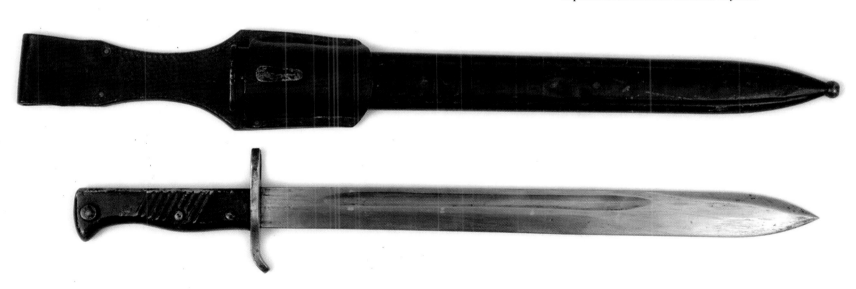

The current German Army weapons are the G3 and the G36 rifles. However, the German armed forces no longer issue bayonets. Under the auspices of the *Haager Landkriegsordnung*, the use of gas, anti-personnel mines, flamethrowers and bayonets has now been banned by the German military.

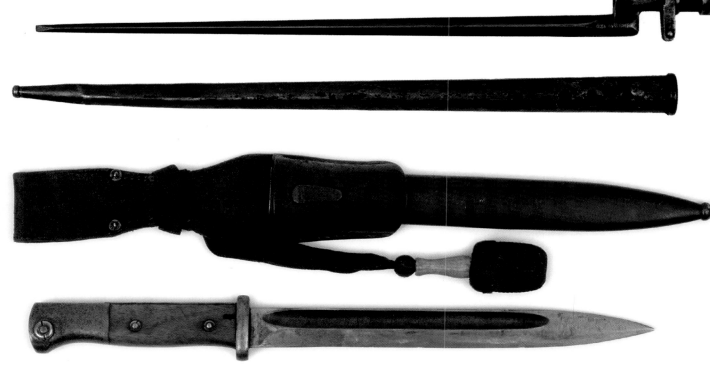

FAR LEFT A German pioneer from the 27th Battalion, he has an interesting combination of *Pickelhaube* and ersatz bayonet. Steel helmets were replacing the *Pickelhaube* at the time that the ersatz bayonet was being issued.

LEFT This mounted German soldier wears the standard World War II S84/98 bayonet on his left side.

LEFT In addition to ersatz bayonets, Germany utilized many captured weapons. This Russian 1891 socket bayonet was provided with a German-made scabbard for issue to second-line units. The Imperial eagle was frequently stamped on such captured bayonets.

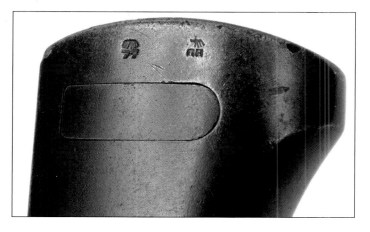

BELOW LEFT This S84/98 bayonet is dated 38 on the blade back and marked "Coppel g.m.b.h." on the ricasso, whilst the scabbard is stamped "S/239.k." The *trodell* (bayonet knot) attached to the frog would have been worn for walking-out and on parades in safe rear areas and in the Fatherland. As viewed, the knot has five sections: the strap (in green for battalion staff and 13th and 14th Companies, or gray for all others); slide (company color); stem (battalion color); crown (mirroring the slide, showing the company color); and tassel (like the strap, only in green or gray). Each section was individually colored, the combination serving to indicate the wearer's company. Battalion staff wore a green *trodell*, with only the stem colored to indicate the battalion number. The example here is colored to indicate infantry battalion staff of the 3rd Battalion (yellow stem).

ABOVE RIGHT S84/98 "*WaA*" *Waffenampt* mark. This early inspector's mark shows an eagle with "drop" wings, this is a pre-1938 stamp. The marking is on the pommel of a bayonet dated 1935, all major components can be found with inspectors' stamps.

CENTER RIGHT In 1938, a Nazi-type eagle with spread wings replaced the old drop-wing *waffenampt* eagle. The new mark is shown here on the pommel of a S84/98 bayonet dated from 1943.

RIGHT The S84/98 bayonet fitted to the K98 rifle. The long bayonet bar was considered to give sufficient support to the bayonet without the use of a muzzle ring.

LEFT S-code "S/175.G." It is believed that S/175 was allocated to Eickhorn and that the "G" indicated manufacture in 1935. Some manufacturers omitted the date coding and instead stamped the date on the blade back.

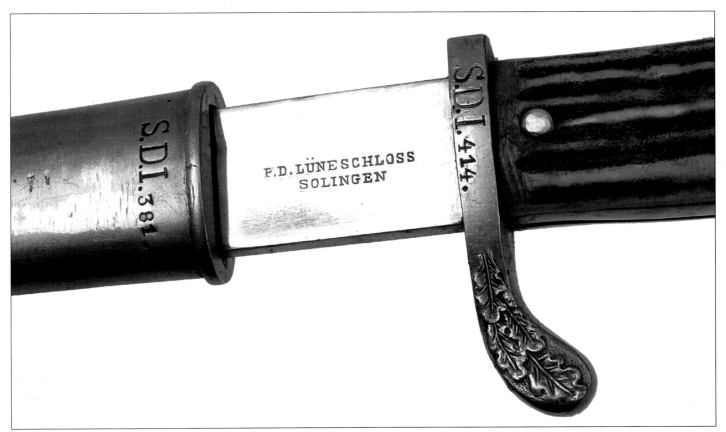

S.D.I.381.

P.D. LÜNESCHLOSS
SOLINGEN

S.D.I.414.

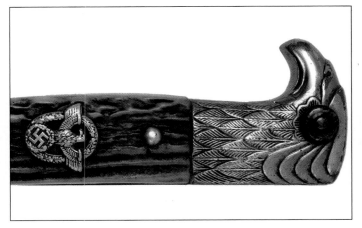

TOP The German police bayonet was possibly the most ornate regulation-issue bayonet. This bayonet was originally Weimar issue, with long blade and a clamshell guard. The guard has been removed and the blade shortened to conform to Third Reich specifications.

LEFT The reverse of the police bayonet quillon and scabbard top-mount bore unit markings typical of those used on World War I bayonets. This bayonet was made by P.D. Lüneschloss, Solingen.

ABOVE The highly ornate hilt had an eagle's-head pommel, stag-horn grips and an oakleaf pattern quillon. The police insignia was inset into the right grip.

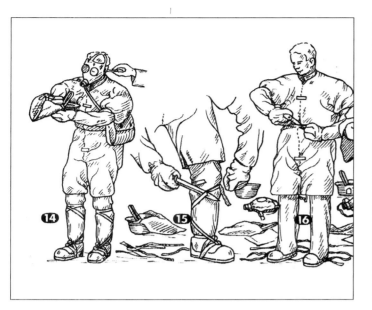

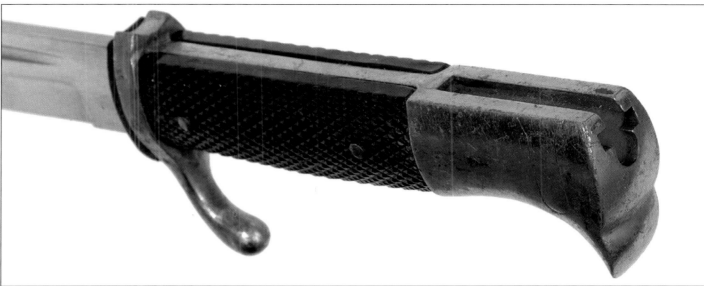

ABOVE An extract from the World War II German instructions for the use of the light anti-gas suit. The bayonet was carried fixed to the rifle when in anti-gas dress. It was an essential item for removing the protective clothing, which had to be cut off using the bayonet (as shown in the two right-hand figures).

BELOW A short "carbine"-bladed walking-out bayonet based on the *Kurzes Seitengewehr* 98. German military ranks were allowed to purchase their own ornate bayonets for use when walking out on a pass. Style depended on spending power, with various grip types, including plastic and stag horn, and blade forms being available. Blades could be purchased with ornate etchings showing military scenes or other decorations. They could also be personalized with the owner's unit or other inscriptions. The frog on this example was originally of patent leather.

ABOVE This "carbine" bayonet has a mortise and functioning press catch. On walking-out bayonets, it was common to find a section of shaped red felt inserted into the mortise.

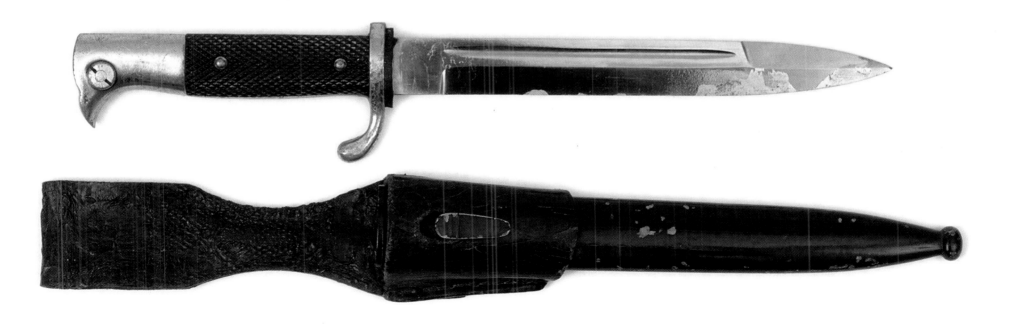

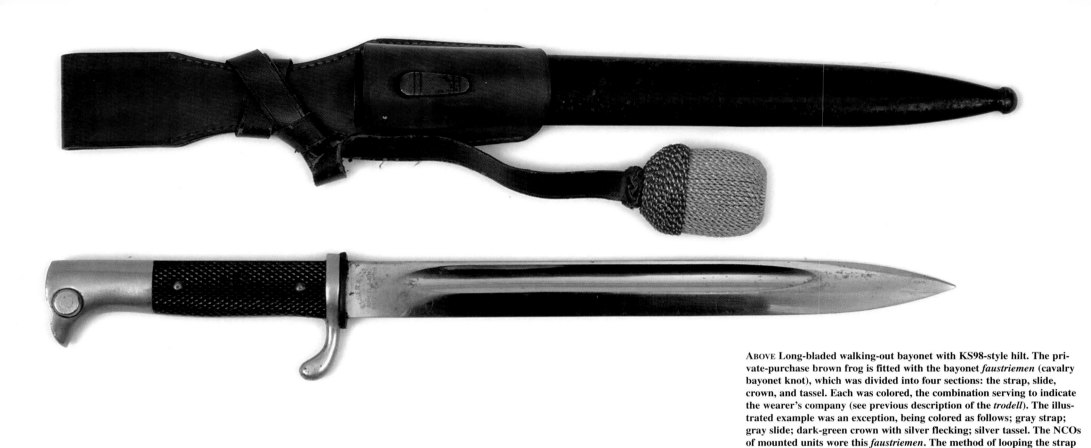

ABOVE Long-bladed walking-out bayonet with KS98-style hilt. The private-purchase brown frog is fitted with the bayonet *faustriemen* (cavalry bayonet knot), which was divided into four sections: the strap, slide, crown, and tassel. Each was colored, the combination serving to indicate the wearer's company (see previous description of the *trodell*). The illustrated example was an exception, being colored as follows; gray strap; gray slide; dark-green crown with silver flecking; silver tassel. The NCOs of mounted units wore this *faustriemen*. The method of looping the strap around the frog was the same for both *trodell* and *faustriemen*.

ABOVE Method of wearing the *faustriemen* (or *trodell*) on a bayonet with a quillon. The strap is looped over the quillon and then hangs parallel with the scabbard. On bayonets with no quillon, it hangs loose from the frog.

FAR LEFT The left ricasso of the long-bladed walking-out bayonet shows the manufacturer's trademark, the squirrel and sword of Eickhorn.

LEFT The right ricasso is also marked, "ESSER & CO., KÖLN A.RH, KREBSGASSE 20," this is the name and address of the retailer.

BELOW The German occupation of Czechoslovakia provided the Germans with a large number of Czech arms and production facilities. The VZ24 rifle and bayonet were issued to German forces. The bayonet was heavily blued and, in keeping with standard German practice, had the muzzle ring removed.

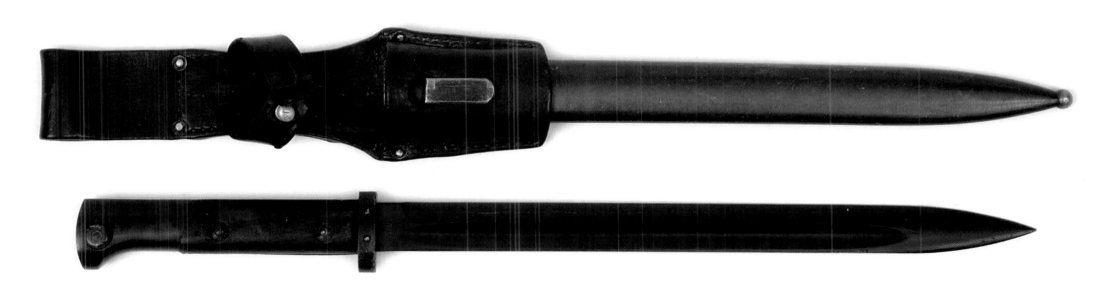

TOP VZ24 bayonet in scabbard showing bayonet frog with hilt loop fastened.

LEFT This bayonet was made for the German forces after the occupation. It bears the "dot" letter code on the ricasso signifying manufacture by Waffenwerke Brunn A.G.

ABOVE The German-issue VZ24 bore typical *waffenampt* markings. This inspector's mark consists of a spread-wing eagle over "65," it is stamped on the left pommel.

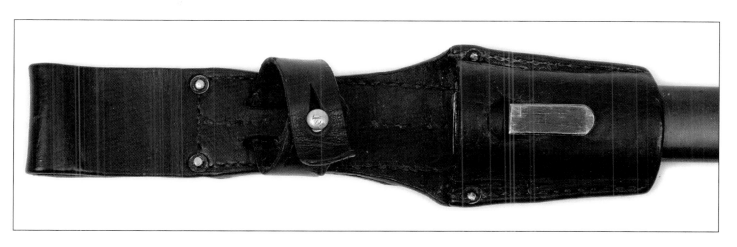

LEFT The Germans re-issued Czech bayonet frogs with the captured VZ24 bayonets. This example has an added hilt loop with alloy fastening stud.

BELOW The West German G3 bayonet. The blade was similar to that used on the American M3 knife, but the hilt was unique. The scabbard is based on the U.S. M8.

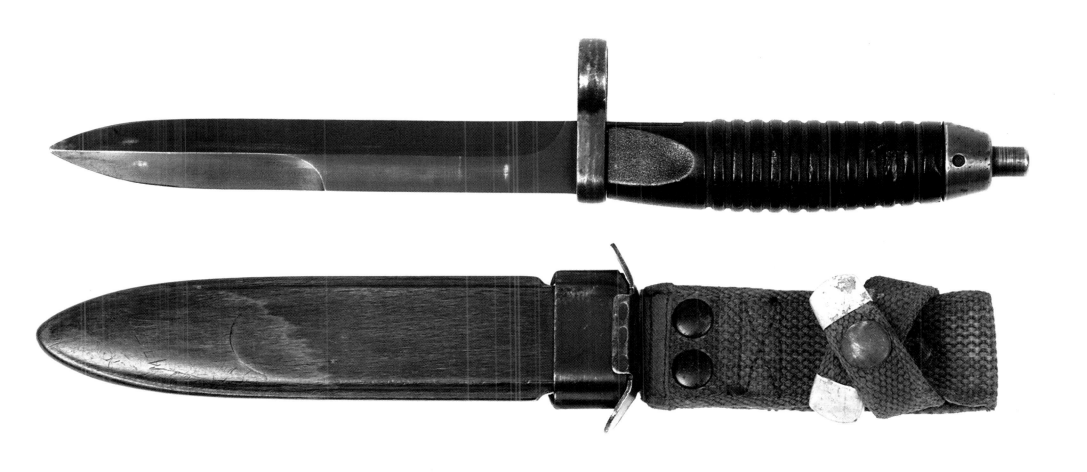

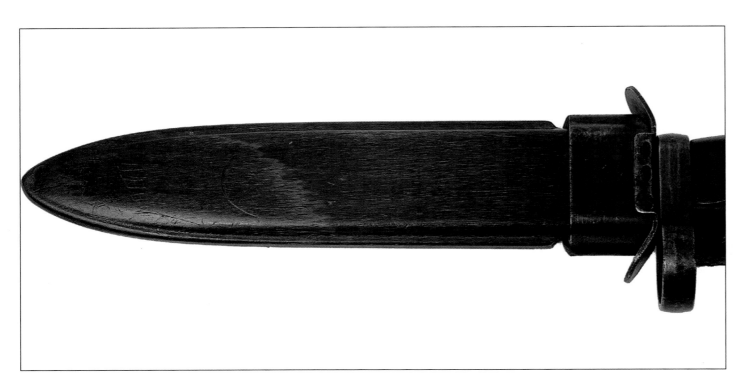

LEFT The scabbard of this G3 bayonet shows the woodgrain finish typical of German-made M8-style scabbards. The color of the finish varied from green to brown.

BELOW The bayonet for the G3 rifle fitted above the barrel in an inverted position. The unusual attachment fitted into the rifle's gas plug.

BOTTOM A bayonet with the standard G3-type hilt mated with a British No. 5-type blade was used on the Pakistani version of the G3 rifle. Prior to the acquisition of the G3, Pakistan relied heavily on standard British and Indian weaponry.

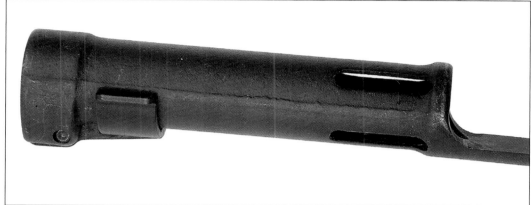

LEFT The blade marking "POF 68" on the ricasso shows that this bayonet was made at the Pakistan Ordnance Factory in 1968. It is typical of German G3-type bayonets made under license.

BELOW FN FAL Type C, known as the *Rohrbajonett* R1. The German-made bayonet has a distinctive roughly finished socket. The prominent seam ridges are sprue markings from the drop forging. The bayonet is parkerized gray overall.

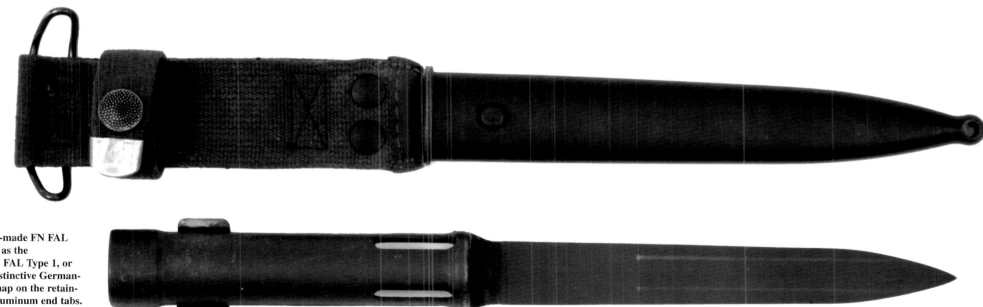

RIGHT Eickhorn-made FN FAL Type C, retailed as the *Rohrbajonett* FN FAL Type 1, or R1. It has the distinctive German-made pebbled snap on the retaining strap, and aluminum end tabs.

LEFT Eickhorn commercial bayonet for the G3 rifle, designated the G3/L in Eickhorn sales literature. The long blade has a distinctive red/brown finish whilst the scabbard has the typical woodgrain finish. The scabbard topmount is marked "U.S.M8A1."

RIGHT A commercial version of the Eickhorn-made Swedish AK4 bayonet, itself based on the West German G3 bayonet, was retailed as the AG3. The scabbard and grips were different from the German Army model.

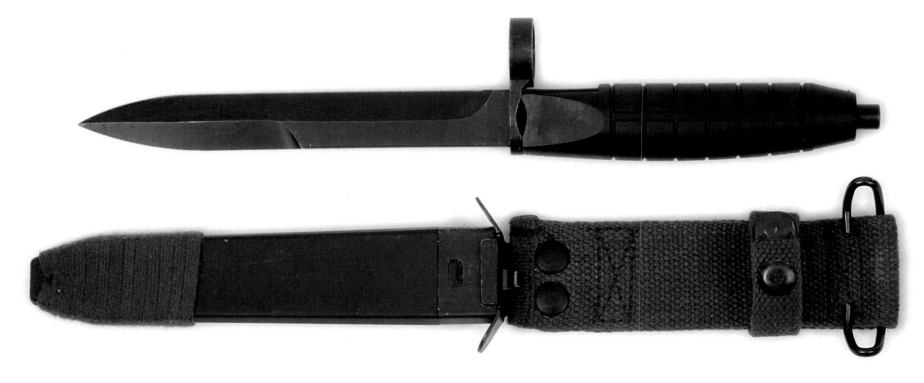

LEFT Eickhorn also produced the EW77S bayonet. It fitted the Swiss Stg. 57, 541, 550 and 551 rifles. The latest Swiss bayonet, the Stg. 90, owes much to the design of the EW77SS.

RIGHT The KCB77M1, which fitted the M15, M16 and AR18 rifles, was aimed at the export market. It has a chunky grip and wirecutter.

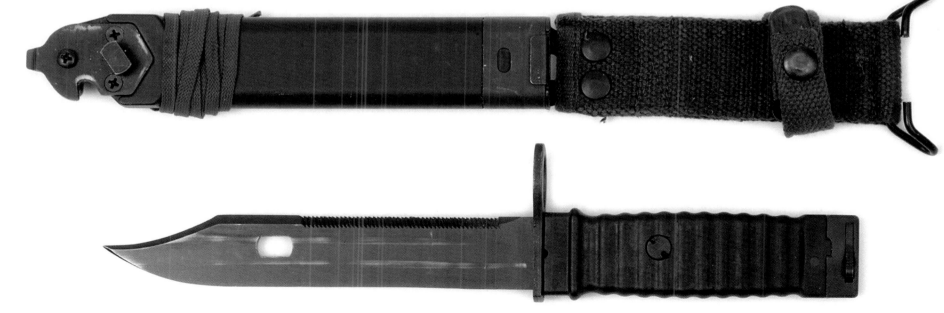

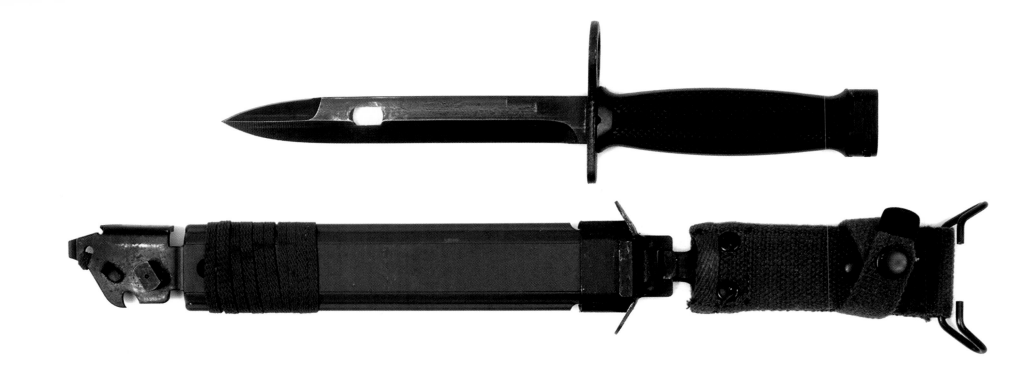

ABOVE The M7/S KH. The M7/S KH improved upon the standard U.S.-issue M7 in having a wirecutter, wire-stripper/nail-puller, bottle-opener and a screwdriver tip to the scabbard. The "KH" in its designation indicated that it had a removable belt loop.

LEFT The metal tip of the scabbard supplied with the M7/S KH provided the user with a wirecutter, wire-stripper/nail-puller, bottle-opener and screwdriver.

East Germany

	Overall length	Blade length	Muzzle ring
MPiK	305mm	203mm	17.5mm
AKM 59	273mm	150mm	17.5mm
AKM 74	270mm	150mm	17.5mm
M1985	365mm	N/A	N/A

The *Deutsche Demokratische Republik* was created by the Allied division of Germany following her defeat at the end of World War II. The western part of Germany was divided under French, U.S. and British control, with the east under Soviet domination. Under occupation by the Russians, the DDR made their own weapons but to Russian design. The first Soviet-type bayonet to be used by the DDR was the folding bayonet of the SKS carbine. A copy of the Russian AK47, the MPiK, soon replaced the SKS. The double muzzle ring **MPiK** bayonet was a copy of the original **AK47** type. It differed from its Soviet parent in having black plastic grips and a webbing belt loop with press fastener. The finish and deep bluing to the metalwork was also noticeably finer. The bayonet issued with the East German version of the AKM, the MPi KM 59, was the same as the Russian AKM Type 1 bayonet, but it had black composite grips, a gray leather suspension strap and gray web hilt strap. Collectors commonly refer to this bayonet as the **AKM 59**. In the early 1970s, the square-pommel second-pattern AKM bayonet was introduced. In East German service, it was issued as the **AK74**. On the majority of DDR bayonets the plastic components were black.

East Germany was one of the few nations to adopt a special training bayonet. The **M1985** consisted of a hollow "socket" hilt, with an external ribbed rubber grip, and a sprung-steel plunger with bulbous rubber tip. They were used on a wood and steel training rifle, the *Modell 4,853*. Internally the socket hilt had a "z"-shaped mortise for fitting to the training rifle, whilst the rubber grip allowed its use as a handheld training weapon. The grips were in black or red rubber.

A modernized bayonet with hollow hilt (containing escape and evasion tools) and a protractor engraved on the blade was made as the AKM 87 bayonet. It was produced in limited numbers. The gray belt loops and grip straps of the East German bayonets matched the color of the East German field equipment. With the collapse of Soviet domination, the wall dividing the two Germanys came down in 1989, and Germany was once again united.

RIGHT Based on the standard AK47 bayonet, the MPiK differed only in detail. It was well finished with deep bluing to the hilt metalwork. The early-production scabbard had a tan web belt loop with hilt strap and press fastener. An identical body with a gray nylon belt loop and hilt strap replaced this.

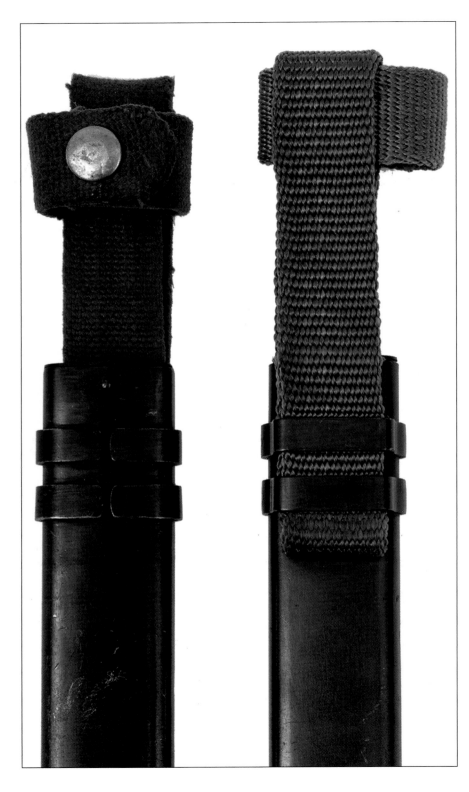

LEFT Detail of the MPiK scabbard throat, the small stud at the top allowed for removal of the blade-retaining spring when depressed. The scabbard's rear belt loop retaining rings were used very differently to other Warsaw Pact AK47-style scabbards. The web strip was normally passed around the scabbard's lower ring and under the upper ring, before being stitched into a belt loop. On East German scabbards, the pre-stitched web loop was passed through both scabbard rings. A short plastic rod was then passed through the end before the slack was pulled taught against the lower ring; this allowed damaged or frayed belt loops to be easily replaced.

RIGHT AKM second-pattern scabbards. At left is an early scabbard with a rudimentary finger guard on the rear of the scabbard. The later, second-pattern scabbard (right) has a larger ridge that runs the circumference of the scabbard edge, visible at the front and rear. This guard is to prevent the user putting their fingers in the arc of the blade when the bayonet and scabbard combination is used as a wirecutter.

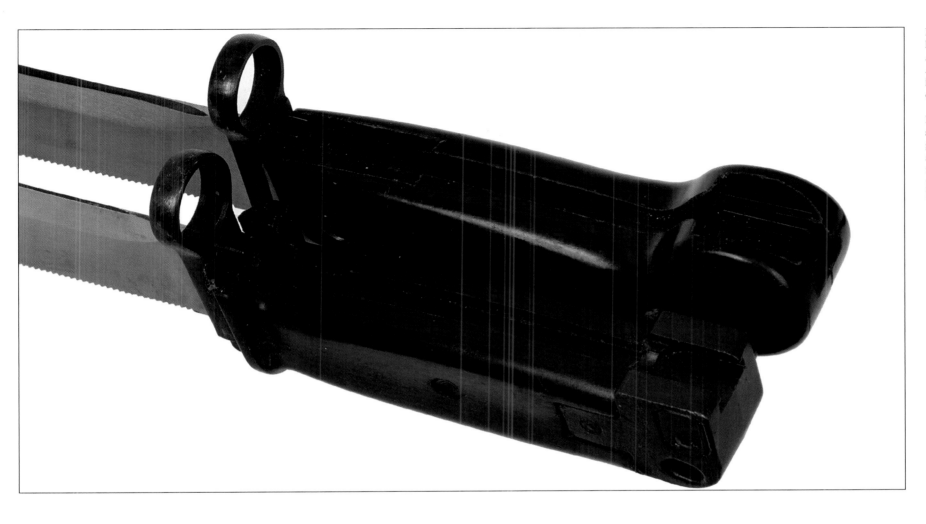

LEFT Comparison between the hilts of the AKM 59, top, and the AK74. The plastic pommel of the AKM 59 could easily be subject to impact damage; the steel pommel of the AK74 overcame this risk.

BELOW The M1985 was a sprung-steel training bayonet with rubber grip. The grip also allowed its use as a handheld weapon. The large rubber tip on the sprung shaft provided a degree of protection in bayonet fencing practice.

Great Britain

	Overall length	Blade length	Muzzle ring
Land Pattern	550mm	433mm	24mm
1815	528mm	432mm	23mm
Elliot type carbine	370mm	278mm	20.5mm
1802 carbine	435mm	326mm	22mm
1838	538mm	432mm	23.5mm
1839/44	551mm	427mm	25mm
1840	426mm	324mm	21mm
1831/44 trials	542mm	420mm	24.5mm
1841 Sea Service	550mm	425mm	24mm
1848	672mm	560mm	N/A
1853	520mm	445mm	21mm
1853/76	520mm	445mm	17.5mm
1855	735mm	610mm	20mm
1856/58	720mm	580mm	20.5mm
1856/58 short	468mm	332mm	18mm
1876	637mm	548mm	17.9mm
1879	794mm	654mm	17.5mm
1887 Mk. III	602mm	467mm	18mm
1888	425mm	305mm	16.5mm
1895	637mm	548mm	17.5mm
1903	425mm	305mm	16.5mm
1907	556mm	435mm	16.5mm
P13	558mm	435mm	15.5mm
No. 4	254mm	203mm	15mm
No. 4 Fannion	883mm	835mm	15mm
No. 5 Mk. I	302mm	202mm	22.5mm
No. 7	311mm	200mm	22.5m
No. 9	257mm	203mm	15mm
X2E1	292mm	162mm	22mm
L1A1	327mm	199mm	14.7mm
L3A3	280mm	180mm	22mm

The most famous musket used by the British was the Brown Bess, although the term is often erroneously applied to any musket of the 18th and early 19th centuries. The **Land Pattern** bayonet was issued to the Guards and King's German Legion, but by the turn of the 19th century **Indian Pattern** bayonets

were general issue. Although the French had adopted a locking ring during the early part of the 18th century, the British were somewhat slow to adapt to the idea, possibly due to its French origins. It first appeared on the socket bayonet for the Duke of Richmond's musket in 1794, but the weapon was short lived and the basal locking ring not particularly well thought of. The design was probably copied from the Hanoverian *Althannoversches Gewehr M/1773*. The design was re-introduced on the .625in Baker rifle bayonet of **1815**. Some 2,000 muskets were modified in 1815 to take a socket bayonet, and an order for 3,000 more followed later. The **1815** bayonet was copied from the Duke of Richmond's type, with 560 of the latter being converted for the Baker rifle. The original bayonet for the Baker had been a fine sword bayonet with brass hilt and knuckle guard. A good handheld weapon, its length and weight made it unwieldy when mounted. After this short-lived foray into the use of locking rings, the idea was forgotten and other methods of securing socket bayonets to muskets were employed.

The type F, or Hanoverian, catch was introduced on the 1838 musket. It consisted of a small hook-shaped spring protruding from the muskets fore-end beneath the barrel. The catch fitted over the large collar of the **1838** musket bayonet. The design was also used on the 1842 musket. The next development in bayonet fixing was Lovell's catch. Once again, a

spring was used to attach the bayonet but the new design was locked onto a lug that protruded from the collar, ensuring a more secure fixing. The design was first used on the 1844 musket, and it was also added to 1839-pattern muskets produced after 1844. The old 1839-pattern bayonets were modified and new ones produced with fittings for Lovell's catch, commonly known to collectors as the **1839/44** musket bayonet. Despite the level of criticism of the heavy and unwieldy sword bayonets, the style remained in use. The Brunswick rifle of 1837 was issued with a long brass-hilted sword bayonet. The **1837** Brunswick bayonet was less practical than the earlier Baker, as the blade form was less efficient and the hilt lacked a guard. The **1848** Brunswick bayonet was similar in general form, though the hilt was different. The improved **1848**, or second-pattern Brunswick bayonet as it is sometimes called, had a new locking mechanism that held the bayonet more securely on the rifle.

As well as being used by the military, bayonets were also issued to some police units of the day. An example of such

BELOW The generic Brown Bess musket was provided with a number of bayonet variants, here a Land Pattern socket bayonet dating to *c*.1780. The brass-mounted leather scabbard is typical of those in use during the early 19th century.

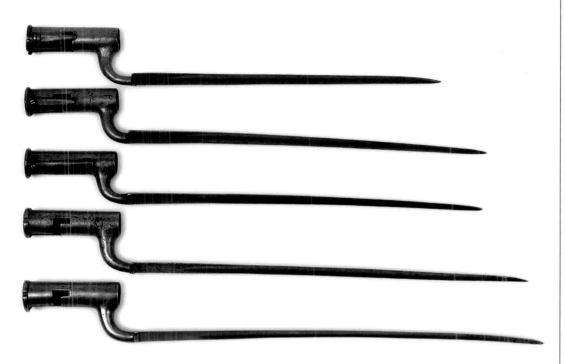

Brown Bess bayonet variants, reverse socket details. From left to right: bayonet for the 1841 Sea Service musket with lug for Lovell's catch; Sea Service trials bayonet; bayonet for "Baker's improved EIC spring bayonet;" India-pattern bayonet with Indian spring; "Windus's Pattern" UEIC India-pattern socket bayonet 1799, made by Makin but also marked by the gun-maker Harrison, who made up the musket and bayonet contracts.

ABOVE The Brown Bess bayonet existed in many variants; a few of the more common types used by the British and in India are shown here. From top to bottom: United East India Company "Windus's Pattern" socket bayonet dated 1799, it has a two-step mortise slot; India-pattern bayonet with India-pattern spring, three step mortise; "Baker's improved EIC spring bayonet" 1818, spring-catch two-step mortise; Sea Service trials bayonet 1831–44, three-step mortise; pattern-1841 Sea Service bayonet for the Royal Marines, the post-1844 type fitted with the lug for Lovell's catch, three-step mortise.

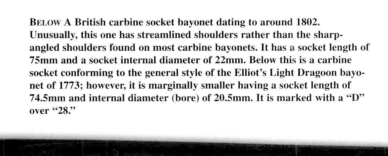

BELOW A British carbine socket bayonet dating to around 1802. Unusually, this one has streamlined shoulders rather than the sharp-angled shoulders found on most carbine bayonets. It has a socket length of 75mm and a socket internal diameter of 22mm. Below this is a carbine socket conforming to the general style of the Elliot's Light Dragoon bayonet of 1773; however, it is marginally smaller having a socket length of 74.5mm and internal diameter (bore) of 20.5mm. It is marked with a "D" over "28."

bayonet use is the small **1840**-pattern bayonet for the Royal Irish Constabulary carbine. The small spring fitted to the ricasso readily identifies the model 1840. The spring secured the bayonet in the scabbard and prevented it being easily snatched from the constable whilst on duty. Early **1840** bayonets for the 1839 carbine had a collar for attachment using the Hanoverian catch, examples made for the 1842 pattern carbine had the distinctive lug that allowed the fitting of Lovell's catch.

The 1841 Sea Service musket, issued to the Royal Navy and Royal Marines, was made up from flintlock parts converted to the percussion cap system. Early **1841** bayonets have provision for the Hanoverian catch; typically, those made after 1844 have the lug for Lovell's spring catch. Many of the preceding bayonet types were used to effect against the Russians during the Crimean War of 1854–56.

The **1853** was the first standard-issue British bayonet with a locking ring, and the first to be entirely made of steel. Although previous British socket bayonets had been provided with a locking ring, that of the **1853** was a median locking ring, unlike the earlier types that had been basal. Earlier bayonets had also only been issued on a limited scale and were not standard. The 1853 rifle and bayonet were the first mass-produced weapons in British service, produced on the "American System" after 1855. For the first time, components were interchangeable between weapons, including bayonets. Much of the machinery used in the mass-production owed its precision to the inventions of Mr. Joseph Whitworth, a Manchester engineer and inventor. The Board of Ordnance had approached Whitworth in 1854 requesting that he design and build machinery to mass-produce the 1853 rifle, a task that led to a revolution in production techniques.

Whitworth had seen the shortcomings of the 1853 rifle during the Crimean War, and invented a superior design with an oval bore and excellent accuracy. As good as the Whitworth rifle was, it was dismissed due to the small .45in caliber, considered by the British military to be far too small and lacking in stopping power. The Rifle Brigade later adopted the Whitworth rifle, which also gained widespread acceptance in the flourishing volunteer movement. Joseph Whitworth also gives his name to the Whitworth screw thread, his specifications moving British industry toward standardization.

The publication *Equipment of Infantry 1866* listed the service life of the 1853 rifle and bayonet as 12 years, and the scabbard six years.

The **1853** bayonet remained unaltered during its service life. However, in 1872 the introduction of the lever action .577in Martini Henry rifle saw the old Enfield 1853 bayonet modified to fit the new rifle. Externally identical the **1853/72**

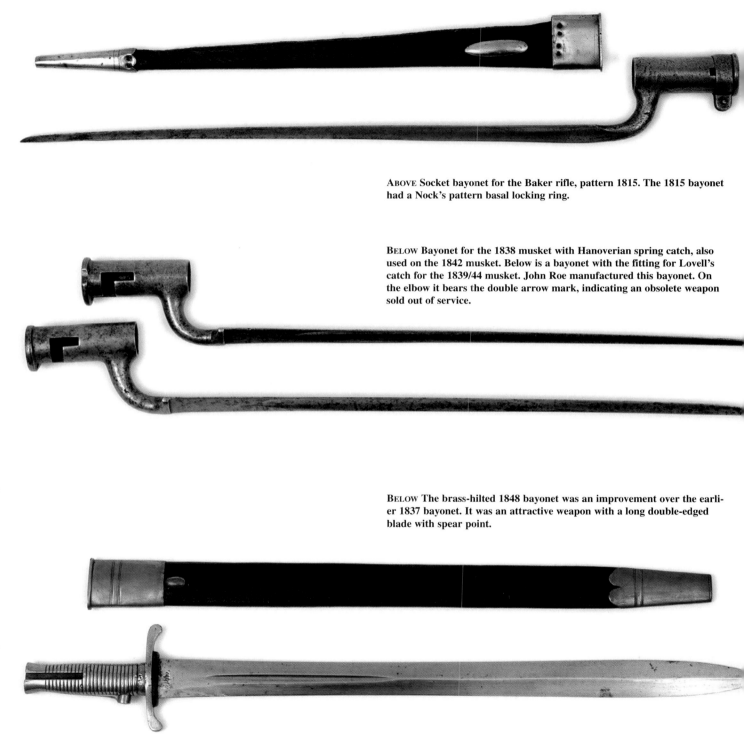

ABOVE Socket bayonet for the Baker rifle, pattern 1815. The 1815 bayonet had a Nock's pattern basal locking ring.

BELOW Bayonet for the 1838 musket with Hanoverian spring catch, also used on the 1842 musket. Below is a bayonet with the fitting for Lovell's catch for the 1839/44 musket. John Roe manufactured this bayonet. On the elbow it bears the double arrow mark, indicating an obsolete weapon sold out of service.

BELOW The brass-hilted 1848 bayonet was an improvement over the earlier 1837 bayonet. It was an attractive weapon with a long double-edged blade with spear point.

socket was bushed to reduce its bore size from the original 20mm to 18mm, allowing it to fit the smaller muzzle of the Martini Henry. The **1853** bayonet had three patterns of scabbard during its service life. The original scabbard had a brass locket and topmount with separate frog stud, as had been in use for decades in British service. The separate frog stud was found to be a weakness and was prone to tearing through the leather if snagged. The second-pattern scabbard remedied this weakness by extending the front face of the topmount and brazing the frog stud directly to it, this pattern was only produced between 1860 and 1866. Additionally, from 1860 the topmount was riveted to the leather body, as was the chape. Prior to this, the topmount and chape had been fixed using indentations, stamped into the brass, with shellac bonding the two together. The second-pattern scabbard also saw the seam in the leather body moved from the edge to the rear. In 1866 the extension was lengthened to meet the topmount at the sides, greatly strengthening it. This modification is the most common scabbard type encountered and was used to replace older or damaged examples as they became unserviceable. The service life of the scabbard was shorter than the bayonet.

Although the 1853 rifle was standard, other arms were authorized for specialist troops. One such weapon was the 1853 artillery carbine. The original bayonet had a brass hilt and yataghan blade, similar to the French 1842 bayonet. This was replaced in 1855 by a second pattern with steel hilt, and leather grips. Both patterns had a steel scabbard.

A further "non-standard" rifle was the .577in Lancaster carbine designed for the Royal Sappers and Miners (engineers).

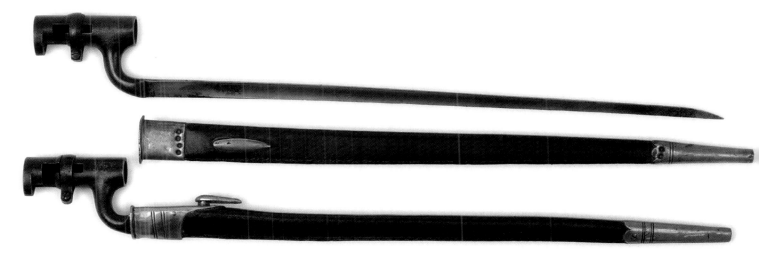

BELOW LEFT **Similar in general form, the hilts differentiated the 1837 from the 1848 Brunswick bayonet. The improved 1848 had a new locking mechanism that held the bayonet more securely on the rifle. The 1848 bears the "Enfield" and "VR" stamps on the ricasso, whilst the pommel shows the double arrow mark, indicating an obsolete weapon sold out of service.**

ABOVE **The 1853 socket bayonet and first-pattern scabbard with separate frog stud. Below is an 1853/72 socket bayonet, a standard 1853 bushed to fit the Martini Henry rifle. It is shown with the third pattern of scabbard with combined topmount and frog stud introduced in 1866.**

BELOW **1840-pattern bayonet for the Royal Irish Constabulary carbine model 1840. The spring on the ricasso secures the bayonet in the scabbard and prevents it being easily snatched from the constable whilst on duty. Early 1840 bayonets had provision for attachment using the Hanovarian catch; this post-1844 example has the lug for Lovell's catch.**

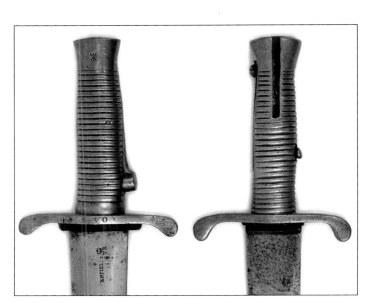

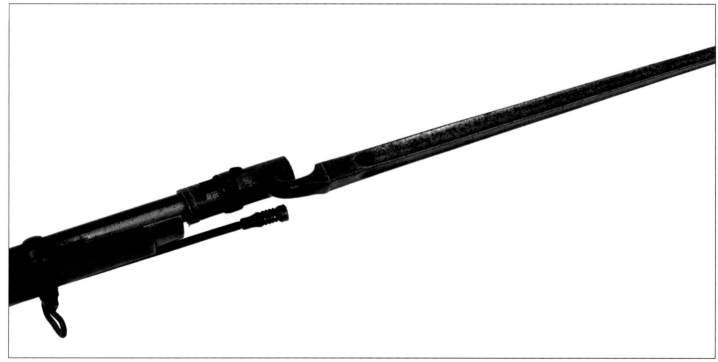

The **1855** bayonet for the Lancaster carbine was a particularly attractive item. It had a long slender pipe-backed blade with a brass crossguard and pommel, leather grips and a brass-mounted black leather scabbard. Many **1855** bayonets may be encountered with "MSC" stamped onto the pommel. This is the marking of the Medical Staff Corps (later the RAMC) to whom the bayonet was later issued as a sidearm. The **1855** fitted to the right side of the rifle, therefore to effect clear sighting with the short foresight the right side of the muzzle ring had a slight depression ground into it.

The 1856 yataghan bayonet was issued to troops armed with the short rifle, including sergeants of infantry and all ranks of the Rifle Brigade. It was similar to the second-pattern 1853 bayonet but had a steel-mounted leather scabbard. The **1856/58** bayonet was almost identical to the earlier 1856. It differed in detail, having the leaf spring secured by a screw rather than a rivet, and having no lead forward of the mortise slot. After 1873, many of the 1856/58 bayonets were converted for use with the Martini Henry rifle. At the end of the 19th century numbers of these were also shortened for issue to cadet units currently armed with the Martini Henry artillery carbine. The **1856/58 short** bayonet can be encountered in a number of minor variants, some having had the muzzle ring finial removed, others can be found without the quillon. The different blade point styles encountered are either rounded or pointed. Some cadet units renovated these bayonets with new grips, an example illustrated has composite grips secured by copper rivets.

The Royal Navy used cutlasses for boarding operations. It made sense therefore to combine the cutlass with a bayonet. The result was the 1859 Naval bayonet, a standard cutlass blade and bowl guard mounted with an 1856-type hilt and muzzle ring. Early types had wood grips, but these were later replaced by leather on the second pattern.

An updated version of the naval cutlass bayonet was adopted in 1871. Based on the 1859 pattern, the **1871** had a straight blade some 30mm shorter and a reduced bowl guard.

In 1859 the "Volunteer Force" came into being, the new force being created under the provisions of the *Volunteer Act*, 1804. The Volunteers were a separate force from the Militia, which was a part-time conscript force that provided a reserve for the regular forces. The Volunteers were authorized their own uniforms and weapons, whilst many adopted standard War Department weapons, others purchased their own rifle and bayonet types. The Whitworth rifle was a highly accurate weapon, yet its small caliber precluded it from widespread acceptance at a time when bullet size mattered. It was, however, popular with the volunteers. A number were used along with the **1863**

TOP LEFT Socket detail for 1853 bayonets. Left, the 1853/72 bushed to 18mm for the Martini Henry rifle, and, right, a standard 1853 bayonet.

TOP RIGHT Bayonet exercise 1857, showing the position of the "Guard."

ABOVE An 1853 socket bayonet fitted to a Snider Enfield rifle. The Snider was a breechloading conversion of the old 1853 muzzle-loading rifle.

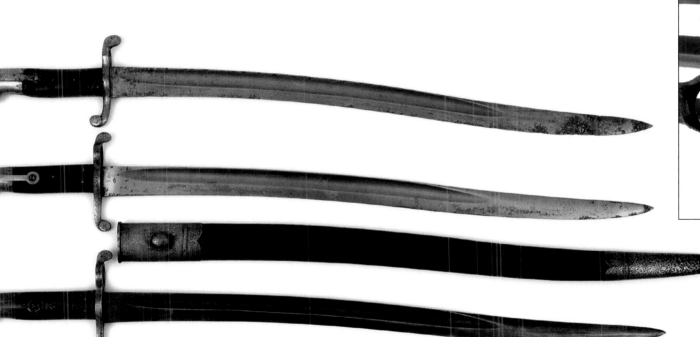

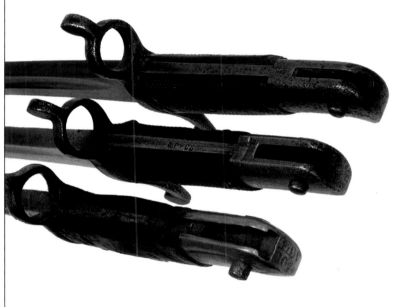

TOP The attractive brass-hilted Lancaster 1855 bayonet. The pommel is marked "MSC" showing that this bayonet was issue to the Medical Staff Corps as a sidearm. The MSC were the forerunners of the Royal Army Medical Corps.

LEFT British yataghan-bladed bayonets. From top to bottom: an 1856/58, (o/a 718, mrd 20.5mm); 1856 volunteer bayonet with brass hilt marked "EDV 107," possibly indicating Edinburgh volunteers (o/a 718, mrd 21mm); and an 1863 bayonet for the Whitworth rifle (o/a 718mm, mrd 20mm).

ABOVE Hilt details, 1856/58: 1856-pattern for rifle volunteers, and Whitworth 1863 with its distinctive round attachment slot. The volunteer pattern has a lead forward of the mortise slot. The 1856 bayonet also had this lead, which differentiates the 1856 and 1856/58 bayonets.

Whitworth bayonet. This was similar to the 1856, but had a yataghan blade and a distinctive round mortise slot.

In 1874, after five years of trials, the .45in Martini Henry rifle was accepted into service as the standard British arm. At first, bushed **1853** sockets were provided for line infantry battalions. These are generally referred to as the **1853/72**. Bushed **1856/58** sword bayonets were issued to infantry sergeants and rifle regiments. In 1876, a new longer-bladed socket bayonet, the **1876**, was approved for issue with the Martini Henry rifle. Unlike previous British sockets the triangular blade form was equilateral. When fixed it was also parallel to the rifle barrel. Earlier bayonets had angled the blade point away from the axis of the bore. The **1876/95** bayonet was a bushed **1876** issued with the .303in Martini Enfield, a Martini action with a

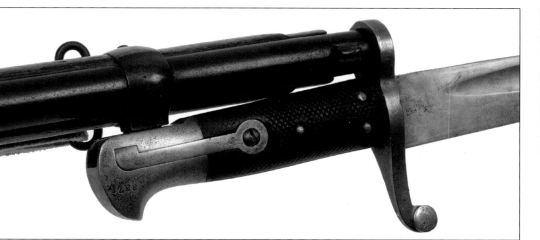

LEFT Martini Henry artillery carbine fitted with a short 1856/58 pattern bayonet, positioned to the right of muzzle.

BELOW LEFT 1856/58 bayonet variants shortened for issue to cadets armed with the Martini Henry artillery carbine. These bayonets were cut down at the end of the 19th century and can be found to vary in detail, as shown here.

reduced-bore Enfield barrel. It was issued to native troops. The scabbard of the **1876** bayonet underwent some modification. It was long and prone to damage, particularly when worn by men of smaller stature. Internally, it had a spring-steel reinforcement running the length of the scabbard. On the **Mk. I** scabbard three rivets held this, visible on the front face. The **Mk. II**, introduced in 1879, only had two rivets. the **Mk. III** was a scabbard issued to colonial units with a single rivet, whilst a further scabbard with an internal chape was specifically for native troops armed with the Martini Enfield rifle. A scarce variant was made without any spring rivets; a little over 100 were made for trials in 1875, but were rejected as they broke when the soldier kneeled.

In 1879, a new bayonet was issued to artillery units armed with the Martini Henry artillery carbine. The **1879** bayonet had a long 616mm blade with a bar guard to the hilt. The locking mechanism is distinctive in that the press catch is on the right side of the pommel, the reverse to that normally found on British bayonets.

During the mid-1880s, serious concerns were raised over the quality of some British **1853**, **1856** and **1876** bayonets following reports of blades bending or breaking when in use during the Sudan campaign, leading to press concerns over the "bayonet scandal." A major investigation concluded that, whilst not a widespread problem, the Naval cutlasses were particularly weak. The report also found that many old Indian Army bayonets had not been inspected by the War Department. Some **1853/72** bayonets were soft. These had reached the Sudan with troops diverted to Aden from India.

In 1887, a new blade-type bayonet was authorized for issue with the Martini Henry, and, in particular, as a replacement for the bayonets that had received criticism following the bayonet

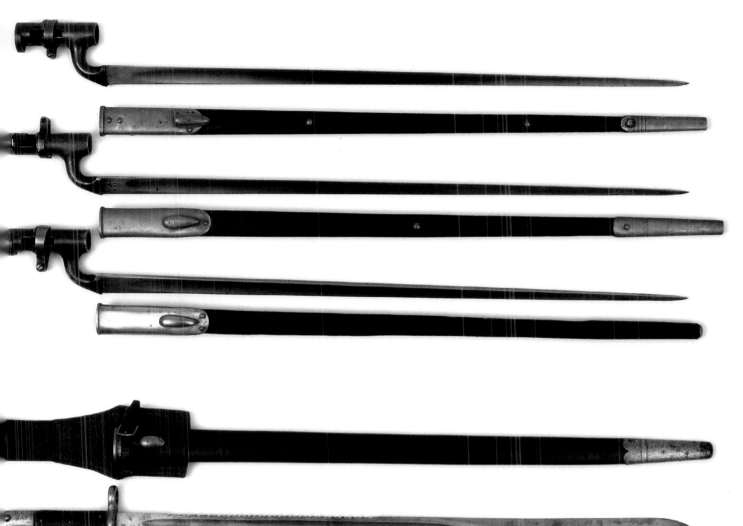

scandal. The 1887 Mk. I had a long fullered blade, leather grips and a leaf-spring attachment mechanism, whilst the Mk. II was a modernized version with the addition of an internal coil-spring attachment. The **1887 Mk. III,** introduced in 1888, was identical except for its plain unfullered blade. The year 1888 also saw the British government conducting trials of a small-caliber magazine-fed bolt-action rifle. The rifle was adopted as the .303in Lee Metford. The bayonet pattern 1888 for the Metford rifle was the first general-issue knife bayonet in British service. It had a double-edged blade and wooden grips secured by one large and two small brass rivets. These were found to be inadequate and weakened the wood. The second-pattern 1888 replaced the three rivets with two, it is referred to as the **1888 Mk. I, 2nd type**. The Lee Metford was soon updated with a new type of barrel, becoming the Lee Enfield. The Lee Enfield did not have a cleaning rod and therefore did not require the clearing hole previously drilled through the grip of the 1888 Mk. I bayonets. Instead the **1888 Mk. II** has a large clearing hole in the pommel making it readily distinguishable from the **Mk. I**. Both the **1888 Mk. I** and the **1888 Mk. II** could be used on the Lee Enfield, but the **Mk. II**

TOP Martini Henry-type socket bayonets. The 1876 was made for the Martini Henry rifle to replace the old bushed 1853/72 bayonets. Top, 1876 with Mk. II scabbard (the Mk. I scabbard had three rivets in the body); native 1895 socket bayonet for the Martini Enfield rifle, which fitted below the barrel, Mk. III scabbard; 1876/95 bayonet (note the filled-in mortise forward of the locking ring), an 1876 bayonet bushed and modified to fit the Martini Enfield rifle. The scabbard is the native pattern, with internal chape, often associated with the Kenyan Tribal Police.

ABOVE An 1879 artillery carbine sawback sword bayonet. This bayonet was issued with the Martini Henry artillery carbine. The orientation of the leaf spring and press catch is opposite to other bayonets of the period, with the press catch being on the right of the pommel rather than on the left as was usual. The frog stud is marked "DOV.A 76," possibly indicating Dover Artillery.

RIGHT The ricasso of the 1879 artillery bayonet, showing typical markings: two inspection markings, a number over "E" surmounted by a crown, showing inspection at Enfield; an arrow over "WD" indicating War Department ownership; and the mirrored "R" showing that the weapon has been condemned as unfit for service.

ABOVE 1887 Mk. III bayonet with its plain unfullered blade and stepped forward muzzle ring. The pommel bears a cancellation stamp just below the press catch. This mark has been stamped over a rack or weapon number that was no longer required.

FAR LEFT Left ricasso markings on an 1887 Mk. III bayonet, a crowned "VR" for Queen Victoria, and "/88" showing manufacture in 1888.

LEFT Right ricasso markings on an 1887 Mk. III, showing an Enfield inspection mark, "WD" and the double-arrow "obsolete" stamping.

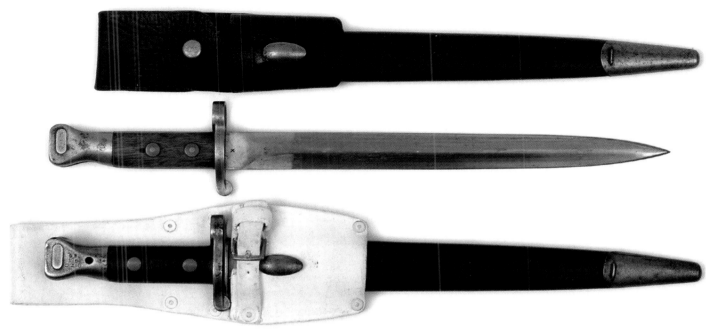

would not fit the Lee Metford with the cleaning rod in place.

The final variant of the 1888 bayonet was the Mk III. On this bayonet, the grip rivets were replaced by screwbolts. The mortise slot of the 1888 was most interesting in that it was on the face opposite the muzzle ring, on the underside of the pommel.

The Lee Metford and Lee Enfield had served well during the Boer Wars, but the authorities were already experimenting with a better design. A new rifle was to be adopted in 1903 and further modified in 1907 as the Lee Enfield Mk. III, better known as the SMLE (Short, Magazine, Lee, Enfield). A short knife bayonet, the **1903**, accompanied it, based on the 12in double-edged blade of the old **1888** pattern. It had a new hilt and, unusually, fitted to a stud and boss separate from, and below the barrel, rather than the muzzle ring fitting over the barrel, as was normal practice. This improved rifle accuracy, as the bayonet was not in direct contact with the barrel. Early models were conversions of the **1888** but new items were soon in production. The SMLE's rifle/bayonet combination was shorter than had previously been in use, and shorter than currently in vogue with other nations. Because of this it was decided to introduce a longer bayonet with a 17in blade. The new bayonet was issued as the **1907** pattern and published in *L of C* January 1, 1908, and March 15, 1908. It had a swept-forward quillon and long spear-pointed blade giving a reach comparable to any likely enemies. The *List of Changes* (*L of C*) were introduced into the British Army in 1860, published monthly and distributed by the War Office with *Army Circulars*, they notified users of new additions and changes to army stores. Numbered sequentially the *L of C* gave details of items new to the stores inventory and also of any modifications and amendments to material already

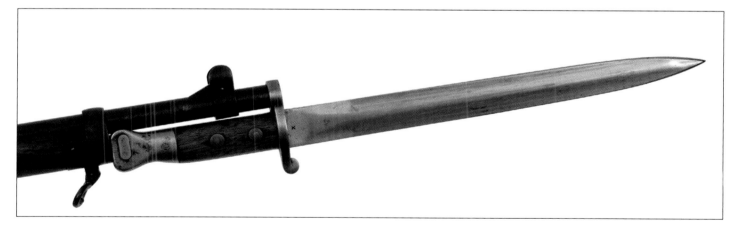

ABOVE LEFT 1887 bayonet blade back inspection stamp, the "E" showing the weapon was inspected at Enfield. Numerous other markings existed, including "S" for Solingen and "B" for Birmingham.

TOP 1888 bayonet types. Top, the 1888 Mk. I second pattern for the Lee Metford rifle. Shown with the 1901 Naval bayonet frog, this example is marked "T.C. Galley" (Thomas Critchfield Galley, a bootmaker and "army contractor" with boot and legging shop in Rickmansworth High St. in 1901); an 1888 Mk. II for the Long Lee Enfield rifle; the Mk. I Land Pattern scabbard carried in a Mk. II General Service buff leather frog. The GS Mk. II frog had a longer belt loop than the Mk I.

ABOVE Long Lee Enfield and 1888 Mk. I second-pattern bayonet. Although the Mk. II bayonet was introduced for use on the Long Lee Enfield, the earlier Metford bayonets were continued in use.

in use. Early **No. 1 Mk. I** scabbards had a brown leather body with steel locket and internal chape; these were later superseded by the **No. 1 Mk. II** with an external chape that gave better protection to the vulnerable scabbard tip, this was notified in *L of C* December 11, 1908. The scabbard, sword-bayonet, pattern 1907, No.1 Mark II was modified by having a new circular stud and square-ended lockets under *L of C* November 19, 1915. The hooked quillon was found to be superfluous and was deleted on all new-production bayonets from 1913 (*L of C* October 29, 1913), with an order that the old type should have the quillon removed. In 1916 (*L of C* January 5, 1916), a further modification was introduced; a small cleaning hole was placed in the pommel. This allowed the easy removal of dirt from the mortise slot, build-up of which could prevent secure fixing of the bayonet to the rifle. Some weapons remained unaltered. 1907 bayonets with hook quillon, no clearing hole and the early Mk. I scabbard command high prices among collectors.

In 1919, it was decreed that the blades of the **1907** bayonet were to be polished instead of sandblasted. The **1907** bayonet was re-named the bayonet **No. 1 Mk. I** in 1926. It was to remain in service during the interwar years and well into World War II, during which the short spike bayonet and No. 4 rifle gradually replaced it. The SMLE was to remain the primary weapon during the campaigns in North Africa and the Far East, where the Indian army shortened the **1907** bayonet to 12in, providing a handier weapon in restrictive jungle terrain. A scarce variant of the **1907** can be found with plastic grips. No official references have been found concerning these grips.

A **practice bayonet** was approved in 1914 under *L of C* December 2, 1914. It consisted of a standard **1907** bayonet, but with the point rounded and "DP" frequently stamped on the pommel. Despite the rounded point, it still presented a dangerous blade. Color parties also later used this type of bayonet, as the rounded point was less of a snag hazard then the sharp **1907** point, which could damage the colors. This bayonet should not be confused with the bayonet fencing muskets. The first musket introduced specifically for gymnasium training was the "Musket with Spring Bayonet" brought into service in July 1863. Based on the 1853, the musket had a spring-loaded bayonet that slid back along the barrel. These muskets went through a number of modifications and updates. Typical of these was the "Musket, Fencing, Short" introduced in 1904 to approximate the reach and weight of the SMLE. The last pattern to be used was the "Musket, Fencing, Mk. X." Introduced in 1913, this pattern remained in service until well after World War II.

The Mauser action had been considered as a replacement

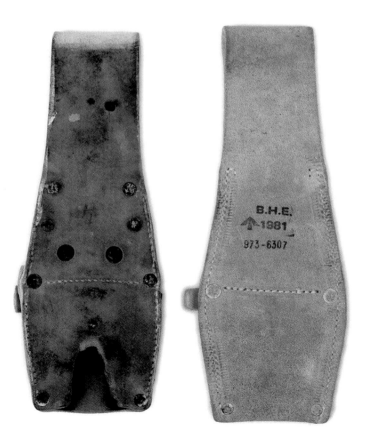

ABOVE British GS buff frogs, showing variants that may be encountered. From left to right: a GS Mk. I with rivets on the fastening strap only; a standard riveted-type GS Mk. II; a GS Mk. II frog that has been modified to fit the 1907 pattern bayonet with quillon. The inserted piece of leather pushed the bayonet away from the frog to give clearance for the quillon, which would otherwise snag; GS Mk. I, a similar example to the first item shown but with added rivets at the lower corners; a 1980s GS frog issued to a Grenadier Guard, the rivets have been removed and replaced by brass paper fasteners, which take a fine polish and are easily replaced. At extreme right is an unissued frog, produced in 1981 for the Brigade of Guards.

LEFT GS buff frog reverse. At left, the GS Mk. II modified for the 1907 bayonet with quillon, showing that, in addition to the leather insert, the rear has also been cut away; the slightly larger insert rivets are also clearly visible. At right, an unissued 1981-dated GS Mk. II frog.

ABOVE A British sentry stands post with his 1888 bayonet fixed to his Lee Metford rifle, the two grip rivets identify the bayonet as the Mk. I second pattern.

for the SMLE. An experimental 7mm rifle was manufactured as the P13, but the outbreak of World War I led to it being shelved. The requirement for small arms during the early stages of the war overwhelmed British production, resulting in the experimental rifle being resurrected in .303in caliber. With British manufacturing at full capacity, the production of the rifle were contracted out to factories in the U.S. Contracts were also placed for a bayonet for the new rifle, by then called the P14. The new bayonet resembled the **1907** pattern but, unlike the modified rifle, retained the original designation **P13**. It differed from the **1907** only in having an extended crosspiece placing the muzzle ring further from the hilt. To avoid confusion over the incompatible bayonet types, two lateral grooves were cut into the wood grips of the **P13**. Winchester and Remington produced the new bayonets in the U.S.; the ricasso bore the manufacturer's marking and the designation 1913. A "crowned A" inspection stamp was applied to all British bayonets made in the U.S. However, America's entry into the war terminated the manufacture of the **P13** bayonet for the British. The U.S. found itself massively short of weapons, as Britain had been in 1914, and all production

FAR LEFT **Prior to World War I, a trio of British soldiers of the 3rd Battalion, the Devonshire Regiment, proudly display their SMLE rifles with fixed 1903-pattern bayonets. These were soon replaced by the longer 1907 pattern.**

LEFT **Gallipoli 1915. A sailor of the Royal Naval Division views the Turkish line through a trench periscope. He is armed with a Long Lee Enfield rifle and 1888 Mk. II bayonet. The scabbard of the 1888 bayonet (and the 1903) were too wide to allow the attachment of the entrenching tool helve holder of the 1908 web equipment, which had been designed to fit the 1907 bayonet. Thus the 1888 scabbard could not be properly seated in the frog, as shown here, when the helve holder was attached.**

BELOW **The 1903-pattern bayonet was the first bayonet type issued with the SMLE rifle. It used the 1888-style blade but with a new hilt style. This example has a production date of July 1903. The Mk. I scabbard is carried in a 1908 web equipment frog. At the turn of the 19th century, short bayonets were popular; however, after its introduction, the 1903 bayonet was considered to be of insufficient length in comparison to bayonets such as the German S98. It was therefore replaced by the longer 1907.**

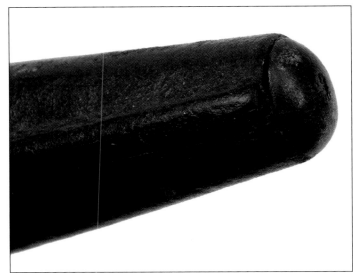

capacity was dedicated to providing for U.S. troops. To ease shortfalls in small arms, the U.S. Army adopted the P14 rifle (in .30-06in caliber) and **P13** bayonet as the models of **1917**. The British and American bayonet types are easily differentiated by the markings and designation stamped on the ricasso as well as the clearing hole in the pommel of the American-issue bayonets. Some late-production British contract weapons were taken up by the U.S. Army, these have the original British markings canceled and over-stamped with U.S. markings. Winchester produced some 225,000 **P13** bayonets and Remington 1,243,000, making the Winchester examples slightly more collectable.

In 1926, a re-categorizing of weapon nomenclature changed the designation of the **P13** bayonet to No. 3 Mk. I. At the outbreak of World War II Great Britain was again very short of weapons, the old P14 rifles and their No. 3 Mk. I bayonets were brought out of storage with many thousands being temporarily issued to newly called-up militiamen. Period images

TOP LEFT 1907 bayonet with hooked quillon and Mk. I scabbard. This bayonet is fitted with a pattern-1914 leather equipment bayonet frog and helve carrier, the wooden helve fitting the 1908 entrenching tool.

LEFT An illustration from the Boer War showing British soldiers fixing 1888 bayonets to their Lee Metford rifles in a gallant "last stand."

ABOVE The Mk. I bayonet scabbard had an internal steel chape rather than an external chape. Less than a year after its introduction (January 1908), it was replaced by the external chape Mk. II scabbard. The internal chape had first been used on the 1888 Mk. II scabbard.

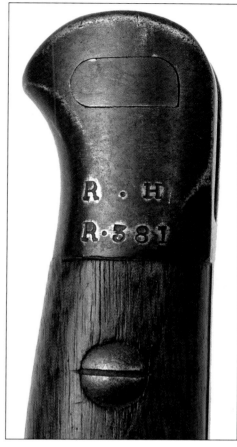

ABOVE LEFT Left side hilt detail of the 1907 bayonet. It bears the "JAC" mark of J.A. Chapman and a December 1908 manufacture date "12 '08." The crowned "ER" shows that it was made during the reign of Edward VII.

ABOVE The right pommel bears the marking "R.H" for the Royal Highlanders, better known as the Black Watch.

LEFT 1914 leather equipment helve and frog reverse showing the method of attaching the helve carrier to the frog.

show a mix of SMLE and P14 rifles in many infantry rifle sections during the 1939–41 period. In 1940, the U.S. sent over 1,000,000 .30-06in P17 rifles and bayonets to Britain. They were issued to the Home Guard and to many overseas units training in Britain, including French and Polish troops. To differentiate the .30-06in P17 rifles from the .303in P14s, the former had a red band painted around the fore-end. There was no need to differentiate between bayonets, as they both fit either rifle. In British service, the U.S. 1917 scabbards were easily carried using the P37 webbing frog or the P39 leather frog. Although the U.S. scabbards had no frog stud on the top mount, the wire belt hook and the mounting lip of the second-pattern scabbard provided sufficient support when the scabbard was carried in the British frog. The first-pattern scabbards with the swiveling leather belt loop required more work. On these, the loop had to be removed and its swivel mounting ground flush with the topmount before the frog was fitted. The frog was sufficiently tight to hold fast against the lip of the scabbard throat.

At the turn of the 20th century, a number of Arisaka rifles and bayonets were purchased for trials. These were passed to the Royal Navy during World War I, at which point Japan was a British ally. In British service, the bayonets were cataloged as the "Sword-bayonet, .256-inch rifle & scabbard P1900."

Their design was to heavily influence the form of the British **1907** bayonet. Most of these Arisakas were later given to the White Russians when British troops were sent to Russia shortly after World War I.

The No. 4 rifle was a lightened and modernized version of the SMLE. Easier and cheaper to produce, it had first been trialed in the early 1920s along with a short spike bayonet. The short bayonet was considered handier than the long **1907** type and equally as efficient at dispatching any enemy. It had been concluded that a blade a little under 8in was adequate to incapacitate a heavily clothed enemy wrapped for winter warfare; the thickness of dress of the Russian winter uniform was used as a test example. Against such clothing, the spike bayonet was considered as having inflicted a sufficiently incapacitating wound during weapon trials. The No. 4 rifle and bayonet were introduced in November 1939, but it was to be some time before production would meet demand and none were issued before 1941, seeing limited service in North Africa and with the first major issues again being made in the Mediterranean in 1943. It had almost fully replaced the SMLE for the assault troops that were to invade Northwest Europe in June 1944, but the SMLE remained in service for some time. The first No. 4 bayonet, the fine-quality **No. 4 Mk. I**, was a one-piece forging. It had a polished cruciform-section blade and deeply blued socket. The small socket-type hilt proved inadequate as a grip, making the No. 4 bayonet wholly impractical to use as a hand-held weapon. The spike-type blade also precluded its use as a knife or tool; it was a stabbing weapon and nothing more. Already far cheaper than the **1907** bayonet, it was to be further modified to reduce cost and labor. Singer Manufacturing Co made the **Mk. I**. The **No. 4 Mk. II**, introduced in 1940, had a simplified circular section blade with "screwdriver" point. Singer also made it, as well as Long Branch in Canada and

ABOVE LEFT The wooden helve showing issue marks for 1916.

LEFT 1914-pattern leather equipment frog types. From left to right: a rare first-pattern frog lacking rivets at the lower corners (the helve strap has been removed on this example); frog for troops not equipped with the entrenching tool, and therefore not fitted with a helve strap; standard 1914-pattern frog with strap for the helve carrier.

BELOW The manufacture of the scabbard for the 1907 bayonet required a number of tools and patterns. One item that was required for the making up of the leather body was the "scabbard mandrel" shown here.

Stevens-Savage in the U.S. In a drive to economize even further, and to broaden the available manufacturers the **No. 4 Mk. II*** was made from separate socket and blade components with a distinct join at the socket where the blade meets. A number of different factories assembled the separate components. Increasing demand for No. 4 bayonets led to the introduction of the **No. 4 Mk. III** in February 1943. The **Mk. III** had a crude socket to which the blade was welded, the whole being left in a partially finished rough state. It was designed by the Birmingham company of Joseph Lucas. Over 196,200 examples of the **Mk. III** were produced before it was declared obsolete in May 1946. Production of the spike bayonet ceased at the end of World War II.

As well as economizing on the bayonet production, the scabbards also received some attention. The early tapering **Mk. I** was supplemented by the **Mk. II** in 1942; it differed in having parallel sides and was thus simpler to produce. In an effort to reduce the use of steel, a plastic **Mk. III** scabbard was also issued in limited numbers, it was similar in shape to the **Mk. II** scabbard. The British No. 4 Mk III scabbard was tapered but the Canadian plastic version was parallel sided, and not a true Mk III. The American **M5** War Aid scabbard was also supplied in some numbers. It had an integral webbing belt loop/frog, riveted in place on early production scabbards it was later affixed with press fasteners, making it removable for replacement or repair. The No. 4 series of bayonets also fitted the Sten Mk. V, issued to airborne forces, and the late-war entrenching tool helve "Helve, Mk. II complete with bayonet

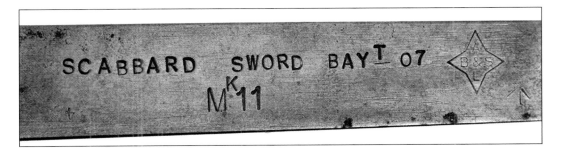

LEFT The mandrel was clearly marked "SCABBARD SWORD BAYT 07 Mk 11." This indicates that it was used for making up the Mk. II scabbard body.

BELOW LEFT During World War II, an RAF guard stands with SMLE rifles at the shoulder. The weapons are fitted with the No. 1 Mk. I (1907) bayonet.

BELOW The 1907 practice bayonet, approved in 1914, consisted of a standard 1907 bayonet but with the point rounded to make it safer in bayonet training. It was still capable of inflicting a serious wound and required care in use. Color parties also used this type of bayonet, as the rounded tip prevented snagging or damage to the colors.

adaptor," adopted in June 1944. The Mk. II helve saw no widespread issue during World War II but it was in limited use with some units from 1944. It was envisaged that the helve would serve as a mine probe or offensive weapon when the bayonet was attached. A No. 4 "Port Fannion" was fashioned from a chromed No. 4 bayonet. It had an extended tubular blade to which was attached two fixing points for a regimental pennant. It is not known how many were produced but at least one example survives. It is believed that the Royal Welsh Fusiliers used this in the immediate postwar years.

The ubiquitous Sten gun was not provided with a bayonet, although a number of differing samples were later made up. A simple tubular socket type was adopted for restricted issue to units such as airborne troops. They were of limited use and the introduction of the Mk. V Sten, with its fitting for the standard No. 4 bayonet, made them redundant as the Mk. V was issued to airborne units as a priority.

Experience gained in the Far East led to many uniform and equipment developments. The long SMLE and the No. 4 were considered unsuitable for jungle warfare and a replacement was produced from late 1944 as the No. 5 rifle, a shortened and lightened carbine version of the No. 4 rifle specifically for jungle use and commonly referred to as the "Jungle carbine." The bayonet **No. 5 Mk. I** was introduced in December 1943, though it was not published in the *Lists of Changes* until September 1944. It was the product of much field research, it had an 8in clip-point blade and an oversize muzzle ring to fit over the enlarged flash hider that was required to reduce the excessive muzzle flash produced by the rifle's short barrel. The mortise slot was round in section rather then the "T" slot normally encountered on British bayonets. Early production examples had the wrap-around wooden grip secured by a single screw. This was soon seen to be inadequate and was replaced by a second type with two grip screws, this retained the designation **No. 5 Mk. I**, with no Mk. II being produced. The early pattern bayonet with single grip screw is extremely rare and it is assumed that many were converted by having new grips added. The rifle and bayonet were first issued to airborne troops training in Britain and destined for the conflict in the Far East. However, the fall of Germany saw them diverted to Norway, where the No. 5 was first used in any number during the spring of 1945. By September, the new rifle and bayonet had reached the Far East with airborne troops, but it was to see little use other than in mopping-up operations. The No. 5 rifle was declared obsolete in 1947, although the **No. 5** bayonet was to see limited service with the postwar Sterling L2A3 SMG issued to second-line troops, such as Military Police and the Intelligence Corps, as well as infantry specialists. It remained

on issue until the SA80 rifle replaced both the L2A3 SMG and L1A1 rifle. Commercial versions were made for export by Sterling, with the company name etched on the blade and the grips made of plastic. The first-pattern scabbard for the **No. 5** was the **No. 5 Mk. I**, it had a steel body, flush throat section and round frog stud. The second type, introduced in 1949, was the **No. 5 Mk. II**. It had a slightly protruding brass mouthpiece. Both types were used on the **No. 5**, **No. 7**, **No. 9** and the **L1** series of SLR bayonets.

The No. 6 bayonet was an experiment to provide the No. 1 rifle (SMLE) with a short-bladed knife bayonet. It had a hilt similar to that of the **1907** bayonet and a **No. 5**-type blade. Very few were made and it is now a scarce bayonet.

The spike bayonets were far from flexible; adequate in dispatching an enemy, they were otherwise of little use. The **No. 7** bayonet was adopted in an effort to provide a bayonet for the Sten SMG that would also provide useful as a knife. It had a

TOP LEFT The naval "N" property mark stamped on the pommel of the 1907 practice bayonet. The Royal Navy trained seamen as landing and boarding parties and took the use of the bayonet seriously in such operations.

TOP RIGHT Right ricasso of 1907 bayonet showing the "X" bending mark applied to show that the blade had passed proofing, Enfield inspection marks, and the "WD" government ownership marking.

ABOVE This 1907-pattern bayonet was manufactured in June 1917. It has the clearing hole in the pommel that was introduced in 1916; prior to the introduction of this simple modification, a build-up of fouling in the mortise slot, common in the trenches, could prevent the bayonet from being fitted to the rifle. It is odd that it was not at first included in the 1907 design, as bayonets preceding that pattern, such as the 1887, 1888 and 1903, all had clearing holes. It is carried in a 1908-pattern web equipment frog with helve holder and attached helve.

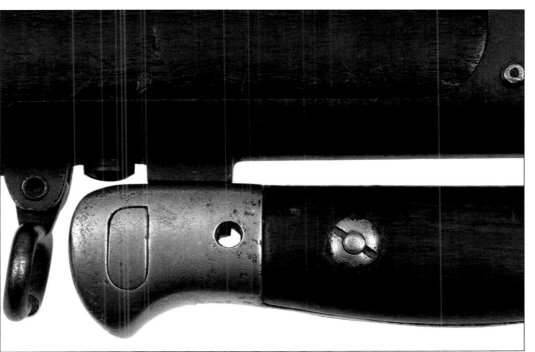

No. 5-type blade, complete with muzzle ring, shaped plastic grips and a swiveling No. 4-type pommel. The unique design was complicated and expensive. When fitted to the weapon, the pommel had to be rotated through 180 degrees and locked in place. Dating to early 1945, the No. 7 saw only limited issue. Guards Division bandsmen later used it as a dress arm long after the issue of the SLR. Following the numerical designations, the No. 8 bayonet for the experimental SLEM self-loading rifle was identical to the No. 5, but for its smaller 14.5mm muzzle ring, this bayonet is somewhat scarce and is unlikely to be encountered. The 7.92mm SLEM (Self-Loading Experimental Model) rifle was made up for trials in 1946, it is believed that only 2,000 rifles and bayonets were manufactured and the design was not adopted. The year 1948 saw the introduction of the No. 9 bayonet, a blade-type socket bayonet marrying the clip-point blade of the No. 5 bayonet with a No. 4 bayonet-style socket. It offered a cheap means of providing the No. 4 rifle with a blade-style of bayonet at considerably less cost than the No. 7.

The 1950s saw a requirement for a self-loading rifle to replace the No. 4. The U.S. had used the Garand since prior to World War II and the majority of industrial nations were looking into replacing their single-shot bolt-action weapons with magazine-fed self-loading rifles. The British toyed with the advanced EM2 bullpup rifle, but, due to political pressure and NATO commitments, they soon found themselves looking at adopting the Belgian FN Fusil Automatic Leger. The FAL was a 7.62mm rifle with a 20-round magazine, firing single shot or fully automatic. A large quantity of the rifles were acquired for trials as the X1 rifle. The accompanying bayonet was the X2E1 (the Belgian FAL Type A also known as the M1953).

LEFT This 1907 bayonet has been fitted with black plastic grips. The exact origin of these unmarked grips is unknown but it is possible they were considered for use in humid jungle terrain where wood grips were prone to deterioration.

RIGHT P13 bayonet right ricasso showing the inspectors marking consisting of an arrow, crow over "33," and a capital "A" showing that the weapon was inspected in America.

The FAL met the needs of the British Army, and, with a few modifications, was taken into service as the L1A1 self-loading rifle, commonly known as the SLR. The SLR had an integral flash hider at the muzzle and therefore the **X2E1** bayonet was not adopted. The new bayonet for the SLR reverted to the well-proven blade of the **No. 5** bayonet with all-steel grips. The first-pattern L1A1 had a protruding release catch that was found to be at risk of accidental operation. A modified version with a recessed catch was adopted as the **L1A3**, with the later **L1A4** representing a manufacturing variant. Most of the L1A1 bayonets were modified to **L1A3** standard and British examples are thus now very scarce. The L1A2 differed from the L1A1 in having the pommel riveted to the tang rather than brazed. Very few L1A2 bayonets were produced in Britain. but it became the standard model used by both Canada and Australia.

The British have used a number of M15 and M16 rifles. They were issued to specialist units and some regiments engaged in jungle warfare, such as the Gurkhas. The bayonets supplied were standard U.S.-issue **M7** with **M8A1** scabbards and carried no British markings other than NATO stock numbers on their Royal Army Ordnance Corps packaging.

After some years of trials, the British adopted a bullpup

BELOW P13 bayonet with standard British-issue Mk II scabbard. This bayonet was made for use with the .303in P14 rifle. The two deep grooves in the grips made it readily distinguishable from the 1907 bayonet. The two bayonets were not interchangeable.

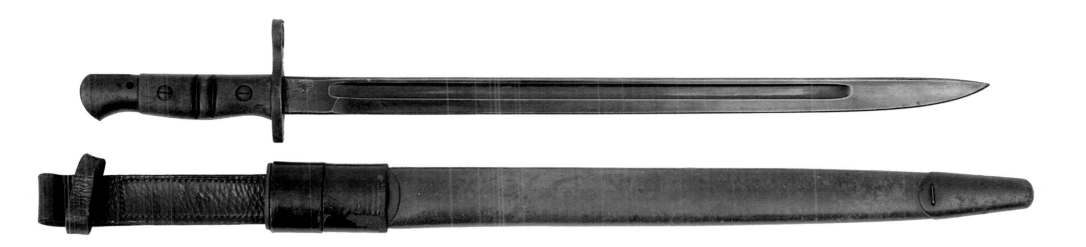

ABOVE A World War I U.S. M1917 bayonet. This example is a Remington-made bayonet marked 1918 on the ricasso. It has a green-painted first-pattern scabbard that has been modified by the British during World War II.

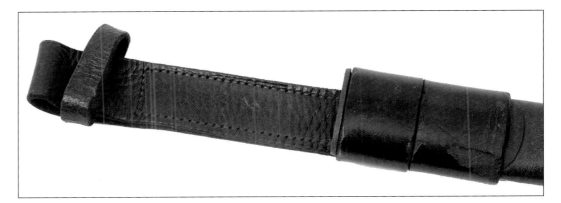

LEFT The leather hanger has been removed from the scabbard and the fixing ground flush with the topmount so that the leather P39 bayonet frog can be fitted. This was one of the many U.S. war aid bayonets issued to the Home Guard.

BELOW The 1939-pattern frog is marked "D.MASON & SONS LTD. WALSALL. 1940" on the reverse.

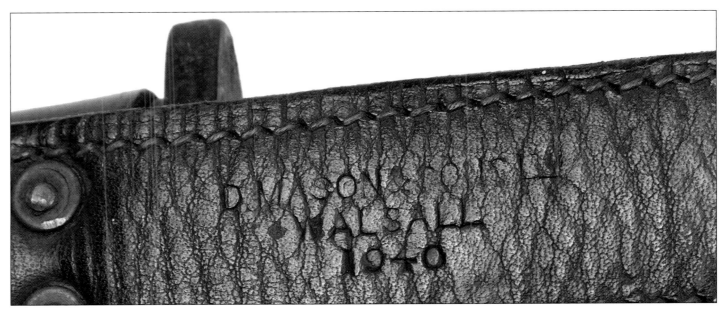

type weapon in 1985. The adoption of the 5.56mm L85A1, better known as the SA80, also saw the introduction of an innovative bayonet design. This bayonet was a great step forward in British bayonet technology, it encompassed a bottle-opener (soon deleted), a serrated blade edge and a saw blade encased in the scabbard, which, in combination with the blade, formed a wirecutter. It also took a major evolutionary step backwards in that it had a hollow hilt that fitted over the rifle's flash eliminator, making it a modern socket bayonet. Early pre-1986 **L3A1** bayonets have a distinct triangular form to the serrated blade edge. Post-1986 **L3A1** bayonets have a parallel-sided serration. Two scabbard patterns can be found with the **L3A1** bayonet. The **L1A1** scabbard has a distinctive beak to the metal tip whilst the **L2A1** scabbard has a flat tip. A number of other minor variations may be encountered such as differing numbers of teeth on the scabbard's integral saw blade. Non "teeth arm" units were issued a simplified scabbard, just the plastic body section without the wirecutter and saw blade. The scabbards were carried in a "frog" that covered the whole scabbard assembly. Early patterns had fixed belt loops on the reverse, later replaced by loops secured with press studs for easy removal without having to dismantle the equipment set.

ABOVE The left ricasso of the
M1917 bayonet showing the
Remington logo and "1918." This
erroneous marking followed the
practice of date-stamping U.S.
bayonets, but the 1917 mark normally encountered was actually a
model designation rather than the
year of manufacture. Applied in
error, the 1918 mark was soon discontinued.

ABOVE RIGHT The right ricasso
bears markings typical of those to
be found on M1917 bayonets: The
"flaming grenade" over "U.S."
ordnance marking, the "X" bending mark and the "eagle" over
'14' inspection stamp.

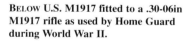

BELOW U.S. M1917 fitted to a .30-06in
M1917 rifle as used by Home Guard
during World War II.

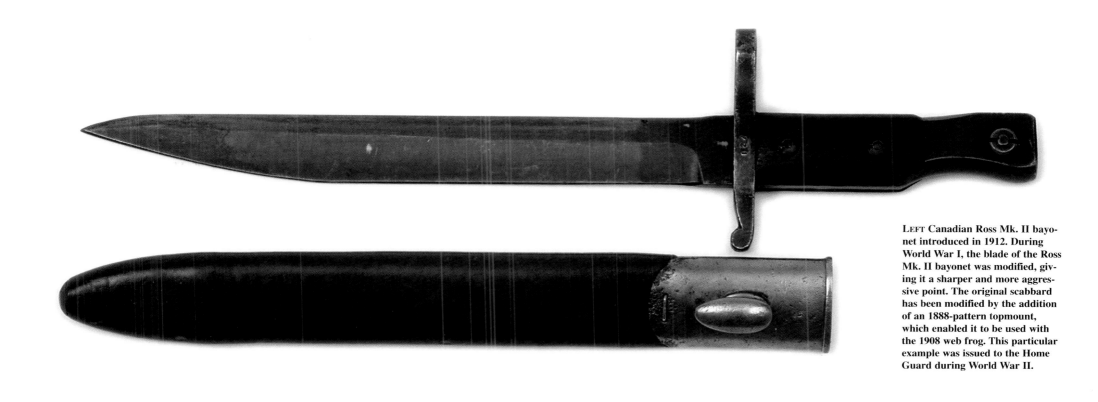

LEFT Canadian Ross Mk. II bayonet introduced in 1912. During World War I, the blade of the Ross Mk. II bayonet was modified, giving it a sharper and more aggressive point. The original scabbard has been modified by the addition of an 1888-pattern topmount, which enabled it to be used with the 1908 web frog. This particular example was issued to the Home Guard during World War II.

RIGHT A Wilkinson-made 1907 bayonet with shortened blade and scabbard. This example was originally made in December 1917.

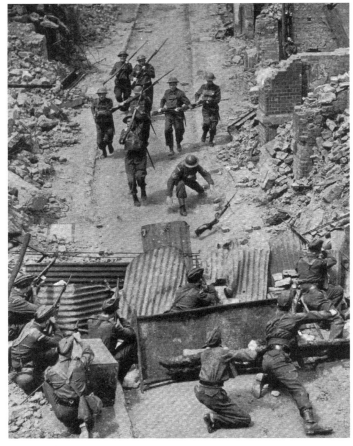

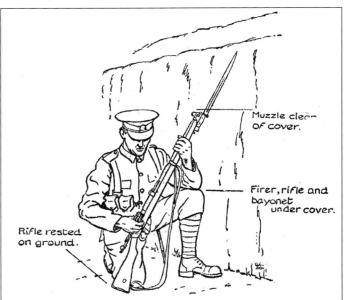

ABOVE LEFT Home Guard members attack a defensive barricade during infantry training. They are armed with American P17 rifles and M1917 bayonets.

FAR LEFT Illustration from the British manual *Small Arms Training volume 1 pamphlet 3, Rifle 1937*. Figure 32 shows the reload from cover and the position of the bayonet in relation to the parapet.

LEFT Photographed during World War I, a Royal Navy guard present arms on the quarterdeck of a warship. They are armed with Japanese Arisaka 1897 rifles and Type 30 bayonets, which had been purchased for trials prior to the war.

ABOVE A No. 1 Mk I (1907) bayonet fitted to a Lanchester machine carbine. The Lanchester was issued to the Royal Navy, and, in smaller numbers, the RAF during World War II. Although somewhat short and of limited practical use, the Lanchester and bayonet combination looked imposing.

Muzzle clear of cover.

Firer, rifle and bayonet under cover.

Rifle rested on ground.

ABOVE Spike bayonet frog and scabbard variants left to right. A Mk. I bayonet by Singer, it has an Enfield inspection mark applied to the fuller by electric pencil. The scabbard has an early (1.5in-wide) P37 frog. This necessitated the use of a "Tabs, Securing, Bayonet" (AA 1819) to secure the scabbard in the frog. The tab was not very effective and instructions were issued to cut a small slit in the frog's upper loop for the frog stud. This soon frayed, so concise orders detailing the cutting of the slit and stitch re-enforcing the cut were detailed in Army Council Instruction 375, issued in the spring of 1944; No. 4 Mk. II bayonet, by Long Branch, with an RAF P25 frog folded back on itself to reduce the width of the frog loops. The instructions for doing so were published in AMO N988 issued on September 28, 1944, as the RAF had not found the cut loop to be satisfactory; Mk II spike made in the U.S. by Stevens, with a late-production thin (1.25in-wide) P37 frog with cut and stitched loop; Mk. II bayonet marked "Yc 306," an unidentified code, with "Frog, Web, Bayonet No. 4." It had two small webbing loops for the body and a web tab that attached to the scabbard boss, it was coded AA5101. The scabbard is the metal-bodied Mk. II; An identical version of this frog was issued to troops armed with the Mk. V Sten gun. The "Frog, Bayonet, Sten Mk V" had a separate pouch that contained the cover plate for the Sten (used when the weapon was broken down). This type was coded AA5508. The Mk. III bayonet is shown with the plastic-bodied scabbard; a U.S.-made Stevens Mk. II bayonet with a war-aid M5 scabbard with integral belt loop; The last bayonet in the line-up is a Singer-made Mk. II, chromed overall and with a blunted tip for use by color parties, it has the early full designation stamping. The Mk. I scabbard is carried in a post-war P37 frog made with an integrally woven slit in the upper loop.

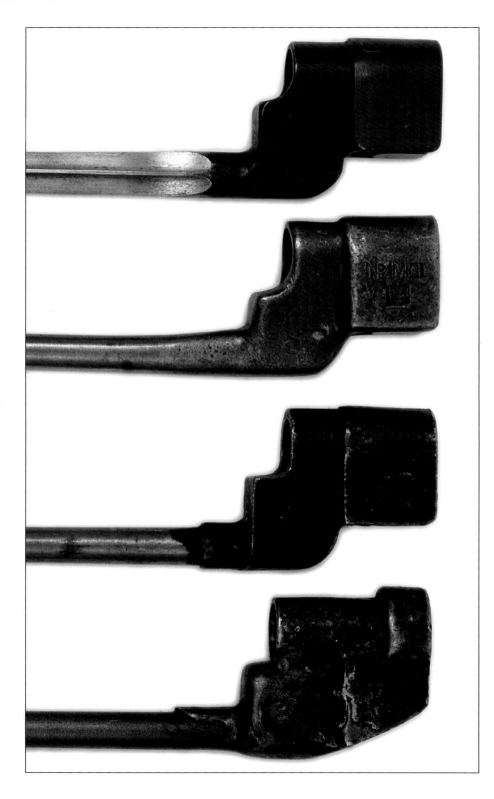

FAR LEFT No. 4 spike bayonet socket details, top to bottom: the Mk. I, only made by the Singer Manufacturing Co.; a Mk. II, this example having the boxed "S" logo showing that it was made in the U.S. by Stevens; the Mk. II* with distinct blade to socket join. The socket is marked "FF" and "SL" for F. Fisher and Sons Ltd., who did not make whole bayonets but provided components; the final, and rather rough, version of the spike was the Mk. III, this example made by J. Lucas. The only marking is a small "1" on the blade.

LEFT Normandy, 1944. German POWs are escorted to the rear by a Tommy armed with a No. 4 rifle and fixed No. 4 spike bayonet.

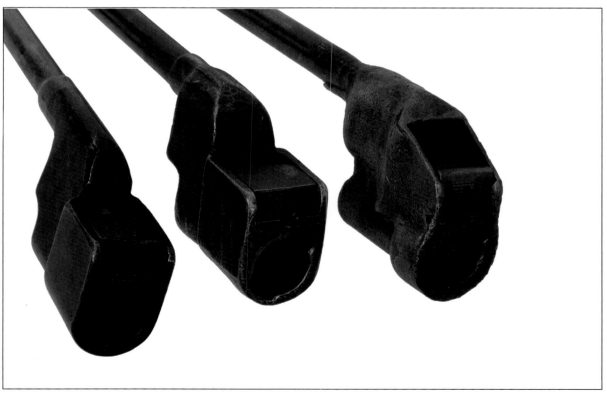

LEFT A No. 4 Mk. I bayonet mounted on a .303in No. 4 rifle. The bayonet blade was short but considered to be of sufficient length to incapacitate any enemy. Its shape made it otherwise of little use, except perhaps for making holes in condensed milk tins.

BELOW LEFT An armorer's drawing of the components of bayonets No. 4 Mk. I and Mk. II* (lower), and scabbards No. 4 Mk. I and No. 4 Mk. II (lower).

BELLOW Arnhem, 1944. A British Para armed with the Sten Mk. V, fitted with a spike bayonet. The Mk. V was designed for airborne troops but was issued as a standard infantry weapon in the post-war years.

LEFT Press-catch detail of a Singer Mk. II. Note the small depression above the press catch, which is present on all Singer-made spike bayonets. The catch is marked "SM;" a Mk. II* stamped "VNS" for Viners of Sheffield. Note the broader socket area forward of the press catch, one of the identifying features of the Mk II*. The rear of the blade is just visible at the back of the socket above the press catch. It was fitted into a hole bored into the socket and then ground flush after fixing by a pin and then brazing or shrinking; at right is a Mk. III marked "m/158≠," the code for Lucas. It has a stamped sheet-steel press catch. The manner in which the outer socket is formed around the machined rifle attachment section is evident.

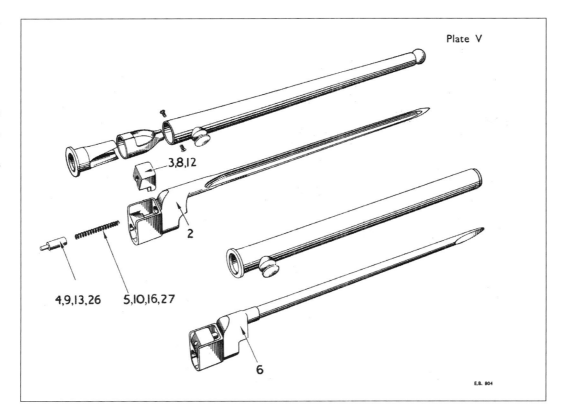

Plate V

3,8,12

2

4,9,13,26   5,10,16,27

6

E.B. 804

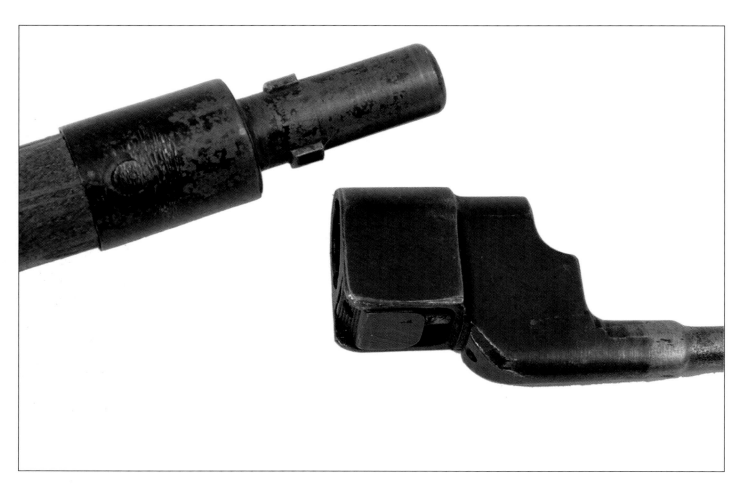

ABOVE The original 1908-pattern entrenching tool helve was coded as JA 5406. Later, a modified Mk. II helve was introduced under ACI 976 of June 1944. An adaptor (JA 6023) incorporating a fitting for the No. 4 spike bayonet was added to the 1908 helve. This was then listed as "Helve, Mk II complete with bayonet adaptor." The Mk. II helve saw no widespread issue during World War II, but was in limited use with some units from 1944.

LEFT Fitting detail of the "Helve, Mk II complete with bayonet adaptor" and No. 4 Mk. II spike bayonet. When fitted, the bayonet could be used as a mine probe or offensive weapon.

BELOW A "Port Fannion" fashioned from a chromed No. 4 Mk. II bayonet in a manner similar to that popular with French regiments. It had an extended tubular blade to which was attached two fixing points for a regimental pennant. It is believed that the Royal Welsh Fusiliers used this example.

ABOVE RIGHT Port Fannion hilt detail. Originally made by Singer (N67), it was probably modified at unit level.

BELOW RIGHT On the outskirts of Arnhem, a PIAT team awaits the enemy. The Para at right is armed with a No. 4 rifle and No. 4 Mk. I spike bayonet; the cruciform blade is clearly evident.

FAR RIGHT British and Indian troops take the surrender of Japanese officers. The soldier with the rifle has an Indian bayonet No. 1 Mk. II fixed to his SMLE, and the shortened scabbard at his side. An officer, at right, with a Mk. V Sten and spike bayonet oversees him. Note also the "Airborne"-pattern frog, complete with pouch, worn at the officer's side.

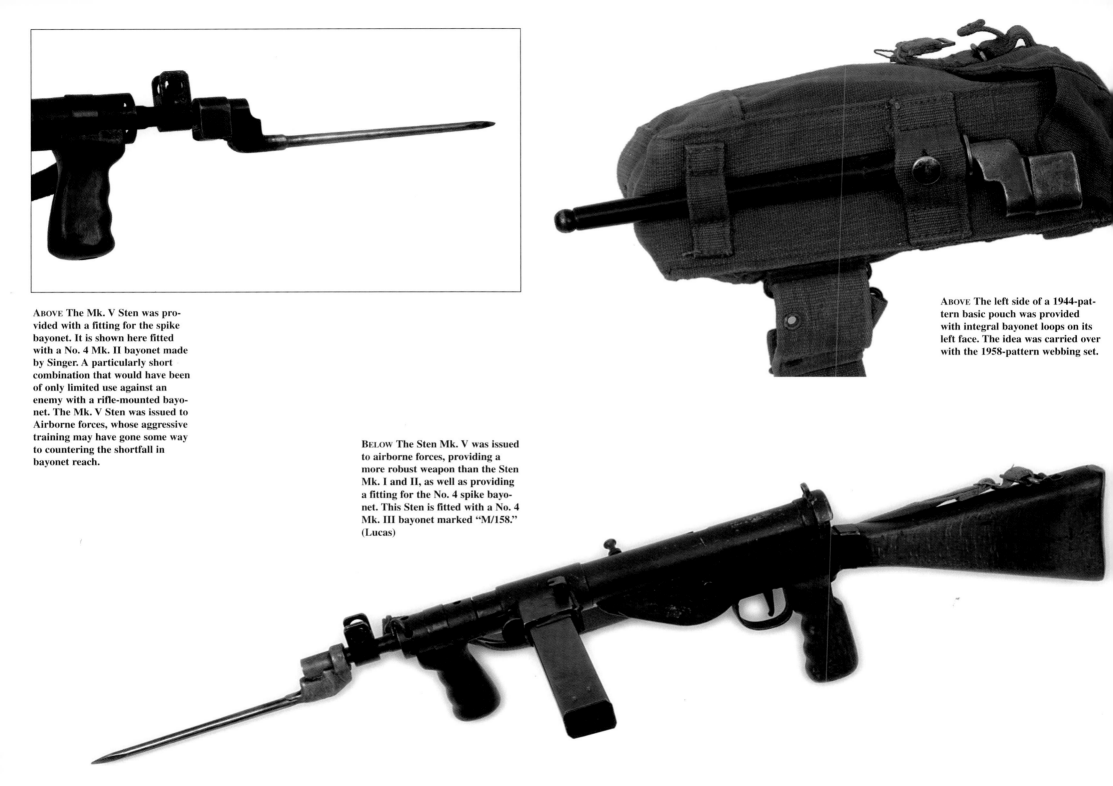

ABOVE The Mk. V Sten was provided with a fitting for the spike bayonet. It is shown here fitted with a No. 4 Mk. II bayonet made by Singer. A particularly short combination that would have been of only limited use against an enemy with a rifle-mounted bayonet. The Mk. V Sten was issued to Airborne forces, whose aggressive training may have gone some way to countering the shortfall in bayonet reach.

ABOVE The left side of a 1944-pattern basic pouch was provided with integral bayonet loops on its left face. The idea was carried over with the 1958-pattern webbing set.

BELOW The Sten Mk. V was issued to airborne forces, providing a more robust weapon than the Sten Mk. I and II, as well as providing a fitting for the No. 4 spike bayonet. This Sten is fitted with a No. 4 Mk. III bayonet marked "M/158." (Lucas)

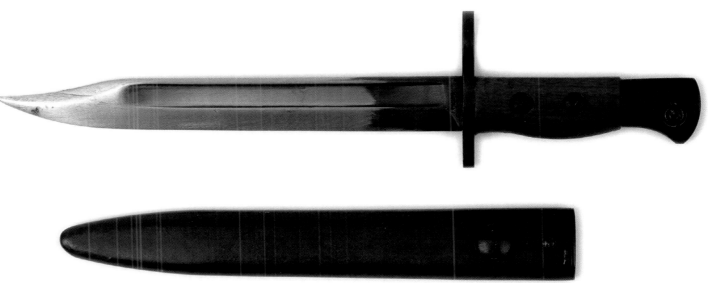

ABOVE No. 5 bayonet for the Jungle carbine was manufactured from early 1944, with first contracts being placed in December 1943. This example is the No. 5 Mk. I second pattern with two grip screws.

LEFT This view shows the enlarged muzzle ring and round mortise slot of the No. 5 bayonet.

ABOVE The skeleton assault jerkin had limited provision for the carriage of ammunition in two pouches; the only other addition was a loop for the No. 4 bayonet. This is the 1944 type of vest; the 1945 version shifted the position of the bayonet to the side of the left pouch.

BELOW The L2A3 SMG, better known as the Sterling. This replaced the Sten in British service, and, like the Mk. V Sten, it had provision for the fixing of a bayonet. The bayonet used was the No. 5, previously used with the Jungle carbine.

RIGHT Korea, 1951. A member of 41 Commando clears a building, armed with a U.S.-issue Garand rifle and M1 bayonet. 41 Commando were equipped from U.S. Army stocks, receiving issues of web equipment, and clothing as well as weaponry.

ABOVE Typical ricasso marks on a No. 5 bayonet showing the "S-294" code for Wilkinson and also the company initials, "WSC." Other manufacturers included ROF Poole, Viners and Elkington.

BELOW Top is a partially finished blade blank; commercially produced by Hopkinsons, it is marked "STERLING." Below this is an unfinished blade blank of the type used on the No. 5, No. 7 and L1 series of bayonets.

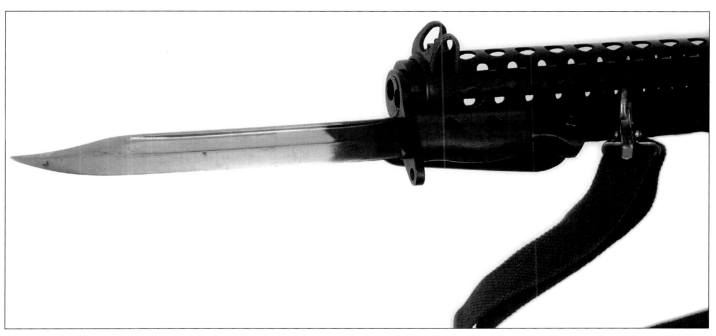

BAYONET & SCABBARD.

Plate F

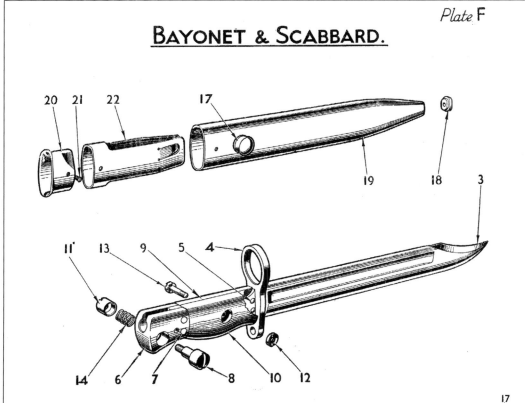

ABOVE The No. 5 bayonet fitted to the muzzle of the 9mm Sterling L2A3 submachine gun. The folding butt rested immediately beneath the barrel, necessitating an offset fixing for the bayonet.

LEFT An exploded diagram of the first-pattern bayonet No. 5 Mk. I with single grip screw. This shows that even in an item as simple as a bayonet there are at least 13 components that could require repair or replacement at unit level.

FAR LEFT The No. 5 scabbard was produced in two variants; at left, the No. 5 Mk. I first introduced with the No.5 bayonet. It is marked S-294 showing manufacture by Wilkinson Sword Co. At right is a No. 5 Mk. II first manufactured in 1949, this one bears the Enfield "ED" marking on the frog stud.

FIG. 3.—THE WITHDRAWAL (USING FOOT)

LEFT *Small Arms Training volume 1, pamphlet 12, Bayonet, 1942.* This illustration shows the No. 1 Mk. I bayonet and the "withdrawal (using foot)," the method of removing the bayonet following a thrust.

BELOW A No. 7 bayonet with GS Mk. II buff leather frog as used by the bandsmen of the Guards Division in the 1980s. The pommel is rotated for carriage in the scabbard and for use as a handheld weapon. The shaped grips provided a firm hold, which is also quite comfortable, unlike when the pommel is rotated for fixing, which makes any method of holding the bayonet quite difficult.

RIGHT Overall view of the No. 7 bayonet with pommel turned for fixing to the Sten. The scabbard is the No. 5 Mk. I. Although red on this example, black grips can also be found on the No. 7.

FAR LEFT Detail of the left side of the No. 7 hilt, showing the fabric-reinforced plastic grips and the pommel rotated for fitting on the rifle. The serrated catch on the hilt back slid forward to allow the pommel to rotate.

LEFT Manufacturer's marking on a No. 9 bayonet showing that it was made at ROF (Royal Ordnance Factory) Poole in 1949. ROF Poole only manufactured the No. 9 between 1947 and 1949, with Enfield then taking over production.

BELOW The No. 9 bayonet was the product of combining the No. 5-style blade with a No. 4 type of socket. The scabbard is the No. 5 Mk. II carried in a "Frog No. 6. Web Equipment Pattern 1937."

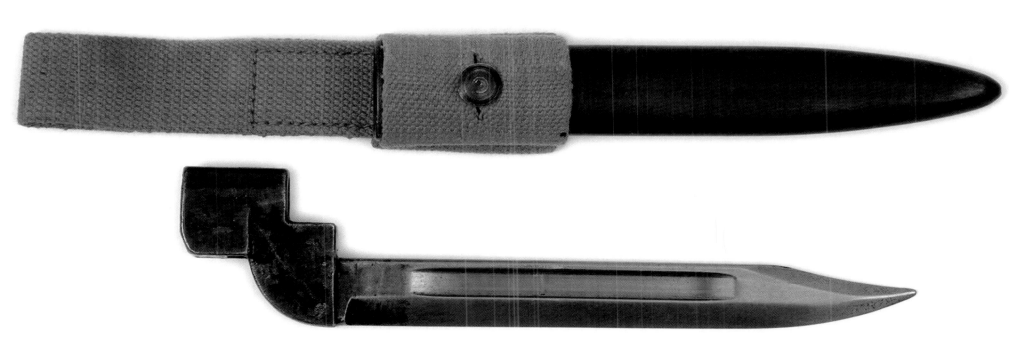

ABOVE The trials bayonet used with the X8 (FN FAL) rifle was the X2E1. The modified rifle was adopted as the L1A1, but the Belgian bayonet with its integral flash hider was turned down in favor of the newly designed L1A1. The X1E1 scabbard is carried in a P44 web frog, as used during trials in Malaya where the rifle and bayonet were field-tested.

FAR LEFT The X2E1 marking was stamped into the lower bayonet tang.

LEFT The typical FAL-type scabbard shows the X1E1 designation stamped into the mouthpiece.

ABOVE 1958-production L1A3 with parkerized blade, long fuller and angled guard, and green polyethylene frog; Birmingham 1960-made L1A3, long fuller and angled crossguard, chromed for ceremonial use, white polyethylene frog; L1A4, long fuller and straight guard, black plastic frog; later production L1A3 with straight crossguard and short fuller, manufactured at Enfield in 1966. The L1A4 differs from the L1A3 in having the pommel secured to the tang using rivets, visible on this example. Brazing is used on the L1A3.

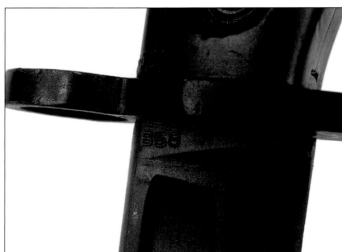

LEFT Port Stanley, Falkland Islands, 1982. A Royal Marine Commando patrols the recently captured town. An L1A3 bayonet is fitted to his SLR, both of which saw use during the close-quarter fighting typical of the conflict.

FAR LEFT, FROM TOP TO BOTTOM: TOP Crossguard detail of L1A3 types. At left, an angled crossguard and, at right, a straight crossguard made in 1966.

CENTER "B58" marking identifying a bayonet made in Birmingham in 1958.

BOTTOM The "ED" marking showing production at Royal Small Arms Factory, Enfield Lock, and the date 1966.

Top An L1A3 bayonet fitted to an L1A1 SLR (self-loading rifle). This early-production bayonet has the angled crossguard and long fullers. The bayonet fixes to the flash eliminator, not the barrel. This is the early-pattern five-vent flash eliminator.

Above The second-pattern flash eliminator had only three vents, thus reducing any effect the flash may have had on the bayonet hilt. The recessed press catch is evident in this image. Used on the L1A3 and L1A4, this is the main point of difference between them and the earlier L1A1 and L1A2. The bayonet designation "L1A3" is stamped into the steel grips.

Left A disassembled No. 5 Mk. II scabbard showing the basic component parts and an armorer's mandrel used to straighten out dents and minor damage to the scabbard body.

ABOVE During infantry weapons trials, an Enfield Weapon System "Phase II" development (EWS 77) bayonet is shown attached to the left pouch of the 1958 webbing set. The British did not adopt this style of socket bayonet with its clipped-point blade.

ABOVE The No. 1 Mk. I bayonet was replaced in British service by the No. 4 spike; however, it was retained in some units for ceremonial use. A bandsman from the Royal Irish Rangers wears it here during the mid-1980s.

LEFT The black PVC frog based on the GS frog. Rifle regiments used this frog on ceremonial occasions.

RIGHT The SA80 bayonet. From left to right, reverse of the frog showing belt loops and belt retaining hook fixings. The early frog could not be removed from the belt without dismantling the equipment. This was remedied on later scabbards by having the lower edge of the two belt loops secured by press fasteners, allowing the loop to be opened for easy removal; the author's L3A1 bayonet carried by him in Iraq during operations with 3 Commando Brigade in 1991. The elastic "bungie" around the hilt was added after having the bayonet dislodged from the scabbard twice during helicopter operations; early pre-1986 L3A1 and L1A1 scabbard with beaked tip. The reverse fuller is marked "86 2101;" post-1986 L3A1 and L2A1 scabbard with flat tip; "Fastex" clip that allowed the scabbard to be carried on the polyethylene belt; DPM frog.

ABOVE L2A1 scabbard with the saw extended for use, and, below, an early L3A1 bayonet attached to an L1A1 scabbard for wire cutting. This pre-1986 bayonet has the early triangular saw teeth on the blade edge. Also shown is the flash eliminator from the SA80 rifle; the bayonet socket fitted to this, locked against the semi circular cut-out.

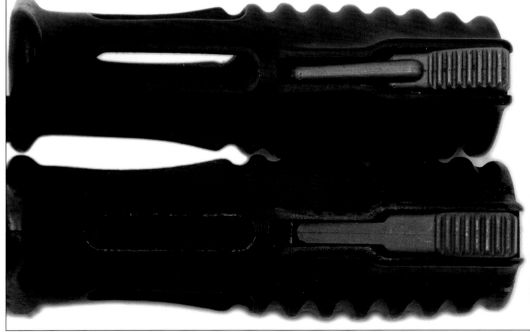

LEFT L1A3 hilt and press-catch detail. Top, a post-1986 re-enforced "pawl" (press catch), below is the early pawl without the reinforcement ridge.

ABOVE British Guardsmen, in winter greatcoats, carry the SA80 rifle with fixed bayonets. The black painted hilt is slightly more worn than one might have expected of the Guards.

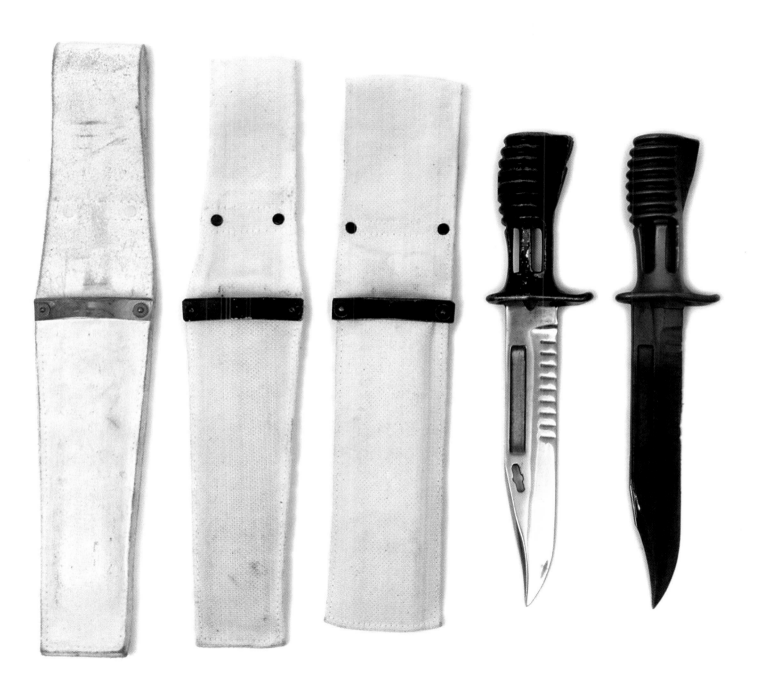

RIGHT L1A3 ceremonial frogs: buff leather Mk. III; white polypropylene Mk. II; white polypropylene, squared-edge variant; chromed L3A1 bayonet for ceremonial use; and an incomplete and unfinished casting, both showing the post-1986 saw teeth on the bayonet blade.

India

	Overall length	Blade length	Muzzle ring
Mysore	345mm	295mm	21mm
"Windus's Pattern"	460mm	340mm	24.5mm
India pattern	510mm	390mm	23.5mm
"Baker's EIC"	495mm	385mm	23mm
1842	500mm	400mm	23mm
1845	698mm	562mm	23mm
1853 type brass	520mm	430mm	21.5mm
Indian carbine	430mm	330mm	20mm
1903	525mm	305mm	16.5mm
No. 1 Mk. I*	424mm	303mm	16.5mm
No. 5	302mm	201mm	22.5mm
L1 long	353mm	253mm	15mm
L1	298mm	197mm	15mm
INSAS	305mm	180mm	22.5mm

ABOVE Indian-made bayonet, originally fitted with an India-pattern spring that has been removed or is otherwise missing. The slot has been extended to allow fitting to an unknown Brown Bess-type musket, but the original, and now superfluous, slot has not been filled. This bayonet is typical of the "make-do" type frequently found amongst the many variants of Indian state bayonets.

BELOW India-pattern Brown Bess-type bayonets with added locking rings. Top, a Land Pattern bayonet with added muzzle ring, retained by small studs rather than a collar; below, an India-pattern bayonet originally fitted with an India-pattern spring, a full collar and locking ring have been added; bottom, the Indian 1842 socket with collar fitting for the pattern F (India) catch.

India covered a large area encompassing different religions and many semi-autonomous and British-ruled states. Since the discovery of India in the late 15th century, the British, French, Dutch and Portuguese had vied for economic and political control. The British gained the upper hand, and the principal economic concern during the 17th, 18th and early 19th centuries was to be the United East India Company, which had formed a vast army to protect its trade, and which also administered Bengal and had three separate armies under the Bengal, Bombay and Madras Presidencies. Both Native and European troops were employed and provided with standard weaponry. The Indian Mutiny of 1857 saw the demise of the UEIC as a military concern. The mutiny prompted the British Crown to take control of India and, in 1858, the British Government took over the company's authority in India. The British continued to administer Indian affairs for the next 89 years. Indian troops fought in the Flanders' trenches during World War I and again provided a great military contribution in the Mediterranean and Far Eastern theatres of World War II. Internal disorder and a new postwar British government saw independence granted to India in 1947, and the country was partitioned on religious lines. The difficult partition saw India losing land in the creation of Pakistan and East Pakistan, which later became

Bangladesh. Post independence has seen conflict in Kashmir, a territory disputed by India and Pakistan, leading to three major wars. A brief conflict in 1962 saw Tibet invaded by China, and Indian forces decisively defeated.

Many of the autonomous Indian states acquired British-type weapons whilst others produced their own arms. An unusual early socket bayonet with octagonal form was issued to native troops in the Indian state of Mysore. It had an "L"-shaped mortise slot and short leaf spring. The **Mysore** bayonet, dating to *c*.1790, was produced in a basic other ranks pattern and a slightly more elaborate NCOs type with added foresight on the socket. Contemporary to this bayonet was the **"Windus's Pattern"** (EIC socket) bayonet with spring catch over the "L"-shaped mortise. The example illustrated has the date 1799 and the UEIC heart-shaped ownership crest on the socket. This pattern was superseded by a version with a longer spring; the UEIC **"Baker's improved EIC spring bayonet"** (1818 pattern) socket, made by Ezekiel Baker.

Sappers of the UEIC company were issued a long sword socket bayonet. The **1845** bayonet for the "Sappers' Carbine" is typical of the type and has a broad basal collar that has a fitting for the musket-mounted pattern F (India) pattern spring catch. This type of catch was first used on the company's **1842** socket bayonet.

Indian states copied many of the British weapons and bayonets. Many variants of the **1853** may be encountered, some of quite good workmanship and others less so. An example of a state-issue **1853** bayonet with a brass socket is illustrated, as is an interesting ornate carbine bayonet.

The latter half of the 19th century saw obsolete British weaponry issued to Indian troops, more modern weapons being provided as production met demand or as they were replaced in British service. During World War I, many Indian troops serving in Europe were issued with the 1903-pattern bandolier equipment. This was used with British-made **1888**- or **1903**-pattern bayonets. Unlike the standard 1908 web and 1914 leather equipment, there was no provision for the carriage of the entrenching tool helve. This was remedied by attaching leather straps to the frog and scabbard of **1888** bayonets and early **1903** bayonets, and to the scabbard body of **1903 Land Mk. I** scabbards issued with later production **1903** bayonets. The straps can also be found on 1907 bayonet scabbards, but all are extremely rare.

India first began production of the 1907-pattern bayonet in 1912 and continued producing the long version until World War II. The rapid fall of Burma and Malaya and the Japanese assault on eastern India provided the Indian Army with many hard-earned lessons. One of the lessons was that a long bayo-

net was not always useful, and that in close jungle terrain a short bayonet was often able to offer an advantage. Therefore, in late 1941, the Indian arsenals began to cut down the blades of the long **No. 1** bayonet from the original 436mm to a more manageable 303mm. Although early examples of the shortened bayonets were carried in standard length scabbards, the scabbards were progressively shortened throughout World War II. By 1943, the bayonets were being made with new unfullered short blades. The exact designations of these short bayonets can be confusing as they were changed by the Indian Government in the postwar years, and also by the Pakistani Government that continued to use Indian weapons. The **No. 1 Mk. I*** was a cut-down **No. 1 Mk. I** bayonet. The new-production short-bladed bayonet retained the original hilt but had a plain unfullered blade; this variant was the **No. 1 Mk. II**. A simplified hilt with squared pommel and parallel-sided grips was in production from 1944. Also with a plain blade, this was designated the **No. 1 Mk. II***. It should be noted that these

BELOW This "Baker's improved EIC spring bayonet" (often called the Baker 1818) for the improved UEIC India-pattern musket of 1818 has been heavily modified. The spring has been removed, the original slot filled and a median collar and locking ring added. This modification dates to the mid-1850s. An unmodified bayonet is illustrated in the British section.

ABOVE The socket of the Mysore bayonet had "flats" rather than the normal round form common to the majority of socket bayonets; the bore remains round. The short "L" slot is a copy of the "Windus's Pattern" spring, often called the India-pattern spring.

designations do not always tie in with the bayonet they are applied to. A typical example being a **No. 1 Mk. II** bayonet erroneously marked "II*" and a **No. 1 Mk. I*** stamped "Mk. I**," somewhat confusing for collectors.

The principal factories involved in the manufacture of the No. 1 bayonet included NWR (North Western Railways), RFI (Rifle Factory Ishapore), MIL (Metal Industries Lahore) and the unidentified "JU." Many of the bayonets were factory refurbished in the postwar years. They are sometimes marked "FR" along with the date of refurbishment, such as "FR 56" for factory refurbished in 1956.

In the post-war period, the SMLE remained on issue for many years. It was supplemented by the Indian version of the SLR, the IASL 1A rifle. Two bayonets were issued with the rifle, differing only in blade length. Both were based on British L1 bayonets but had wooden grips instead of steel. A copy of the **No. 5** bayonet was also made in India and was still being issued with the Sterling SMG in the 1990s.

The 5.56mm Indian version of the Soviet AKM is the INSAS (Indian Small Arms System) rifle. Manufactured at Kanpur, it resembles the AKM II. The **INSAS** bayonet has a longer blade than that standard to the AKM types. It differs in a number of other minor ways, most noticeable is a small screwdriver tip forged at the top of the muzzle ring. Apart from being slightly longer and incorporating a bottle-opener, the scabbard is the same as the second-pattern AKM. However, the finish is noticeably much poorer than Soviet-manufactured bayonets. The press catch is identical to that used on the IASL 1A bayonet, which was copied from the British L1A2 recessed design. The INSAS entered full service in 1997, and is gradually replacing the Indian IASL and AK rifles.

BOTTOM 1845 bayonet for "Sappers' Carbine." This is but one variant of the bayonet type. It has the broad socket base collar for provision of the pattern F (India-pattern) catch that would have been fitted to the musket. The base of the blade retains the leather washer that would have prevented undue wear between the steel bayonet and the brass scabbard throat.

BELOW "John Roe" is marked on the blade back of this 1845 socket bayonet. Roe was a West Bromwich-based parts contractor for EIC between 1842 and 1856.

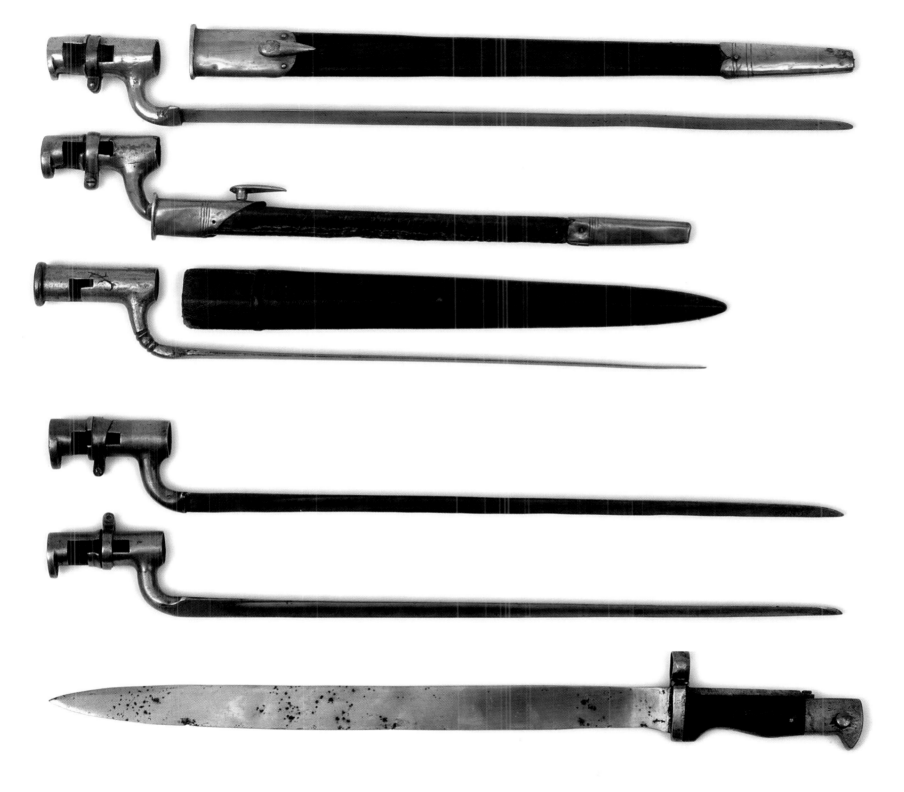

LEFT Two Indian 1853-type socket bayonets. At the top is an unusual brass-socketed bayonet with steel blade and brass-mounted brown leather scabbard; in the center is a short-bladed bayonet with 1853-style socket. The triangular blade of this bayonet is marked with a snake. The lower carbine-type bayonet has a flat double-edged blade and leather-covered wooden scabbard. The elbow of the bayonet is ornately decorated.

LEFT Two Indian copies of the British 1853 socket bayonet. Both fit the Enfield 1853 rifle. The upper example is a straight copy, whilst the example below has a locking ring that is closed when orientated 180 degrees from the normal position. Both bayonets show the ring in the locked position.

LEFT State-pattern sword bayonet dating to the 20th century. Little is known about this item, which may be a fantasy piece. The author's attention was drawn to the odd rust pitting. The blade retains an overall polish whilst small areas have quite deep pitting, possibly indicative of acid-induced pitting. The reverse of the pommel is marked with a "20."

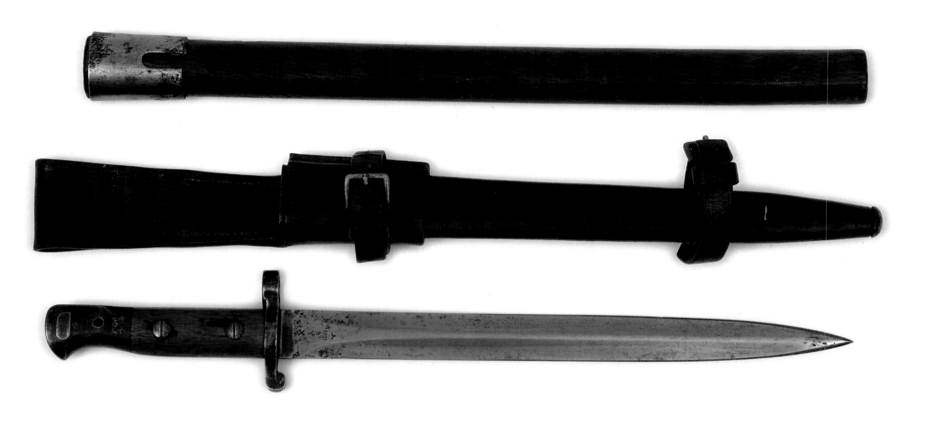

LEFT Indian-issue 1903 bayonet with helve attachment. Whilst British troops serving in France were issued the 1907 bayonet and 1908 or 1914 pattern helve holder, Indian troops were issued this combination. Two small leather loops were stitched to the back of the scabbard and a leather strap was passed through each one, fastening on the front to retain the wooden helve. The pommel is marked "59R"; the 59th Regiment were better known as the Scinde Rifles (Frontier Force).

BELOW The helve was carried attached to the front face of the scabbard, as shown here. Standard Mk. II (long 1907) pattern scabbards have been noted with the two loops on the reverse, suggesting that they too were used in this manner.

LEFT Indian bayonets for the SMLE rifle: No.1 Mk. I* (actually marked Mk. I**). Originally a Wilkinson 1907, this example bears a factory refurbishment mark (FR) for 1956; a Mk. II made by NWR (North Western Railways) in 1944 is marked "II;" a Mk11*, again marked "NWR 44," and stamped "II*." The first two frogs are standard Indian P37, the third one is a late-war jungle green example.

LEFT Typical markings on a North Western Railways Mk. II made in 1944.

BELOW An Indian Mk II* with squared pommel fitted to an SMLE rifle. The SMLE was provided with a nose cap, the bayonet muzzle ring fitting to this rather than directly to the barrel.

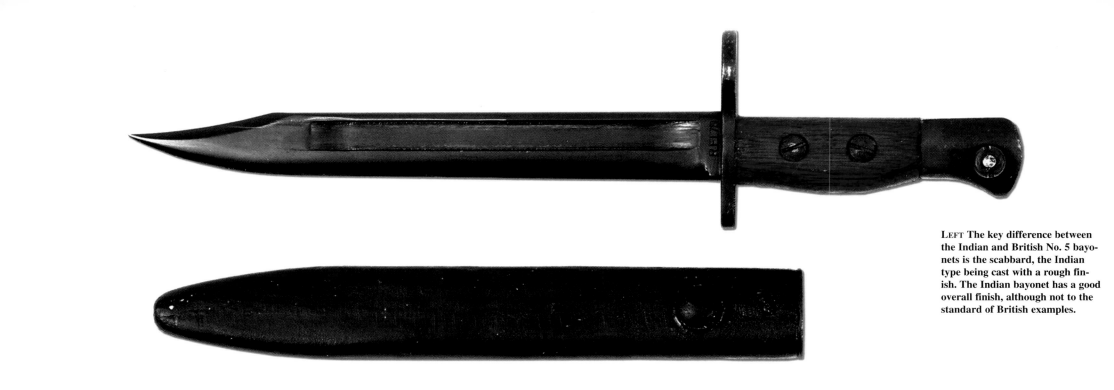

LEFT The key difference between the Indian and British No. 5 bayonets is the scabbard, the Indian type being cast with a rough finish. The Indian bayonet has a good overall finish, although not to the standard of British examples.

LEFT India adopted the British L1A1 version of the FN FAL rifle in 1963. The L1 bayonet is based on the British SLR bayonet but with wood grips; two different blade lengths were issued with this, the shorter, being the same as the British type.

BELOW Two different scabbard types were issued with the long-bladed L1 bayonet: a shortened Mk. II (1907 bayonet) scabbard, as used here, and an all-steel type, which was an extended version of that issued with the short bayonet. The pommel of this example is marked "83."

FAR LEFT "R.F.I. 78" is stamped deeply into the left ricasso of the Indian No. 5 bayonet. This indicates manufacture by the Rifle Factory Ishapore in 1978.

LEFT Indian troops in North Africa search for mines, showing the No. 1 Mk. I in use as probe.

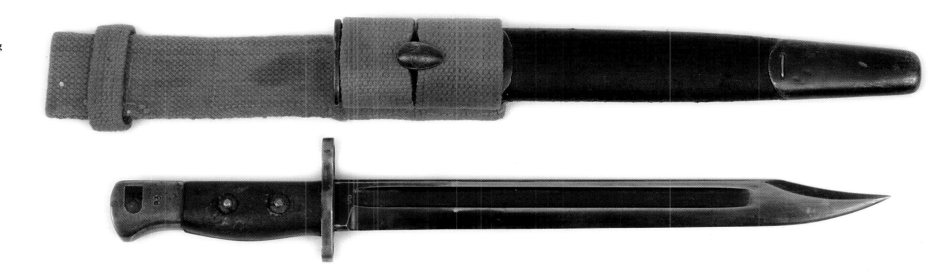

BELOW Similar to the AKM II in general form, the INSAS bayonet has a poor finish. Most noticeably, it has a longer blade and a screwdriver tip on the muzzle ring. The grips and scabbard are made from a cream-colored composite material that has been sprayed orange.

ABOVE Indian officer cadets parade with the IASL rifle and long pattern L1 bayonet. (DGI Indian Army)

RIGHT The INSAS has a press catch and fixing mechanism copied from that used on the L1 bayonet. The prominent screwdriver tip on the muzzle ring is evident in this view, as is the painted finish, overlapping the base of the ring.

Israel

	Overall length	Blade length	Muzzle ring
Mk. IA (S84/98)	384mm	251mm	15mm
Mk. IA	379mm	246mm	15mm
VZ24	432mm	298mm	14.9mm

The State of Israel came into being on the May 14, 1948, on Palestinian land that had formerly been under British mandate. The fledgling Israeli military forces were initially armed and equipped with British material. The world arms market was awash with weaponry and Israel soon bought up countless numbers of surplus German K98 rifles and bayonets. The **S84/98** bayonets and the Israeli copies, designated the **Mk. IA**, have generally and erroneously been called the M49 by collectors. The **S84/98** were refurbished and given muzzle rings as well as the Israeli Star of David inspection marking, which was applied to the bayonet and scabbard. The Israeli arms industry-produced version of the **Mk. IA** differed in the blade style as well as its noticeably inferior quality of manufacture. The ricasso of the Israeli-made bayonet was stamped in Hebrew with

the weapon designation in three lines "Bayonet Mk.IA. Manufacturer 101. 1949." The scabbard throat was similarly marked "Scabbard Mk.IA. Manufacturer 101. 1949." The original modified German bayonets can be found with plain wood or ribbed plastic grips, but the Israeli bayonet was only produced with ribbed plastic grips. In addition to the K98, numbers of Czech VZ24 rifles and bayonets as well as Yugoslavian rifles and bayo nets were purchased. The Israeli **VZ24** bayonets are readily identifiable as they were stamped with typical Israeli issue marks. Most of these imported rifles were later rechambered for the NATO 7.62mm cartridge. Typical Israeli markings applied to bayonets included the Star of David previously mentioned and the "*Tsadi*" symbol within a circle; this was the Israeli Defence Force's property mark and used in the same way as the British War Department arrow. Israel also produced a copy of the British No. 6 type bayonet for the SMLE. The finish is quite poor by comparison with the British original.

The Israeli Defence Force was later to purchase the 7.62mm FN FAL rifle, which was initially issued with the **FAL**

Type A bayonet. Later weapons were provided with the tubular **FAL Type C** bayonet. The native 5.56mm Israeli Military Industries Galil rifle also used a modified **FAL Type C** socket. The Israelis have also used a number of other weapons, including the U.S. M16 rifle and M7 bayonet. In Israeli service, the M16 can also be found fitted with a modified **FAL Type C** bayonet.

The 9mm Uzi SMG was to become synonymous with the IDF, being the preferred weapon of commando and special forces units. It was issued with a bayonet similar to the FAL Type B, but had a standard press catch arrangement. The **Uzi** bayonet is uncommon.

BELOW The Israelis purchased a quantity of K98 rifles and S84/98 bayonets. The bayonet was issued in Israel as the Mk. 1A, commonly referred to as the M49. It was modified from the original S84/98 by the addition of a muzzle ring. The locally produced scabbard has a British P37 frog. Israeli forces used British and U.S. webbing during their formative years.

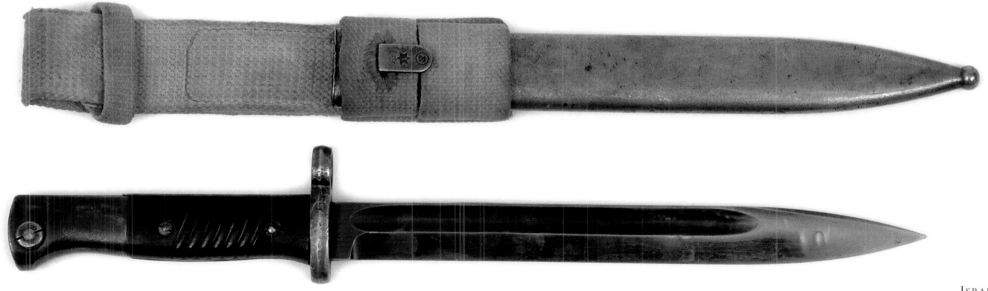

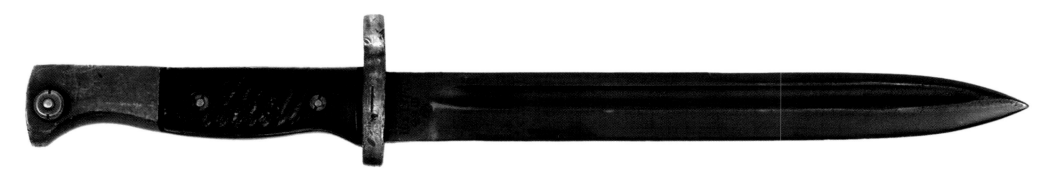

ABOVE Israel produced their own Mk. 1A (M49) bayonets, noticeably cruder than the German originals. Israeli weapon inspectors had highly flexible tolerances. The grips fit particularly poorly.

LEFT Israeli Mk. 1A markings. At left, the scabbard throat marked in Hebrew "Scabbard Mk.1A. Manufacturer 101. 1949" and, at right, the ricasso stamped "Bayonet Mk.1A. Manufacturer 101. 1949." Although correctly the Mk. 1A, this bayonet is generally referred to as the M49 by collectors. Both the ricasso and the frog stud bear the "*Tsadi*" military property symbol.

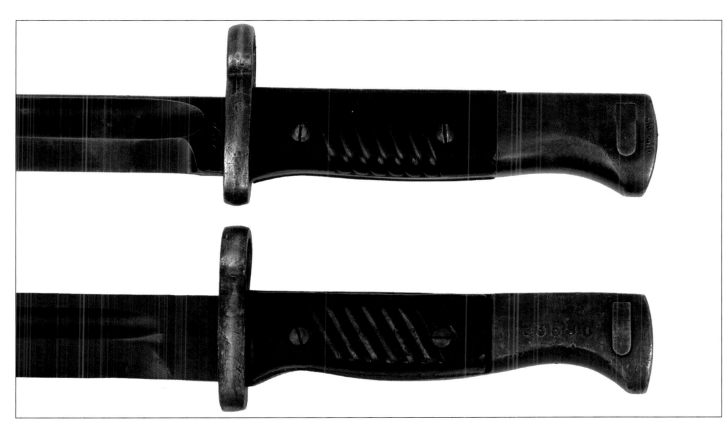

BELOW A Czechoslovakian VZ24 bayonet as used by Israel. It differs from the original Czech bayonet in being heavily blued overall and in having Israeli markings added. Many Czech rifles and bayonets were acquired during Israel's early years.

ABOVE LEFT Comparison of the hilts of a German S84/98 conversion and an Israeli-made Mk. 1A bayonet. With the exception of the added muzzle ring, the German-made bayonet (above) is vastly superior in its finish. Of note are the two *waffenampt* eagle marks above the locking bolt.

ABOVE Although faint, the markings on the frog stud of the VZ24 bayonet clearly identify its use by Israeli forces. The markings include the Star of David and the "*Tsadi*" symbol within a circle; this is the Israeli Defence Force's property mark and is used in the same way as the British War Department arrow.

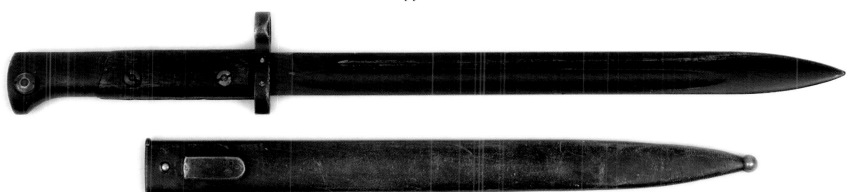

Italy

	Overall length	Blade length	Muzzle ring
1836	602mm	463mm	N/A
M1870/87	644mm	517mm	17.5mm
M1870/87/15	360mm	232mm	17.5mm
M1891	414mm	302mm	12.5mm
1891TS	420mm	300mm	12.9mm
1891 folding carbine	347mm	N/A	N/A
1891/38	289mm	177mm	13mm
M1	349mm	248mm	16mm

Italy was unified under the House of Savoy in 1870. Prior to this time, each state had decided upon its own individual armament requirements. One weapon that remained in use following unification was the Piedmont rifle and **1836** bayonet that was also later used on the 1860 rifle and Carcano 1868 rifle. However, following unification and weapon standardization, Italy was to adopt the Swiss-designed 10.35mm Vetterli rifle in 1870. The bayonet chosen was the long sword-bladed *baionetta* M1870. It had a straight blade, long forward-curved quillon and a distinctive, long leaf spring. The scabbard was of brass-mounted leather. 1887 saw a Vitali box magazine added to the 1870 rifle and the long leaf spring of the M1870 bayonet reduced in length to produce the otherwise identical **M1870/87** bayonet for the Vetterli-Vitali rifle. During World War I, Italy modified many M1870 and **M1870/87** bayonets by removing the hook quillon and reducing the blade length from 518mm to 235mm. The resulting knife bayonet was issued as the **M1870/87/15** bayonet with the M70/87 rifle. The

barrel was sleeved to 6.5mm to conform to the caliber of the M91 rifle. Interestingly, a number of the blade tips from the shortened bayonets were re-used with brass hilts to make up new bayonets.

The standard Italian rifle of the two world wars was the 6.5mm Mannlicher Carcano 1891. The **M1891** bayonet was first issued in a brass-mounted leather scabbard, with steel mounts being used later. Two patterns of all-steel scabbards were also used, one plain and one with raised decorative ribs. Some World War I-era bayonets can be of particularly poor finish with numerous heavy grinding marks. In 1897, the Italians introduced a modified bayonet for use on the rifle issued to *Truppe Speciali* (specialist troops). It differed from the standard **1891** in having a modified locking mechanism with an unusual transverse mortise and a press catch located on the end of the pommel. The **1891TS** can be found in any of

the scabbard types issued with the **1891** bayonet. The Carcano cavalry carbine, *Moschetto per Cavalleria 1891* was provided with a folding bayonet permanently fitted below the barrel. Despite the designation, its use was not restricted to mounted units. The same bayonet style was also used on the **1938** carbine.

Italy was one of the few nations to introduce a submachine gun with a bayonet mounting. The M1938 folding-blade knife bayonet was unusual in not having a muzzle ring but a "T" bar, similar to the mounting lug normally found on the rifle but that

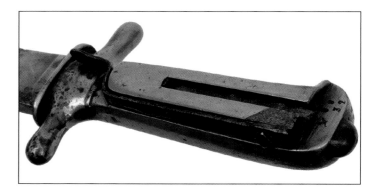 

BELOW LEFT The Piedmont 1836 hilt showing the long side-mounted leaf-spring locking mechanism.

BELOW Piedmont 1836 hilt showing the smooth grip; however, the fixing mechanism on the reverse made the weapon uncomfortable to use as a handheld weapon.

ABOVE Piedmont 1836 bayonet. It is believed that this was used on the Piedmontese 1860 rifle and the Italian Carcano 1868 artillery carbine, and remained in service after Italian unification. The ricasso is marked with the gothic letters "W&C."

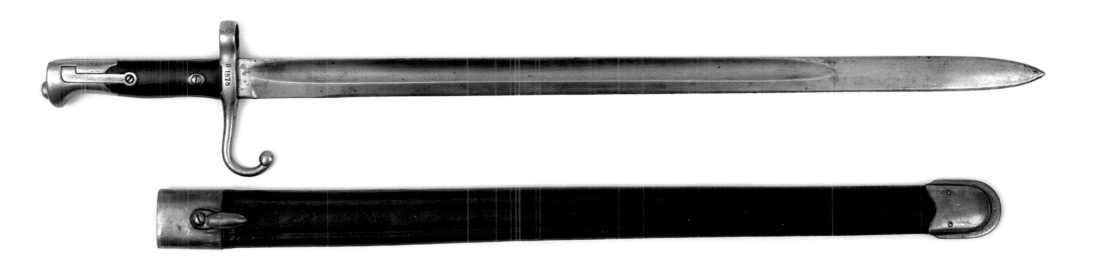

fitted into a slot on the gun. The bayonet was only made prior to World War II and then in limited numbers.

The 1891/38 rifle upgraded the small 6.5mm round to the more powerful 7.35mm. However, the onset of World War II saw the majority of weapons manufactured in the old and readily available 6.5mm. The short knife bayonet for the new rifle was based upon that issued with the machine gun, but with a slightly shorter blade, though it had a standard muzzle ring. Like the SMG bayonet, the blade of the **1891/38** folding bayonet could be folded back into the hilt and carried thus folded on the rifle, although scabbards were provided for belt carriage. The folding mechanism was soon found to be too fragile for the rigors of wartime service, with the blades soon becoming loose. The modified **1891/38** fixed-blade bayonet was therefore introduced. This added a new crossguard to the older components, providing a fixed blade but retaining the old-style hilt with blade recess. By 1943, the **1891/38** fixed-blade bayonet was being made in a new configuration with a solid hilt, providing a true knife bayonet with fixed blade. The same patterns of scabbards were issued with the M38 and **1891/38** bayonets. They can be found with either a standard frog stud or a fixed metal belt loop fitted diagonally across the upper part of the scabbard.

After World War II, Italy was provided with both British and U.S. firearms and bayonets including the **No. 4** spike and the **M1** Garand. Italy later produced bayonets of both types, the spikes being rarely encountered. The Garand pattern is

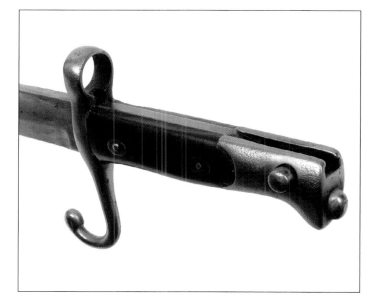

more common. The Italian version of the **M1** was identical to the U.S. type, bar markings and the fact that a short web belt loop was attached to the throat of the **M7**-pattern scabbard. Some early production scabbards used a U.S. style throat with a typically Italian-style brass chape leather scabbard. The U.S. M1 carbine and **M4** bayonet were also used in quantity, the **M4** bayonet providing the basis for the BM59 and later Beretta rifle bayonets.

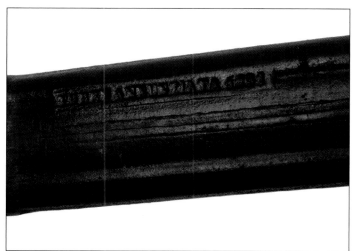

TOP The 1870/87 bayonet differed from the earlier 1870 model in that it had a short leaf spring. The scabbard is the second pattern, the first having longer brass mounts and no lip on the chape.

ABOVE LEFT 1870/87 bayonet showing the left hilt. The composite grips meet the pommel in a distinct curve; note also the nut securing the pommel to the blade tang.

ABOVE 1870/87 bayonet scabbard, it is marked "TORRE ANNUNZIATA 1891"

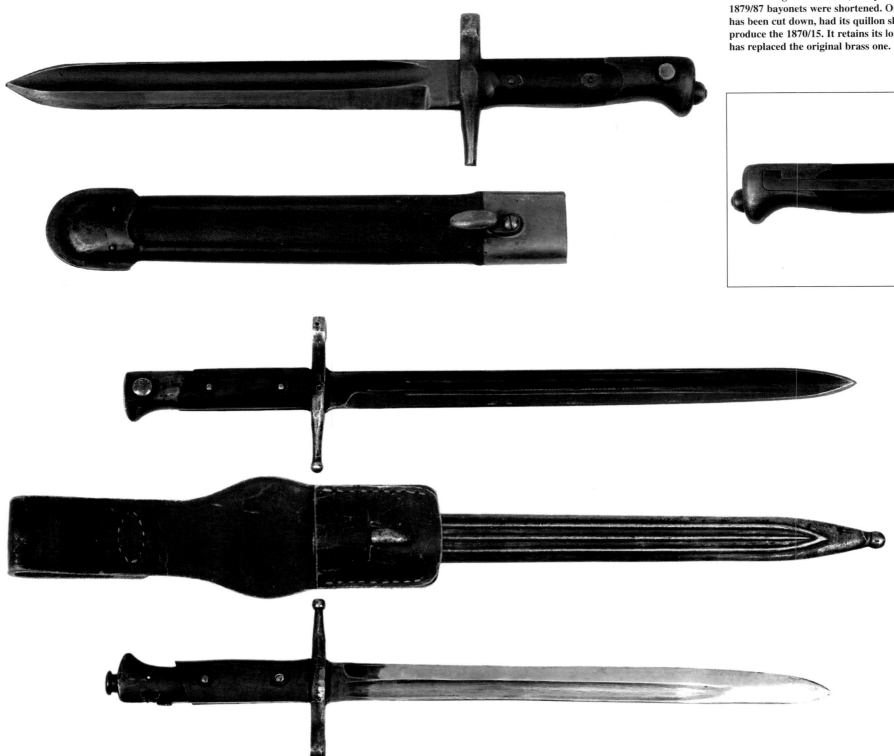

LEFT During World War I, many of the long and unwieldy 1870 and 1879/87 bayonets were shortened. Originally an 1870 pattern, this bayonet has been cut down, had its quillon shortened, and been blued overall to produce the 1870/15. It retains its long leaf spring. A steel economy chape has replaced the original brass one.

ABOVE The right hilt of the 1870/15 bayonet showing the original long leaf spring.

LEFT M1891 and M1891TS (*Truppe Speciali*). At top is an 1891 bayonet, left side. It has a standard internal coiled-spring press catch. The 1891TS below, showing the right side, differed in having a lateral mortise and a press catch at the pommel end. The blue-gray leather frog was common to the majority off Italian bayonets. It is fitted to a decorative fluted-steel scabbard; plain steel and brass- or steel-mounted leather scabbards were also used.

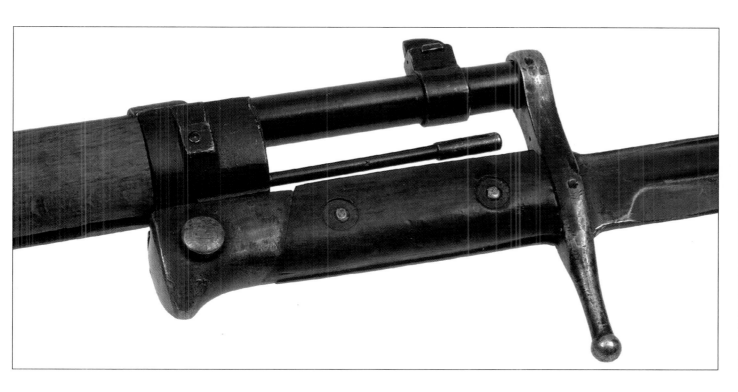

LEFT An 1891 bayonet fitted to a *Fucile di Fanteria Modello 1891*, better known as the Mannlicher Carcano.

BELOW The 1891TS bayonet hilt showing the unique lateral mortise slot and the press catch located on the end of the pommel.

BELOW The M1938 carbine had a permanently attached folding bayonet, shown here in the fixed position. The same bayonet was also used on the earlier 1891 carbine.

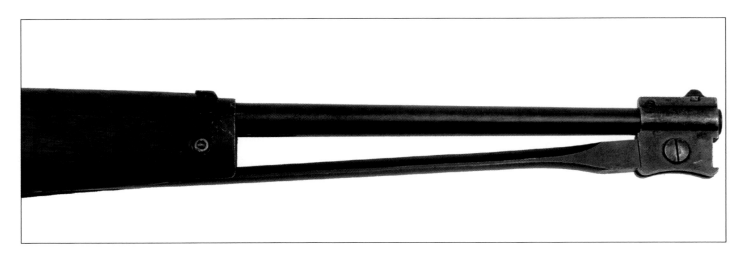

ABOVE The 1938 carbine bayonet in the folded (closed) position.

BELOW The Carcano 1938 carbine and folding bayonet. The 1938 carbine was similar to the 1891 carbine, but had a fixed rear sight rather than the adjustable tangent sight.

ABOVE M1938 carbine. This shows the bayonet in the folded position, and the left side of the locking catch and sight block, which are integral with the bayonet fitting.

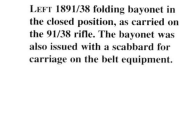

LEFT 1891/38 folding bayonet in the closed position, as carried on the 91/38 rifle. The bayonet was also issued with a scabbard for carriage on the belt equipment.

LEFT 1891/38 folding bayonet hilt, left side, with the blade extended. This shows both the standard mortise and press catch, and the ancillary press catch, behind the crossguard, that operates the folding blade.

LEFT The folding 1891/38 bayonet was found to be a poor design. The blade frequently wore loose and it was expensive and time-consuming to produce. This led to the manufacture of a fixed-blade version, and a number of folding bayonets were converted to fixed blades. From left to right: 1891/38 scabbard with belt loop; 1891/38 folding bayonet; 1891/38 scabbard with frog stud; 1891/38 bayonet newly made with a fixed blade; 1891/38 folding converted to fixed blade by the addition of a new crossguard.

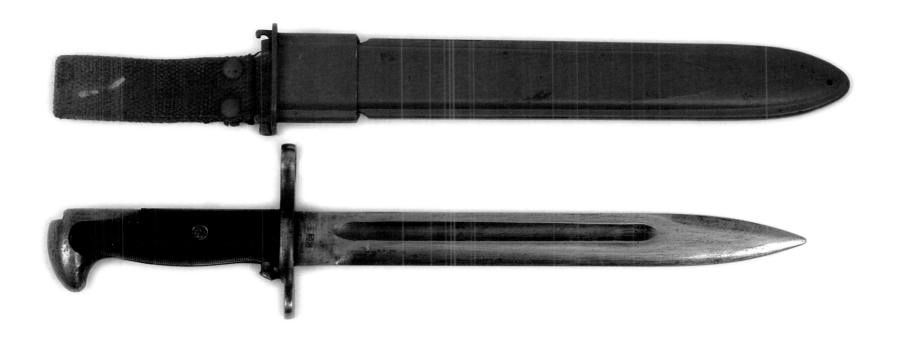

ABOVE Like many nations in the post-war era, Italy purchased a quantity of U.S. M1 Garand rifles for issue to her troops. This bayonet, an Italian copy of the U.S.-made bayonet, is identical but for the markings. On the right ricasso is a cartouche bearing a star over "FAT" over "55," for the year of production. The scabbard is also a copy of the U.S. M7 scabbard but with a web belt loop instead of the U.S. M1910 belt hook.

LEFT The left ricasso of the Italian-made M1 bayonet bears the military property star mark over "55," for 1955 manufacture, above the serial number "146792."

Japan

	Overall length	Blade length	Muzzle ring
1897 Type 30	508mm	397mm	14mm

Unlike much of the world, Japan remained free of Western domination until 1853. In that year, the American Commodore Perry infamously sailed into Tokyo Bay and persuaded the Japanese of the benefits of trade and links with the Western world through the power of his ship's guns. Under powerful Western "diplomacy," Japan soon fell into line with Western ideals. In 1871, production of modern firearms began at the state arsenal in Tokyo, but it was not until 1881 that the first indigenous rifle was introduced, the 11mm Murata Type 13. A note on the method of providing designations to Japanese arms is useful. Although Japan used their own calendar, the *Jimmu Nengo*, that started in 660 BC, Japanese weapons classification was generally, but not always, based upon a new *Nengo* instituted in 1868, the year of the ascension of the Emperor Meiji. The new time-period corresponded to the years of the reign of each emperor. Emperor Meiji acceded to the throne in 1868, Meiji year 0, and thus the Type 13 rifle was introduced in the western calendar year 1881, the 13th year of Meiji's reign. In 1912, the *Taisho Nengo* became standard when Meiji's son Prince Yoshito became the Emperor Taisho. Prince Hirohito replaced Taisho, his father, in 1926, beginning the *Showa Nengo*. Thus the end of the World War II came in the year Showa 20, 1945 being the 20th year of the reign of Emperor Hirohito, or 2605 on the Japanese *Jimmu Nengo* calendar.

A series of Murata rifles followed the Type 13, including the Types 16, 18, 20, 22 and 27, all using bayonets showing much western influence with long blades and hook quillons. Possibly thanks to the initial U.S. "influence," Japan rapidly rose to become the dominant power in the Far East, later defeating the might of the Russian Army in the Russo-Japanese war of 1904–05. This was perhaps the first major conflict of the 20th century, and one that could have had far-reaching implications. Great Britain had signed a pact with Japan stating that if Japan and Russia went to war, Britain would automatically ally itself to Japan if any other nation entered the war on the Russian side. The pact with Japan was not called upon, but

ABOVE Manchuria. Japanese troops, with fixed bayonets, advance past destroyed railway stock. (Courtesy R.F. Stedman)

BELOW Standard early-production 30th year (1897) bayonet. It has a rounded pommel, shaped grips and a hooked quillon. The scabbard and hilt are heavily blued with the blade left bright. The leather frog has been modified, the loop being re-stitched to enable fitting to a wider belt than originally allowed.

Britain's propensity for forming mutual defense pacts would later lead her into two world wars, one of them against Japan. The 6.5mm Type 30 rifle entered service in 1897, having been designed around the new small-caliber cartridge that had been accepted into Japan's military service two years previously. The 1897, or **Type 30,** *Juken* (bayonet) that accompanied it is frequently called the Arisaka bayonet. It was to serve the Japanese army until the end of World War II. The original **Type 30** bayonet was well made with a bright blade and heavily blued hilt. It had an equally well-made steel scabbard. During World War II, the quality of finish of Japanese bayonets rapidly deteriorated. The contoured hilt gave way to a squared finish pommel with square-sided grips, and the hooked quillon was deleted, as was the blade fuller. Metalwork was only partially finished with grinding and machining marks left and blued over. Wooden scabbards replaced steel and even rubber scabbards were pushed into service as the need for weaponry outstripped resources. The **Type 30** bayonet was also used on the Meiji 38 rifle and the squad light machine guns Type 96 and 99. The Japanese were the only nation to fit bayonets to squad LMGs.

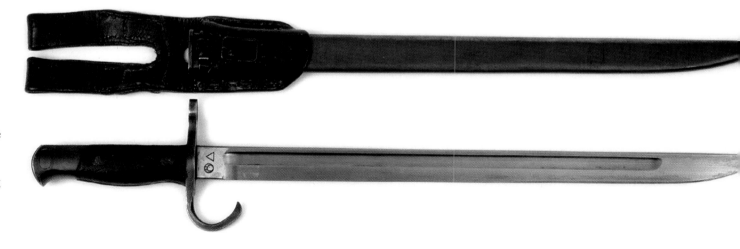

As well as providing weapons for the nation, Japan also produced weapons for export, including the Siamese 51st year (1908) bayonet manufactured by the Tokyo Arsenal. This bayonet resembled the **Type 30** but had a shorter 295mm blade.

The Type 44 (designated by Meiji's 44th year—1911) was a short 6.5mm carbine with a permanently attached folding bayonet with a blade length of 350mm. It was originally intended as a cavalry weapon, but its actual use was not so restricted. The fixed bayonet overcame the problem of having a long bayonet hanging at the wearer's side, but was of little use other than as a thrusting weapon. However, this fitted with the principal Japanese doctrine that taught that the bayonet was the primary weapon of the soldier. In battle the Japanese normally had bayonets fixed, and the aggressive use of the weapon by Japanese troops is well documented.

Japan was one of the few nations to provide a fitting for a bayonet on its submachine guns and squad level light machine guns. The 8mm SMG Type 100 was designated under the *Jimmu Nengo* calendar year 2600, or 1940. It was standard practice to use only the last two numbers of the year when the calendar designation was used. However, in this instance a "1" was added rather than use the "00" alone. The Type 100 bayonet was a short 198mm-bladed bayonet, similar to the **Type 30**. It had no quillon and was carried in a steel scabbard. The Type 100 SMG saw only a limited issue, seeing service only with selected units as well as Japanese army and navy paratroops.

The **Type 30** bayonet was used by a number of nations in the postwar era, mostly without change. Korea added a U.S.-style webbing belt loop to the standard Japanese scabbard so that it could be used with U.S. web belts. With large stocks of Japanese weapons scattered throughout the Far East at the end of World War II, many formerly occupied nations used them for their own forces. The Japanese defense forces, formed in 1950, were initially armed with U.S. weapons, but a modern 7.62mm assault rifle was issued as the Type 64, later being replaced by the Type 89 in 5.56mm. The bayonet for the latter was based on the U.S. M7.

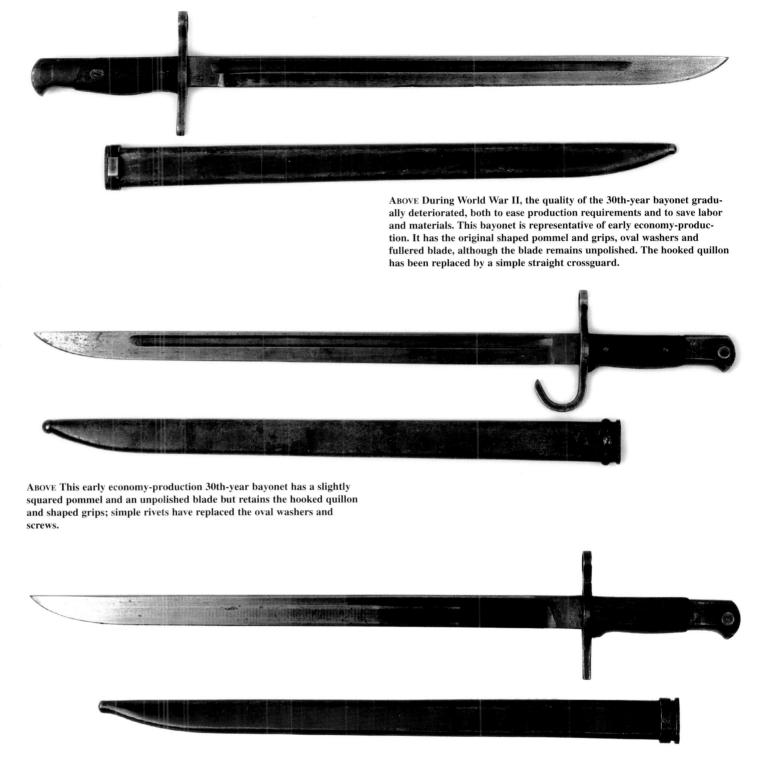

ABOVE During World War II, the quality of the 30th-year bayonet gradually deteriorated, both to ease production requirements and to save labor and materials. This bayonet is representative of early economy-production. It has the original shaped pommel and grips, oval washers and fullered blade, although the blade remains unpolished. The hooked quillon has been replaced by a simple straight crossguard.

ABOVE This early economy-production 30th-year bayonet has a slightly squared pommel and an unpolished blade but retains the hooked quillon and shaped grips; simple rivets have replaced the oval washers and screws.

RIGHT Late-production 30th-year bayonet with slightly squared pommel, straight crossguard and no fuller to the blade. The grips are less well shaped than earlier examples and are, again, retained by rivets. The 30th year was to deteriorate further, late-war examples having a square pommel and straight slab grips. By the end of the war, examples were being made with no rifle attachment, they were lashed to poles as pike-type weapons.

FAR LEFT Comparison of typical hilt variants of the 30th-year bayonet. All are marked on the ricasso with the manufacturer's stamp. From left to right: Nagoya Arsenal and unknown sub plant; Nagoya Arsenal and Toyada *Jidoshoki Seisakusho* (Toyada automatic loom works); Kokura Arsenal and unknown sub plant; National *Denki* (National Electric) and Kokura Arsenal.

LEFT Arisaka rifles and bayonets form a stand of arms for the colors of a Japanese unit. Note how the bayonet's quillons have been used to "stand arms."

FAR LEFT BOTTOM A late-war economy 30th-year (1897) bayonet fitted to an Arisaka 1897 rifle. The "arrow" and "M" mark show that the bayonet was made by National *Denki* (National Electric), the second ring marking being that of the Kokura Arsenal, the contracting and supervisory arsenal.

LEFT Mounted patrol, Manchurian style. A Japanese private 1st class carries his Arisaka rifle shouldered; the 30th-year bayonet is worn on his left side, suspended from its leather frog. (Courtesy R.F. Stedman)

North Korea (Korean Democratic Peoples Republic)

	Overall length	Blade length	Muzzle ring
Type 68	292mm	168mm	17.6mm

BELOW Although the Type 68 rifle bayonet resembles the early AK47 bayonet, the fittings are of the standard AKM type. The scabbard owes its design to the AK47 type, being of the same form; however, the two are not interchangeable.

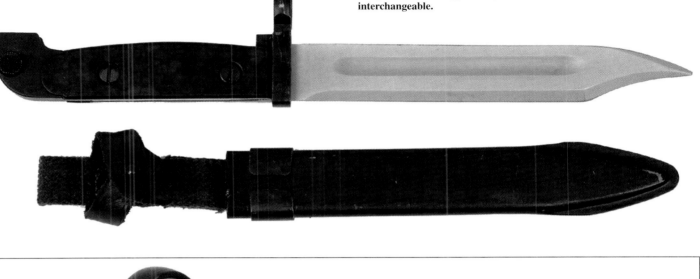

For many years, Korea was occupied by China before being annexed by Japan in 1910. After the defeat of Japan in 1945, the Russians occupied the northern part of the country and the Americans the South. Korea, or "Chosen" as it was known, was formally divided along the 38th parallel in 1948, a move that led directly to the Korean War (1951–53), where the United Nations fought against the Communists in a bitter conflict that still remains unresolved. Soviet influence in arms is obvious in the KDPR, with the majority of weapons being supplied by Russia and China during the early years prior to establishment of a domestic arms industry. Weapons in use have included the Russian PPsh, M1944 carbine, and 91/30 rifles, as well as their Chinese-made counterparts.

North Korea eventually took on its own weapon production. Early weapons copied those supplied by Russia and China, and later progressed to national variants of other foreign weapons. The AK series were popular and a new bayonet was designed for the KDPR copy of the AKM rifle. At first glance, the **Type 68** bayonet for the North Korean Type 58 rifle (AKM) looks similar to the early double-ring Soviet AK47 bayonets, but it differs in a number of respects. It has the typical red composite grips, a shorter reversed-edge clip-pointed blade and, instead of the double-ring attachment mechanism, it has the standard forward muzzle ring and a "T"-slot in the pommel. It is best described as being a hybrid of the AK47 and AKM bayonets. The scabbard is very much like the original Russian AK47. It has a web belt loop and leather hilt-retaining strap. The scabbard side-seam is very pronounced and has distinct spot-weld joining marks along its length.

RIGHT Whilst the grips give the appearance of the AK47, this view of the hilt shows the unmistakable AKM muzzle ring and pommel fitting.

South Korea (Republic of Korea)

	Overall length	Blade length	Muzzle ring
K-M1 short	285mm	168mm	16mm
K-M5/M4	289mm	169mm	15mm

Whilst the weapons of North Korea owed much to their Soviet origins, the Republic of Korea relied heavily on the United States for its armaments. In the immediate post-war era, Japanese weapons predominated, but these were rapidly replaced by U.S. equipment. A number of Arisaka **30th-year** bayonets had their scabbards modified by the addition of a U.S.-style webbing belt loop to the throat. This enabled the Japanese scabbard to be carried on the American M1910 equipment belt. During the Korean War, the .30-06in Garand rifle predominated, and continued to provide the mainstay in the following years. The **M1** bayonet was used in great numbers by the Koreans who also made their own copy, the K-M1. Although many **M1** bayonets had already been shortened from the original **1905** bayonet, a number of the **M1** and **KM-1** bayonets used by the Koreans were later cut down further and had their blades ground to conform roughly to the dimensions of the U.S.-issue **M3** blade. The scabbard used with this short bayonet was a modified U.S. **M7,** with a steel sleeve added to the plastic body. The Koreans also used the U.S. M4 bayonet, and a number were manufactured in Korea as the **K-M4**. Some **M5A1-**style bayonets, also made in Korea, were crudely modified to fit the M1 carbine by having a new muzzle ring added. Still under U.S. influence, the M16 rifle has also been issued in large numbers along with the **M7** bayonet.

ABOVE RIGHT A Korean-made K-M1 Garand bayonet, with the blade crudely cut down to dimensions similar to the M3 blade. The scabbard is a standard U.S. M7 cut down to suit the smaller blade, the U.S. flaming grenade still visible beneath thick, dark olive-drab paint. A thin metal sleeve has been fitted over the plastic body and pinned in place at each edge seam below the original throat.

ABOVE This bayonet, originally a Korean-made M5A1, has been modified to fit the M1 carbine. The finish is very crude, with poor forging and grinding marks evident throughout. The grips are made from dark-gray black plastic with fabric reinforcing, giving a mottled finish under close inspection. The grips were made by the same manufacturer as produced those for the cut-down K-M1 bayonet.

The Netherlands

	Overall length	Blade length	Muzzle ring
1871	581mm	513mm	18mm
1895	478mm	356mm	13.7mm
AR10	305mm	189mm	21.5mm

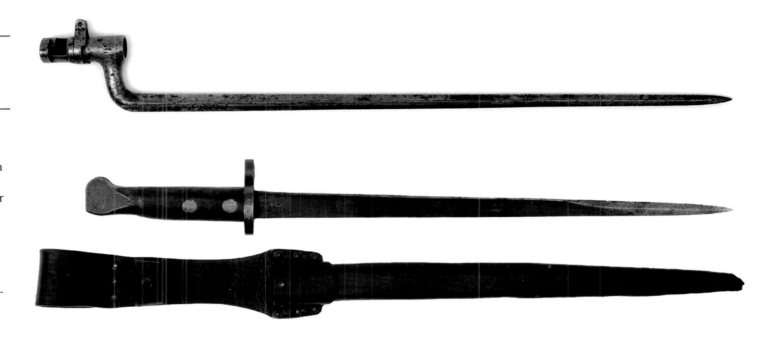

The low countries of Europe had been under the rule of the Spanish Hapsburg Empire until the northern (Dutch) area won its independence in 1648. The nation's power grew, and in 1814 it was united with the southern (Belgian) lowlands under a new monarchy. This union remained until 1839 when the southern region broke away as an independent Belgium. Typically, French weapon design predominated and this trend continued into the latter half of the 19th century. In 1871, the Dutch adopted the 11.4mm Beaumont rifle, which was used with the **1871** socket bayonet. A yataghan-bladed sword bayonet was issued to the Navy and Marines. This bayonet was almost identical to the French **1866** Chassepot, but bore the Dutch manufacturer's name inscribed on the blade back. The Beaumont rifle was converted to the Vitali magazine-feed system in 1888. The new Beaumont-Vitali 1871/88 rifle used the old **1871** socket, but also used the bayonet with a new two-piece locking ring that could be easily dismantled.

In 1895, the Netherlands adopted a 6.5mm Mannlicher-action rifle and carbine. A number of variations of bayonet may be found, but the standard **1895** bayonet has a long "T"-section blade and the same Lee Metford-style pommel as found on the British **1888** bayonet. The wood grips are secured with two rivets. Early **1895** bayonets were made in Austria by OEWG, but in 1902 production began at the Dutch arsenal at Hembrug. After World War I, the quillon, used as a stacking hook on Dutch arms, was deleted from production.

Just prior to the opening of the conflict in the Far East, the Marines of the Netherlands East Indies were provided with the American Johnson rifle and the crude **1941** bayonet.

After World War II, the Dutch made an effort to gain a foothold in the international arms market. This effort produced the self-loading Armalite AR10 rifle and bayonet. The Artillerie Inrichting-produced AR10 gained little interest and

was not used by the Dutch forces, although the rifle and bayonet were exported to Burma, Nicaragua, Sudan and Portugal. The Sudanese adopted their own interesting bayonet design for use with the AR10. It is illustrated under that nation. The Dutch **AR10** bayonet, first produced in the early 1960s, was based upon that originally issued with the FN-made 1948 gendarmerie carbine. It differed in having a larger muzzle ring and the press catch on the left of the hilt, rather than on the right as on the 1948 bayonet. The 1948 carbine bayonet is very rare.

Whilst British and U.S. weapons were issued immediately after World War II, the Dutch soon adopted the NATO-standard FAL rifle and the **Type C** socket bayonet. The Canadian 5.56mm C7 rifle has now superseded this.

The Dutch forces adopted the Buck M9 bayonet in 1996, for issue to the air mobile brigade. In 2004, it was decided to look for a replacement for the US M9 bayonet, for issue to all infantry units. The main contender under consideration is the Eickhorn Model 2000.

TOP The quadrangular 1871-pattern bayonet for the 11.4mm Beaumont rifle. The rifle was a single shot breechloader, allowing the bayonet to be fitted below the barrel. The socket is marked with the serial "E 345."

ABOVE The Dutch 1895, introduced at a time when most nations were adopting the knife bayonet, was one of the few bayonets to use the "T"-section blade, a pattern that was never universally popular.

FAR LEFT The pommel of the 1895 bayonet used the same fixing mechanism as the British 1888 bayonet. The "T" mortise is on the lower face of the pommel, a secure fixing method that positioned the pommel between the barrel and bayonet bar, but was nonetheless not widely used. This bayonet was made at Hembrug.

LEFT The AR10 rifle had a barrel flash eliminator, which required a large muzzle ring. The heavily contoured wood grips were retained by screwbolts.

BELOW Produced for export only, the AR10 bayonet was made by Artillerie Inrichtingen. It had an M3-style blade and a scabbard based on the M8A1.

Norway

	Overall length	Blade length	Muzzle ring
1894	330mm	208mm	N/A
S84/98	384mm	251mm	N/A

Formerly a part of Denmark, Norway was ceded to Sweden in 1812. Despite Sweden's quite aggressive intentions in Scandinavia, Norway managed to retain a degree of autonomy, particularly in its choice of weaponry. This autonomy helped allow Norway to gain independence from Sweden in 1905. Rather than adopting Swedish arms, Norway chose to produce her own weapons. One of the most commonly encountered bayonets of the 19th century is that for the Krag 1894 rifle. The **1894** *bajonett* was made either at the Norwegian Kongsberg Arsenal or in Austria. Kongsberg productions bear the crowned "K" marking, whilst Austrian-made bayonets have the typical "OEWG" stamp. The 1894 bayonet was standard when Norway was overrun by Germany in 1940, and it continued to be produced for issue to German second-line and security troops during the occupation.

During World War II, many Norwegians escaped the German occupation and fled to neutral Sweden. Once there, many were recruited into the *Norske Polititroppene*, a Norwegian gendarmerie unit armed by the Swedes. While politically sensitive, towards the end of the war, the *Polititroppene* nonetheless undertook some military operations in the far north of Norway and were among the first units to enter Oslo following the German surrender. They were uniformed and equipped by the Swedes who provided a large number of 1896 rifles and bayonets. The rifles and bayonets continued in use in the immediate postwar period of reorganization of Norwegian forces.

The German capitulation in Norway left countless arms and equipment in barracks and armories. Much of the equipment was issued to the Norwegian Army, and, later, to the reserve forces, including K98 rifles and **S84/98** bayonets, the scabbards often being modified by the addition of a U.S. M1910 belt hook. The original German scabbard had the frog stud removed and the belt hook added in its place, thus when worn on the belt the modified scabbard was essentially

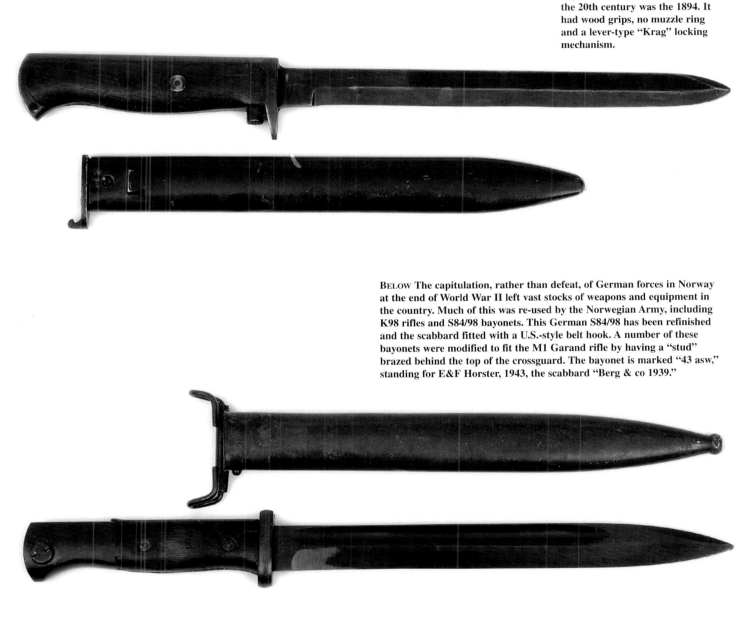

BELOW The standard Norwegian bayonet during the first half of the 20th century was the 1894. It had wood grips, no muzzle ring and a lever-type "Krag" locking mechanism.

BELOW The capitulation, rather than defeat, of German forces in Norway at the end of World War II left vast stocks of weapons and equipment in the country. Much of this was re-used by the Norwegian Army, including K98 rifles and S84/98 bayonets. This German S84/98 has been refinished and the scabbard fitted with a U.S.-style belt hook. A number of these bayonets were modified to fit the M1 Garand rifle by having a "stud" brazed behind the top of the crossguard. The bayonet is marked "43 asw," standing for E&F Horster, 1943, the scabbard "Berg & co 1939."

reversed in orientation. The United States provided many arms to Norway during the 1950s; both the M1 carbine and the M1 Garand rifle were issued to Norwegian units. The old **1894** bayonet was modified in the mid-1950s by the addition of a stepped forward muzzle ring, added to the crossguard, and a small step cut in the pommel. The resulting **1894/M1** bayonet utilized its original scabbard modified with an added webbing belt loop similar to that used on the U.S.-issue **M8A1** scabbard. It fitted the U.S. M1 carbine. In 1957, a quantity of the German **S84/98** bayonets were converted to fit the M1 Garand resulting in the 84/98/M1, often referred to as the M1957. A rearward extension was added to the crossguard, this held a small stud that engaged in the gas plug of the rifle in the same manner as the **M5** Garand bayonet. The scabbards were also modified with the U.S. belt hook. Examples of the U.S. M1 Garand rifles and M1 bayonets have been retained for ceremonial use and can be seen used by the Royal Guards.

The Norwegian 7.62 *Automatisk Gevaer* 3 (AG-3) rifle uses a standard above-barrel German-made G3 bayonet. The AG-3 bayonet is recognizable as it has green plastic grips with a stippled finish. It is carried in an M8A1 type scabbard. A variant used by the officers' academy, *Krigsskolen*, has black grips and a black leather belt loop to the scabbard.

LEFT A Norwegian officer armed with the 7.62mm *Automatisk Gevaer* 3 and bayonet. This is based on the German G3 and differs only in detail. (Norwegian Army).

BELOW Norwegian forces used the U.S. M1 carbine after World War II. It was issued with a conversion of the 1894 bayonet, the 1894/M1. This was the basic 1894 bayonet, but with an added muzzle ring and a small step cut into the pommel at the mortise. The original scabbard was retained, but fitted with a U.S.-style webbing belt loop.

Peru

	Overall length	Blade length	Muzzle ring
1909	654mm	521mm	N/A
1935	430mm	300mm	15.5mm

Peru was the home to an ancient Inca civilization but, like much of South America, was conquered by the Spanish in 1532. Independence was gained only in 1821. The 1930s and 40s saw numerous conflicts with neighboring Chile, Colombia and Ecuador, during which time the Peruvian Mauser rifles and bayonets saw much use.

At the turn of the 19th century, Peruvian troops were armed with the 1891 rifle, a copy of the Argentine 1891 rifle. A quantity of Chilean 1895-type rifles and bayonets were also in use. In 1909, a large number of German G98 export rifles were procured along with **1909** bayonets, copies of the original German **G98** type. These bayonets were identical to the German issue but can be identified by the national *Republica Peruana* crest on the pommel. The crest shows a shield sur-

RIGHT 1909 bayonet showing the manufacturer's marking "SIMSON & Co, SUHL," and weapon number "7799" stamped onto the crossguard.

FAR RIGHT The pommel end of the 1909 bayonet is marked with the Peruvian national shield ownership stamp.

BELOW The Peruvian 1909 rifle was a direct copy of the German G98. Similarly, the accompanying 1909 pattern bayonet was a copy of the S98, the two being distinguishable from each other only by the applied markings.

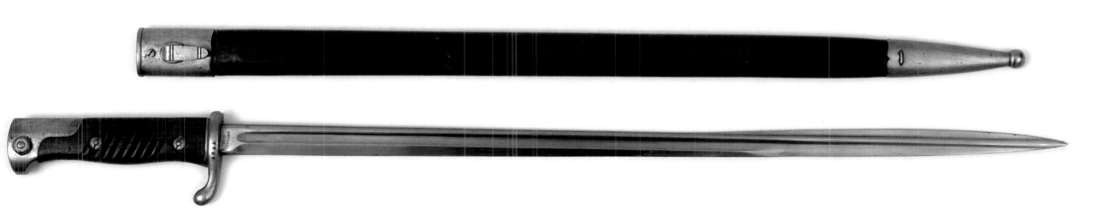

mounted by smiling sun. The shield bears a representation of a llama and a tree above a goat horn. Czech VZ24 rifles and bayonets were purchased during the early 1930s. In the mid-1930s, the Belgian FN 1924 export rifle was also purchased, along with M1935 short rifles. The **1935** bayonet is quite distinctive in having a Belgian **1924**-type hilt with a Czech-style blade and crossguard. Two distinct scabbard types can be found with these bayonets, both Czech in appearance.

During the early 1950s, Peru acquired a small quantity of Ingram submachine guns. These were equipped with the U.S.-designed **Ingram M6** spike bayonet. The same decade also saw the 7.62mm FN FAL and **Type A** bayonet brought into service with Peru.

BELOW The 1935 bayonet as supplied with the 7.65mm M1935 short rifle made in Belgium by FN. Although the hilt generally conforms to the Belgian M1924 bayonet style, the blade and crossguard are similar to those used on the Czech VZ24, as is the protruding reverse to the press catch. Two scabbard types have been noted with this bayonet, differing in frog stud and finial shape.

RIGHT The two scabbard variants used with the 1935 bayonet, showing the unusual frog stud form of the scabbard at left, and the Austrian styling of the frog stud at right.

Poland

	Overall length	Blade length	Muzzle ring
WZ22/29	387mm	249mm	N/A
KBK 47	273mm	150mm	17.5mm
6H4	270mm	150mm	17.5mm

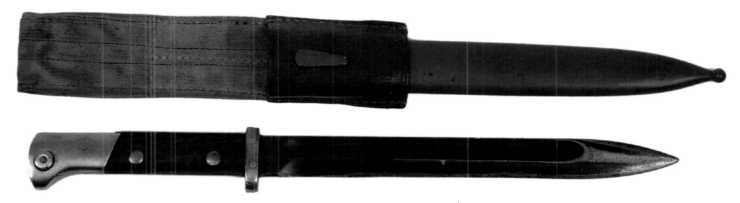

Poland has a long history, first becoming a true nation in the 11th century and a major power by the 1500s. A later decline in her fortunes saw Poland partitioned in the 18th century, but with the end of World War I, Poland was once again re-united as a republic. But the widespread division of European nations had sown the seeds of discontent. Germany invaded Poland in 1939, followed soon after by the Russians, effectively dividing Poland once again. The German refusal to withdraw from Poland led to a declaration of war that was to plunge the world into conflict once again. Poland suffered heavily during World War II, emerging from the struggle under Soviet domination that did not end until 1989.

After World War I, the first weapons in use with the new army were ex-Russian Mosin Nagant and German Mauser rifles. These were soon supplemented by newly produced copies of the Mauser rifles made at the state factory at Radom, using German G98 machinery awarded as war reparations. Four bayonet patterns were also made, differing only in detail. All resembling the German S84/98, they can be found with a muzzle ring and no flashguard, a muzzle ring and flashguard, no muzzle ring and no flashguard, and no muzzle ring but with a flashguard. Added to these are Polish bayonets taken up by the Germans during World War II and modified by the removal of the original muzzle rings. The exact designations are therefore open to some debate. Various markings can occasionally be found on the pommels: WZ22, WZ24, WZ27 and WZ29, although all four types are generally referred to as the **WZ22/29**. The WZ prefix is for *Wzor*, meaning model. The bayonets are normally marked with the Polish eagle over WP (*Woisko Polski*—Polish Army) and the manufacturer's stamp. Both "FB RADOM," *Fabryka Bronie Radomiu* (Radom arms factory) and Perkun, a private company based in Warsaw, manufactured bayonets.

ABOVE Polish Mauser bayonet WZ22/29. This example, with a flash guard and no muzzle ring, owes much to the German S84/98 bayonet in its design. The right ricasso of the heavily blued blade bears the maker's mark "PERKUN." The pommel and crossguard remain polished metal.

LEFT The left ricasso of this WZ22/29 bayonet bears the polish eagle over "W.P." This was an abbreviation of *Woisko Polski*, meaning Polish Army.

BELOW The Polish bayonet frog is made up from double layer canvass with a leather front. The rear is heavily stamped including the date "19.V111.25" (August 19, 1925).

The post-war era saw Polish arms production dictated by the Warsaw Pact, and therefore Russian weapons were standard. However, the Poles produced their own weapons rather than purchasing Russian-made material, and were initially armed with the SKS and later the AK47. The Polish copy of the standard double-ring AK47 bayonet is the **KBK 47** issued with the early AK47 rifles. The key difference between the Russian and Polish examples is in the scabbard. The Polish scabbard differs in having no lip to the scabbard tip, and a different method of attaching the removable belt loop to the top of the scabbard. Unlike the Russian version of AK47 bayonet scabbard, the belt loop of the **KBK 47** is all leather rather than webbing and leather. The Russian AKM-type bayonet replaced the **KBK 47**. The original Polish-issue AKM bayonet was the 6H3, it was based on the first-pattern Soviet AKM with bulbous grip. The Poles called the second-pattern square-pommel AKM the 6H4 bayonet. This was a copy of the Russian AKM II. In Polish service, it was issued without the serrated saw to the blade back. Poland also issued a training bayonet with the standard **6H4** hilt and a rubber-tipped retractable plunger in place of the blade.

As with many former Soviet satellites, the Polish Army has retained the SKS rifle and bayonet for parade and ceremonial use.

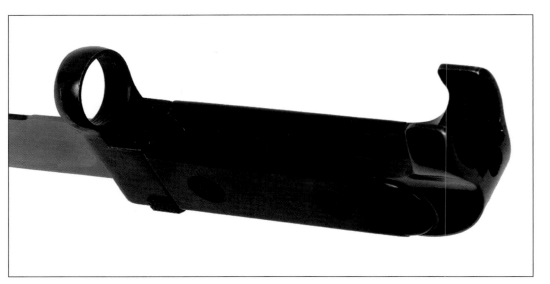

LEFT Left side detail of the KBK 47 hilt, showing the rear "ears" and forward fixing pawls positioned just behind the muzzle ring.

BELOW LEFT The Polish version of the AK47 bayonet was the KBK 47. It was a well-made bayonet that was almost identical to the Russian weapon. The main differences lay in the scabbard detail. The tip was void of the "fins" typical of this variant, and the belt loop was unique to the Polish pattern.

BELOW The leather belt loop on the KBK 47 scabbard was easily removed, being retained by a leather tongue passing through two loops.

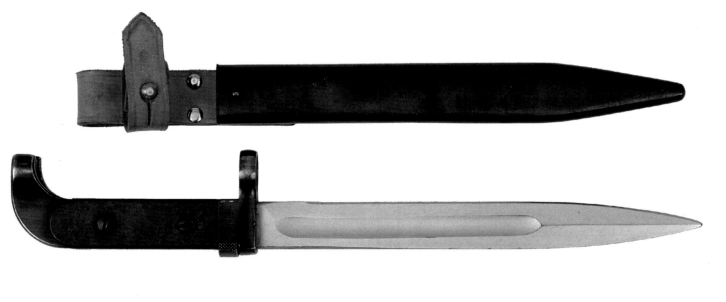

ABOVE, FROM LEFT TO RIGHT:
LEFT Radom-produced KBK 47 bayonets bear the factory's "11" marking on the left side of the crossguard. Note the hatched finger grip on the release catch.

CENTER The right side of the crossguard on the KBK 47 shows the year of production, in this case 1958.

RIGHT The weapon issue number of the 6H4 bayonet, "3329," is stamped on the scabbard body and the crossguard.

LEFT Based on the Soviet AKM II, the Polish 6H4 bayonet did not have a saw-back edge to the blade. The scabbard is the first model previously issued with the 6H3 (AKM I). The rubber section provides a hand grip with electrical insulation for use when cutting live cable.

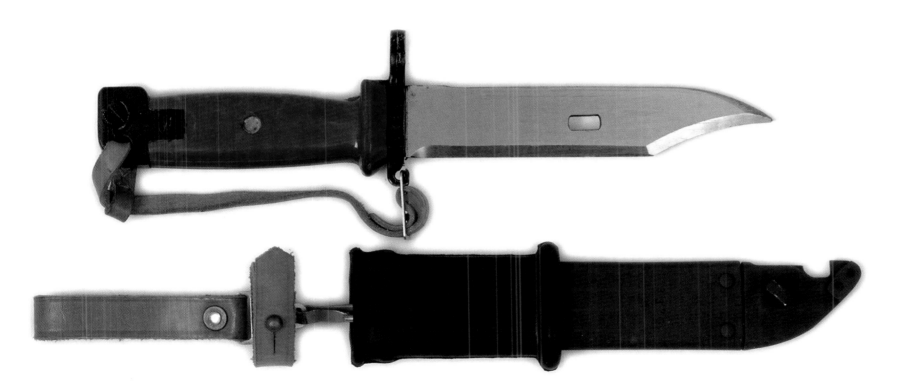

Portugal

	Overall length	Blade length	Muzzle ring
1885	597mm	470mm	15.5mm
1904	406mm	283mm	15.5mm
1904 long	552mm	397mm	15.4mm
1948	295mm	175mm	N/A

Having long been a major colonial power and monarchy, Portugal, founded in 1143, became a republic in 1911. Portugal fought with the Allies during World War I but remained neutral during World War II. A military coup in 1974 saw Portugal withdraw from many of its African colonies, though still retaining a degree of military influence in some.

The Portuguese had used a number of foreign weapons from the early 19th century. British muskets predominated, with 10,000 Snider rifles and bayonets being made for supply to Portugal in 1875. By the latter part of the century Portugal was looking to manufacture its own pattern of weapons and the 1885 Guedes-Castro rifle was developed along with a short yataghan-bladed bayonet. Before production had gotten underway at the Steyr factory in Austria, the Portuguese government decided against the Guedes-Castro, opting instead to adopt the 8mm bolt-action Kropatschek rifle. It was the first small-caliber bolt-action rifle to be adopted by any army. The new rifle was

LEFT Portuguese troops on the Western Front in World War I. The soldiers have been issued with the British SMLE rifle and 1907 bayonet. The bayonets have been thrust into the sacking training dummies, typical of those used to teach offensive bayonet techniques worldwide.

BELOW LEFT Made in Austria, and based on the 1873 bayonet, the 1885 Guedes is often referred to the Kropatschek bayonet. It was originally designed for the Guedes-Castro rifle, which was not adopted; it was, however, issued with the Kropatschek rifle.

BELOW 1885 Guedes hilt left side detail. The crossguard is marked "HH 747."

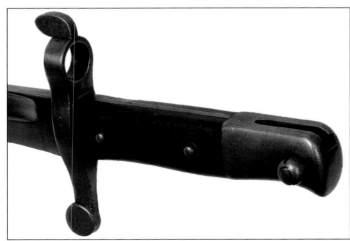

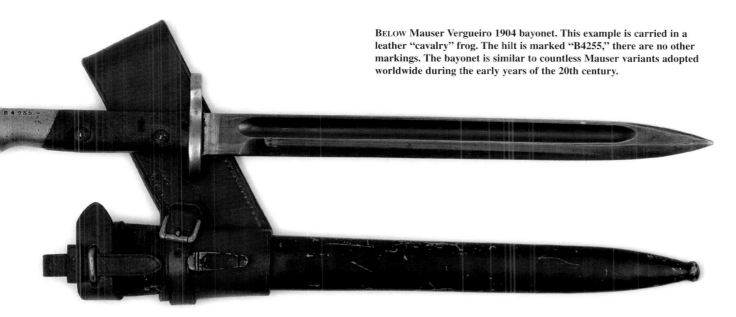

BELOW Mauser Vergueiro 1904 bayonet. This example is carried in a leather "cavalry" frog. The hilt is marked "B4255," there are no other markings. The bayonet is similar to countless Mauser variants adopted worldwide during the early years of the 20th century.

taken into service as the 1886; however, it utilized the bayonet that had been designed for the lever-action Guedes-Castro rifle. The *baioneta* **1885** was typically Austrian in appearance, resembling the Austrian 1873 but with a different crossguard. Depending on reference source, the bayonet can be found referred to as either the Guedes or Kropatschek **1885**. At the beginning of the 20th century, a new rifle, the 6.5mm Mauser Vergueiro, was taken into service by the Portuguese Army. The **1904** bayonet that accompanied the new rifle was available in two blade lengths, the shorter being for the standard rifle and the longer for the carbine. Although Portugal was neutral during World War II they adopted a German-made rifle, based on the K98, in 1937. A copy of the K98 was later adopted as the M41, but supplies from Germany ceased in 1943. A copy of the **S84/98** bayonet was used on both weapons. In Portuguese service this was known as the model 1937.

Very few submachine guns were ever issued with a bayonet, but the Portuguese FPB was one of them. The double-

ABOVE LEFT The complicated "cavalry" frog retained the scabbard using a buckle and strap. The bayonet hilt was held by a quick release tab that could be undone, and the bayonet removed, with one hand.

LEFT A white dress variant of the 1904 bayonet frog. Now discolored with age, it was originally highly polished.

ABOVE The long version of the 1904 bayonet. The hilt was identical to the short pattern, with the wooden grips being retained by rivets and round washers. In keeping with normal Portuguese practice, the crossguard on this bayonet is marked with a serial number, "6330." The scabbard is fitted with a black leather frog, typical of those used with the 1904 bayonets.

edged **1948** bayonet was designed specifically for use with the FBP submachine gun, manufactured by the Government arsenal Fabrica Braco de Prata. The hilt was of the **1904** type mated with a short, sharply spear-pointed, double-edged blade. Scabbards were of blued steel. Typically, bayonets attached to short weapons such as the submachine gun are unsuited to bayonet fighting, but the blade profile of this weapon would have made it deadly as a handheld weapon. Portugal was later to use the AR10, FN FAL and G3 rifles and bayonets. Many being used in the postwar colonial conflicts in which Portugal found herself.

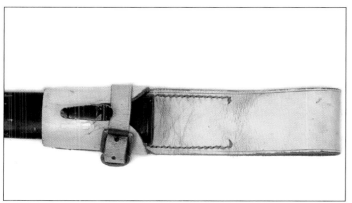

BELOW The FPB submachine gun was provided with fittings for a bayonet. The FPB 48 bayonet had a Mauser-type hilt mated with a sharply pointed double-edged stiletto blade. From left to right are the FPB 48 scabbard with standard web frog; the left side of the bayonet; the bayonet mounted in a variant scabbard, without ball tip, and a web "cavalry" frog.

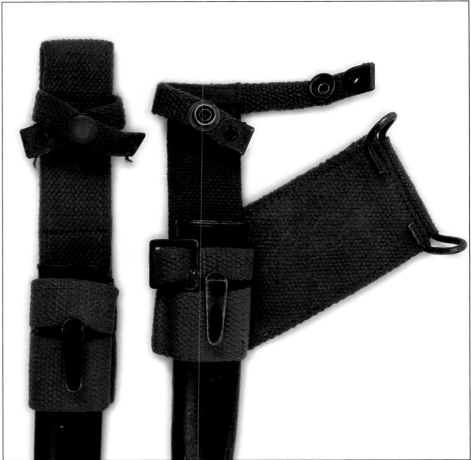

ABOVE The webbing frogs used by Portugal were based on the leather types used with the Mauser Vergueiro bayonets. The "cavalry" pattern frog presented the bayonet at an angle of 45 degrees rather than vertically.

Russia

	Overall length	Blade length	Muzzle ring
1856	576mm	510mm	20.5mm
1891	502mm	428mm	15mm
SVT 1940	362mm	243mm	14mm
M1944	387mm	N/A	14mm
SKS	312mm	227mm	14mm
AK47	305mm	203mm	17.5mm
AKM	273mm	150mm	17.5mm
AKM II	270mm	150mm	17.5mm
AKM III	286mm	160mm	17mm

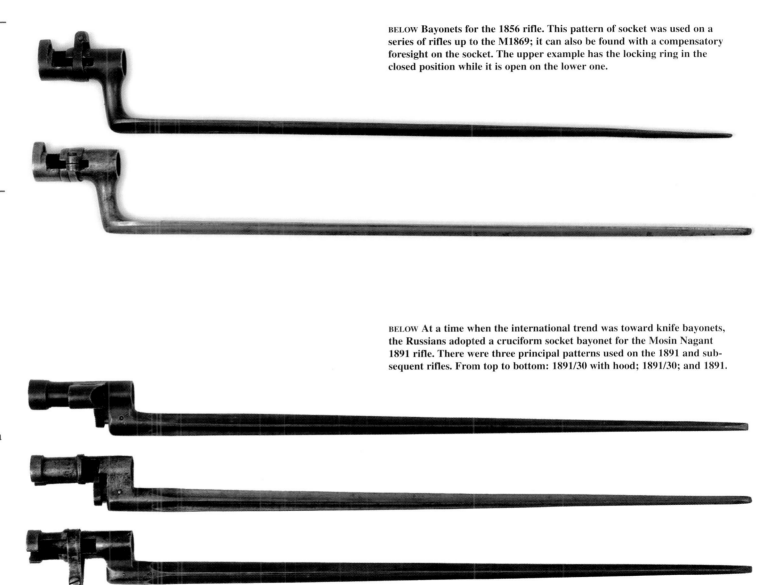

BELOW Bayonets for the 1856 rifle. This pattern of socket was used on a series of rifles up to the M1869; it can also be found with a compensatory foresight on the socket. The upper example has the locking ring in the closed position while it is open on the lower one.

BELOW At a time when the international trend was toward knife bayonets, the Russians adopted a cruciform socket bayonet for the Mosin Nagant 1891 rifle. There were three principal patterns used on the 1891 and subsequent rifles. From top to bottom: 1891/30 with hood; 1891/30; and 1891.

Early 19th-century Russian arms were copied from those in use with other major nations, such as the French and English. Models dating from 1808 were copied from French AN IX socket bayonets. Further patterns followed in 1826, 1827, 1828, 1845, 1847, 1854 and 1856. These were all similar to the French Mle. 1822 pattern.

The Russian 1843 musket and bayonet were copies of the British Brunswick patterns. Similarly the 1845 musket had a bayonet that was a direct copy of the French 1822, complete with locking ring. Both of these types were used against Britain and France during the Crimean War. This reliance on foreign designs continued into the second half of the 19th century when the Russians produced the 1856 rifle based on the well-proven British 1853. The **1856** *Schtik* can be found with a pointed blade tip or a flat screwdriver point, and the socket bridge is on the upper face of the socket, an uncommon practice. A variant of the **1856** has a small long-range sight fixed on the socket. In 1869 the 1856 rifles were converted to the Krnka breechloading system, but retained the old bayonets, which were also used on the 1865 and 1869 Albini Baranov rifles.

In 1868, the Russians took delivery of the American-made .42in Berdan rifle. It was purchased from the well-known U.S. arms company Colt. The Berdan rifle was soon under production in Russia, this version being the Berdan II. Both rifles were issued with a socket bayonet, the former being the 1868 and the latter Berdan II type being the 1870.

During the Russo-Turkish war of 1877–78, the Turks were defeated by the might of the Russian Army, supported by Bosnia and Herzegovina. During this conflict, the superiority of the Ottoman weapons, mainly imported from the U.S., was readily apparent as the Russian casualties mounted. The 1856 Krnka and Berdan rifles were no match for the Turkish Winchester and Remington repeaters, which were only overcome by the sheer weight of Russian troops.

The weapon that was to see the Russian troops through World War I and the Revolution was the 7.62mm Mosin Nagant 1891 rifle. It was made in Russia and, to keep up with demand, Remington and Westinghouse in the U.S. also produced it as did Chatellerault in France. The bayonet supplied with the new rifle was an uninspired quadrangular-bladed socket bayonet with a screwdriver tip that could be used in stripping the rifle. A heavily reinforced collar at the rear of the socket allowed for an open slot with no bridge. The slot can be found with different angles of rotation, varying from 90 degrees on early examples to both 60-degree and 30-degree rotations. It was intended that the bayonet would be carried permanently attached to the rifle and therefore no scabbard was issued. After the Revolution, an improved version of the Nagant bayonet was issued with the 1891/30 rifle, a slightly shorter and modernized 1891 with an integral foresight hood. The **1891/30** bayonet was a minor improvement on the original in that it had a new catch in the form of a spring-loaded plunger at the short elbow. A modified version of the **1891/30** bayonet was fitted with an integral foresight hood. The scarce second-pattern hooded **1891/30** was used with the standard 1891 rifle and provided the foresight with a hood not present on the original rifle. All three patterns were used during the "Great Patriotic War."

ABOVE RIGHT **1891 socket showing the standard locking ring and heavy collar. The bayonet has a short elbow with the blade positioned just below the rifle muzzle when fitted. This example bears the pre-1917 Ishevsk Arsenal marking of a bow and arrow.**

RIGHT **The 1891/30 bayonet was an improvement over the 1891 in that the median locking ring was deleted and a press catch was placed in the rear of the elbow. A median collar added strength to the wide attachment slot.**

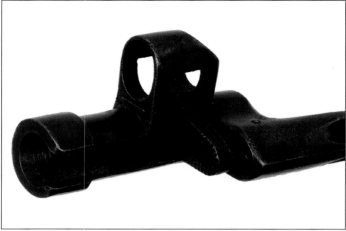

ABOVE LEFT **Comparison of the 1891 bayonet sockets: 1891 with median locking ring; 1891/30 with press catch; and 1891/30 socket with press catch and foresight hood.**

ABOVE **1891/30 bayonet with the distinctive foresight hood. This bayonet is otherwise almost identical to the 1891/30.**

In the early 1930s, the Russians had made moves to issue self-loading rifles to their troops. The first rifle issued in any quantity was the AVS (Simonov) rifle M1936, but it was deemed not to meet requirements and production was discontinued. The 1936 AVS bayonet had a 332mm blade and 465mm overall length; it is rarely encountered. The replacement for the AVS was the SVT (Tokarev) rifle. The first bayonet to be issued with the new rifle, the SVT 38, had a new hilt design but the same long blade as the earlier AVS. The more commonly encountered **SVT 1940** bayonet had a shorter 244mm blade but the same hilt as the SVT 38. On both weapons a raised collar, preventing accidental activation of the catch and subsequent loss of the bayonet, protected the press catch. The scabbards of both the SVT 38, **SVT 1940** and AVS bayonets were similar. Of sheet steel they had leather or webbing belt loops without a hilt strap. They provided the basis for the later **AK47** bayonet scabbard. This series of weapons were primarily intended for issue to NCOs. The old Mosin Nagant 1891 and 1891/30 rifles remained the principal weapon of the Soviet infantryman during World War II. From 1944 a new carbine version of the 1891 rifle was on issue. The Mosin Nagant M1944 carbine had a short cruciform-bladed folding bayonet. The **M1944** was permanently attached to the rifle and folded back against the right side of the stock when not in use. The design principle provided the basis of the later folding bayonets. The SKS (Simonov) rifle was the first postwar development in Russian arms, providing the Soviet infantryman with a self-loading rifle with equal firepower to the U.S. M1 Garand. The **SKS** bayonet had an identical locking mechanism to the **M1944** bayonet but a 222mm blade similar to that previously used on the **SVT 1940**. It was permanently attached to the rifle but folded beneath the barrel rather than to the side.

The SKS was used by all of the Warsaw Pact nations, supplied by Russia or home produced as copies or variants. But soon after the adoption of the SKS the ubiquitous AK47 (*Avtomat Kalashnikova* 1947) assault rifle came on the scene. The Kalashnikov in its various forms is recognized worldwide, it has been used in more wars and caused more casualties than any other small arm. A simple weapon, easy to maintain and equally robust, it was the immediate replacement for the SKS. The **AK47** bayonet used the same blade style as the **SKS** but with a slightly shorter blade length of only 200mm, the blade edge being uppermost, in the style of the Austrian **M1895** bayonet. Red plastic grips were fitted to the heavily blued hilt, which had a standard muzzle ring at the crossguard and a second open top ring or "ears" at the pommel. This arrangement made use of the bayonet as a hand weapon uncomfortable unless the user had small hands. The release catch was just behind and below the crossguard. When the bayonet was fitted to the rifle the catch was not particularly easy to operate, especially with cold or gloved fingers, and may have required two hands to effect its release. The design of the **AK47** scabbard owes much to that used with the Tokarev **SVT 38** bayonet, it differs in having a pronounced lip around the tip but is otherwise very similar in design. In 1959, a modified AK47 rifle appeared, the AKM (*Avtomat Kalashnikova Modernizirovanyi*). It differed from the AK47 in minor detail, having a stamped receiver and, on later models, a lug beneath the gas port for the **AKM** bayonet. Introduced in the mid-1960s, the bayonet for the **AKM** was a major development in bayonet thinking. It had a saw to the blade back, the blade itself engaging with a lug on the scabbard to form a wirecutter; both the hilt and scabbard were electrically insulated so that live cable could be safely

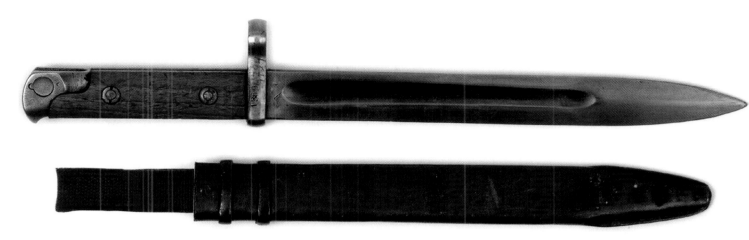

RIGHT An Estonian soldier armed with a Mosin Nagant 1891 rifle and bayonet. The Russian rifle and bayonet were used by a number of other nations, including Latvia, Lithuania and Finland.

ABOVE The SVT (Tokarev) bayonet was the first Russian knife bayonet to be issued. It did not replace the 1891 socket type but supplemented it, being issued to some NCOs and specialist troops.

LEFT The pommel of the SVT 40 was fixed to the tang using a key and groove fixing evident in this view of the underside of the pommel. Note also the short collar, protecting the press catch from accidental operation.

BELOW Left side view of the SVT 1940 hilt. This shows the chamfered mortise slot and protective press catch collar.

cut. Insulation of the steel scabbard was effected by the use of a heavy rubber sleeve at the top of the scabbard body whilst the entire hilt was made from an insulating red composition material. An adjustable leather strap was threaded through a hole in the hilt and attached to a small hook on the crossguard. Adjusted to fit across the back of the hand, this provided a secure hold when the weapon was held. To enable the bayonet to be attached to the soldier's equipment, a simple leather belt loop and hilt strap were attached to a ring on the upper rear of the scabbard using a "carbine" clip. The second-pattern **AKM II** bayonet differed from its predecessor in having a square hilt section with metal pommel; the leather strap was later replaced by one of webbing. The scabbard was also redesigned. Instead of the rubber sleeve, a full-length ribbed-plastic outer to the scabbard provided insulation. It utilized the same steel tip for the wirecutter and the belt loop was the same as that used on the first-pattern scabbard. Later production AK74 rifles initially used the **AKM II**, but a new bayonet was introduced in 1984. The third-generation **AKM III** (AK74) bayonet retained the second-pattern AKM scabbard but was otherwise a new design. The hilt owed little to the earlier patterns. The hand strap was deleted and the new shape black plastic grips had three concentric ridges to provide a better hold. The clip-pointed blade was replaced by a new spear-point style, which retained the familiar saw edge, now located on the lower part of the blade.

The **AK47** and **AKM** bayonets made by Soviet satellite nations differ in minor detail from the original Russian versions, as do the scabbards, but they are often difficult to differentiate. Bulgaria, East Germany, Hungary, North Korea, Poland and Romania have all made their own rifles and bayonets.

Note: For the sake of brevity, images of a number of AKM bayonet types have been grouped under Russia regardless of the nation of manufacture. Readers should also see under China, East Germany, North Korea and Poland for further variants.

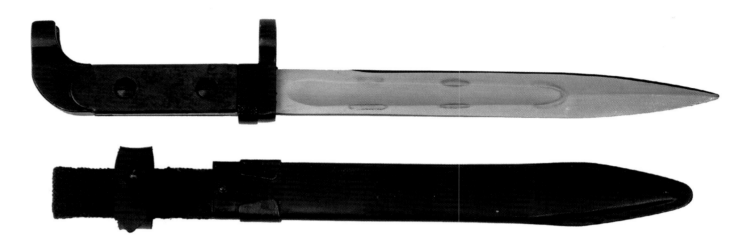

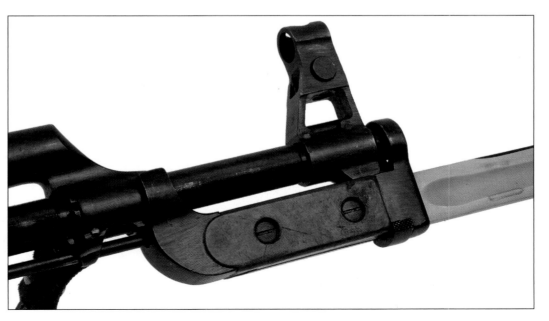

TOP The model 1944 carbine had a permanently attached folding bayonet. It had a short quadrangular blade similar to the 1891 type.

ABOVE Russian-made AK47 bayonet and scabbard. The scabbard is similar to that used with the SVT, having the distinctive lip around tip and web belt loop. It has an added leather hilt strap. Many of these bayonets were supplied to Soviet satellite nations, but a number of countries made their own versions that differed in detail.

LEFT AK47 bayonet fitted to an AK rifle.

LEFT AK47 variants: East German early web hilt loop; East German nylon hilt loop; Russian; Polish.

BELOW Hilt detail of the muzzle ring and pommel ears of the AK47 bayonet.

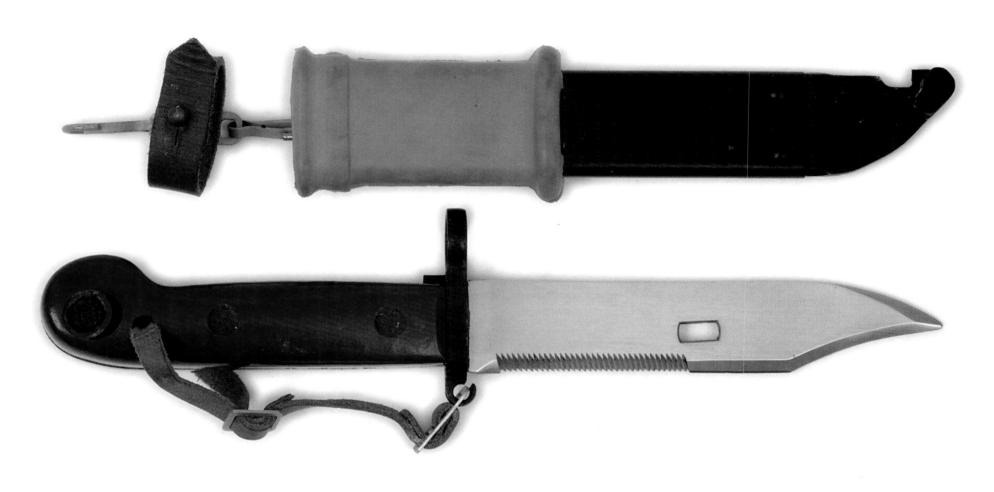

ABOVE Romanian-made AKM I bayonet. A Peshmerga Guerrilla gave this bayonet to the author during operations in Iraq. The bayonets appear well made; however, several bayonets were encountered where the blade had broken at the cut-out used to join the blade with the scabbard for wirecutting.

RIGHT Romanian-made AKM II. The distinctive feature of the Romanian bayonet is the wrist strap that has a double buckle rather than a riveted loop and buckle. Otherwise it is identical to Russian production.

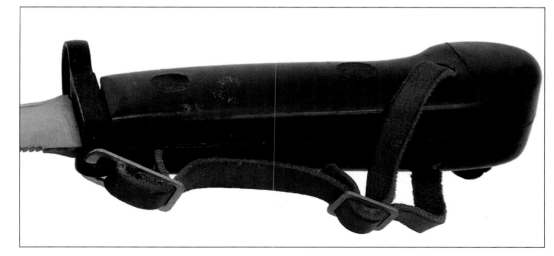

Above AKM bayonet types. These bayonets were collected by the author whilst serving in Iraq, with all but the last example being Romanian made; AKM with brown grips; AKM with red grips; AKM II with Romanian frog; Russian-made AKM II with Romanian frog.

ABOVE Bulgarian-made AK74 NBV bayonet, a copy of the Russian AKM III (AK74). The AKM III used a new hilt and blade design but retained the AKM II scabbard. This scabbard is based on the early Soviet type with only a rudimentary finger guard on the rear. The Bulgarians were obviously not unduly troubled by finger loss when the bayonet was used as a wirecutter!

BELOW LEFT Detail of the right side of the AKM III hilt. The grips have three raised ridges and a stippled finish to aid grasp.

BELOW The belt loop attaches to the rear face of the scabbard using a small carbine clip. The carbine clip attachment was standard on Warsaw Pact AKM bayonets.

BELOW The distinctive ringed "10" marking applied, by the manufacturing arsenal, to the Bulgarian scabbard and hilt.

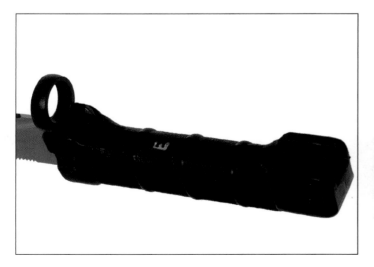

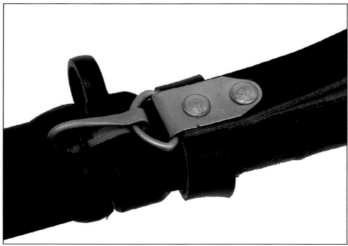

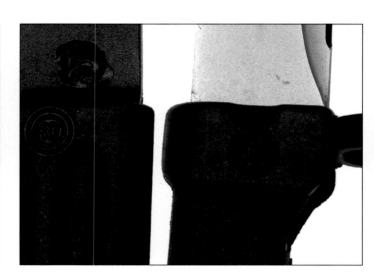

South Africa

	Overall length	Blade length	Muzzle ring
SA No. 9	222mm	168mm	15mm
R1	288mm	166mm	22mm
Uzi S1	292mm	170mm	18mm

As a Commonwealth nation, South Africa had always followed the lead of Britain with regard to its armaments. Prior to becoming a republic, standard British small arms and bayonets had been used, with weapons such as the 1907 bayonet being imported from Britain and Australia. The postwar **SA No. 9** bayonet, produced in South Africa, differed from its British counterpart in having a plain unfullered blade similar to that used on the **FAL Type A** and Uzi bayonets. The Belgian **FAL Type A** bayonet was adopted as the M1 bayonet

for the early FAL rifles acquired by South Africa. The national armaments company, Armscor, then concentrated domestic production on their licensed version of the FAL, the R1. The R1 rifle had a flash eliminator and thus required the **FAL Type C** tube/socket bayonet. The South Africans adopted this bayonet as the **R1** bayonet. Early scabbards were Belgian Type A metal scabbards similar to that used on the **FAL Type A**. Plastic scabbards later replaced these. The final scabbard type used with the **R1** had a dual-slot mouthpiece, having a "D" shape imposed over a rectangle allowing the scabbard to take both the **R1** bayonet, the Uzi **S1** and the **SA No. 9** bayonet. Armscor also made the bayonet for the Israeli-designed Uzi SMG under license. The **S1** was made entirely of metal, with steel slab grips retained by screws; only the scabbard was of plastic.

The South African Army introduced their own version of the Israeli Galil rifle, the 5.56mm R4, as a replacement for the FAL. Some consideration was given to the subject of a bayonet, and it was felt that there was no requirement for one because of the nature of operations undertaken by the armed forces. However, some of the old **R1** bayonets were modified to fit the new weapon; these bayonets being used for "policing" duties. Heavily parkerized in a light-gray finish, the R4 bayonets have a different release catch and no flash eliminator holes. Only 1,000 examples of this rare pattern were produced, the conversion being undertaken under drawing numbers HAG-20-R4B-01 and 02 of September 2, 1992.

Early South African bayonets are marked with an arrow within a "U," this was later changed to an "M" within the "U," both signifying ownership by the South African defense department.

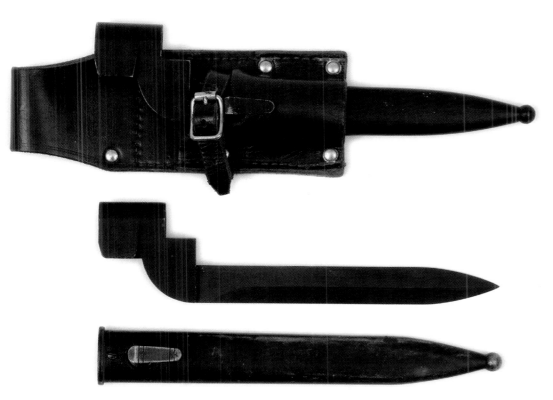

FAR LEFT **South African No. 9 bayonet. This bayonet has the same socket as the British No. 9, but the blade form of the Uzi S1 bayonet. Three scabbard types can be found in use with the SA No. 9: a short steel scabbard as shown mounted in the leather frog used with this bayonet type; an over-length scabbard, originally used with the M1 bayonet (FAL Type A); and the plastic scabbard used with the R1 and S1.**

LEFT **Socket detail of the SA No. 9, showing the fitting for the lugs on the barrel of the No. 4 rifle.**

TOP This R1 bayonet has been painted brown over sand, but the paint to the blade has been worn off by the scabbard. The plastic scabbard is fitted in a web frog with hilt-retaining loop and press stud, allowing fixing to the belt to prevent lateral movement.

ABOVE The form of the third-pattern plastic scabbard meant that the socket was orientated toward the body of the frog when the bayonet was seated in the scabbard.

ABOVE RIGHT The second-pattern plastic scabbard supplied with this R1 bayonet has a dual-purpose throat fitting. This allows use with both the R1 bayonet blade with its flat/convex section and the rectangular blade section of the Uzi S1 and SA No. 9 bayonets.

RIGHT R1 bayonet carried in the basic pouch. This type of bayonet carriage was first used on the British 1944-pattern basic pouch and then carried over with the 1958 web set.

LEFT The S1 was a licensed copy of the Uzi bayonet. This small knife bayonet had metal grips that were heavily blackened, as was the pommel and blade. The accompanying scabbard was the standard South African model that fit the R1 and S1 bayonets.

BELOW LEFT The distinctive pommel mortise slot of the S1 bayonet.

BELOW South African leather frogs. From left to right: a frog for the No. 1 bayonet; a variant with narrower belt loop; frog for the No. 4 bayonet. Similar to that used on the SA No. 9, it has a narrow body, as the side has been stitched down.

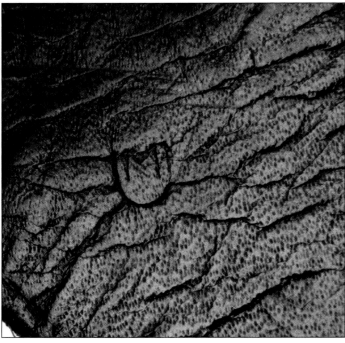

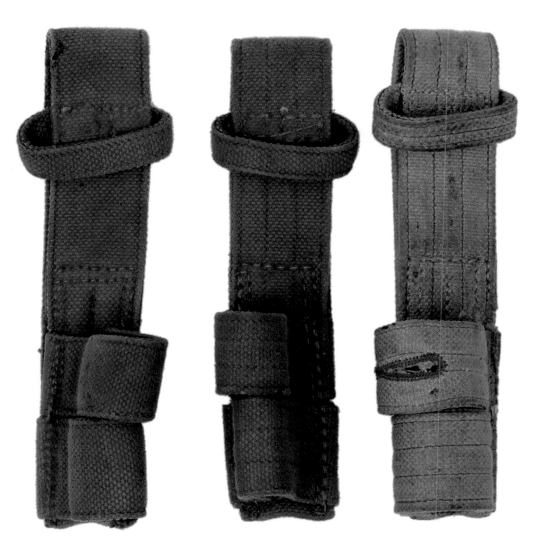

LEFT South African World War II P37 web equipment frogs. Two standard P37 frogs for the No. 1 bayonet, both showing typical SA construction, being made up of thin webbing stitched up into thicker sections. At right, a standard frog modified in 1944 by having a button hole stitched into the upper loop section, which enabled use of the frog with the No. 1 bayonet or the No. 4.

BELOW Typical marking on a World War II P37 webbing frog. It has the "U" and arrow, stamped in purple, with the makers marking "D.I.F & CO LTD." This shows that it was made by D.I. Fram of Johannesburg.

TOP Maker's marking on the No. 1 bayonet frog, showing that Fraser and Son Ltd made it in Cape Town in 1942. It is marked with a "U" and arrow device representing the Union of South Africa.

ABOVE The second frog has no maker's mark, but bears the post-union "U M" stamp of the South African defense forces.

Spain

	Overall length	Blade length	Muzzle ring
1857	545mm	455mm	20mm
1871	615mm	545mm	18mm
Remington quadrangular	525mm	495mm	18mm
1893	373mm	249mm	15mm
1893/16	514mm	384mm	15.3mm
1941	373mm	249mm	15.5mm
1943	381mm	249mm	N/A
M69 or CETME	336mm	224mm	22mm

The 16th century saw the rapid rise of Spain as one of the dominant powers in Europe. This rise was accompanied by the creation of a major empire in South America (which encompassed the whole of South America, except for Brazil), the Philippines and elsewhere. The empire was largely lost in the 19th century, independence being given to, or won by, many South American nations; with other colonies, including the Philippines and Cuba, being ceded to the United States following the Spanish–American War of 1898.

One of the principal infantry weapons of the 19th century was the breechloading Remington rifle; this replaced the earlier muzzleloading 1857 rifle and bayonet. The **1857** *bayoneta* was similar to the British **1853,** which had undoubtedly inspired its design. It was also used on the 1859 and 1867 rifles. The American-made Remington rolling-block was tested by Spain in 1869 and accepted as the standard Spanish arm in 1871. A number of bayonet types were used on the new rifle. The standard **1871** pattern was a U.S. export, but variants were also produced in Spain, including a quadrangular-bladed bayonet (similar to the Swedish **1867** pattern). During the Spanish–American War, the Spanish used American-made weapons to great effect; U.S. forces suffered greatly at the hands of the Remington rifle. At the Battle of San Juan Hill, in 1898, the Spanish showed the Americans the effectiveness of the Remington rifles at much longer ranges than the U.S. rifles could counter. Despite this advantage, Spain lost the war. The 7mm 1893 rifle was also used in the Spanish–American War.

This was a standard Mauser rifle. The **1893** bayonet was a short knife type. The longer **1893/16** bayonet was used on the 1893/16-pattern short rifle, a shortened version of the 1893 rifle that replaced earlier carbines that had no provision for a bayonet fixing. A bolo-bladed bayonet, the **1941** pattern, was later produced for use with the short rifle. It was distinctive in having a curved "bolo" edge to the blade. The 1941 bayonet is normally found with wood grips, but these were later occasionally replaced with plastic grips when the original wooden ones were damaged. The **1893** and **1893/16** bayonets were standard during the Spanish Civil War of 1936–39. The war caused widespread loss of life and allied Franco's Spain to Germany. Although neutral during World War II, Spanish volunteers fought with the Germans and Nazi Germany temporarily influenced Spanish arms and equipment. The 7.92mm 1943 short rifle was a close copy of the German K98, and the Spanish-made **1943** bayonet was itself based on the German

BELOW The *Modelo* 1857 bayonet has a sharp angle to the bayonet's elbow. It bears more than a passing resemblance to the British 1853, but differs at the shoulder, the join of the blade and shank.

RIGHT South America, *c.*1870. Spanish soldiers of the 5th Infantry Regiment pose with muzzle loading M1859 rifles and fixed *Modelo* 1857 bayonets.

BELOW A Spanish bayonet with quadrangular blade for the Remington rolling-block rifle. It is similar to the Swedish 1867, and was one of the generic export patterns produced for use with the Remington rifle.

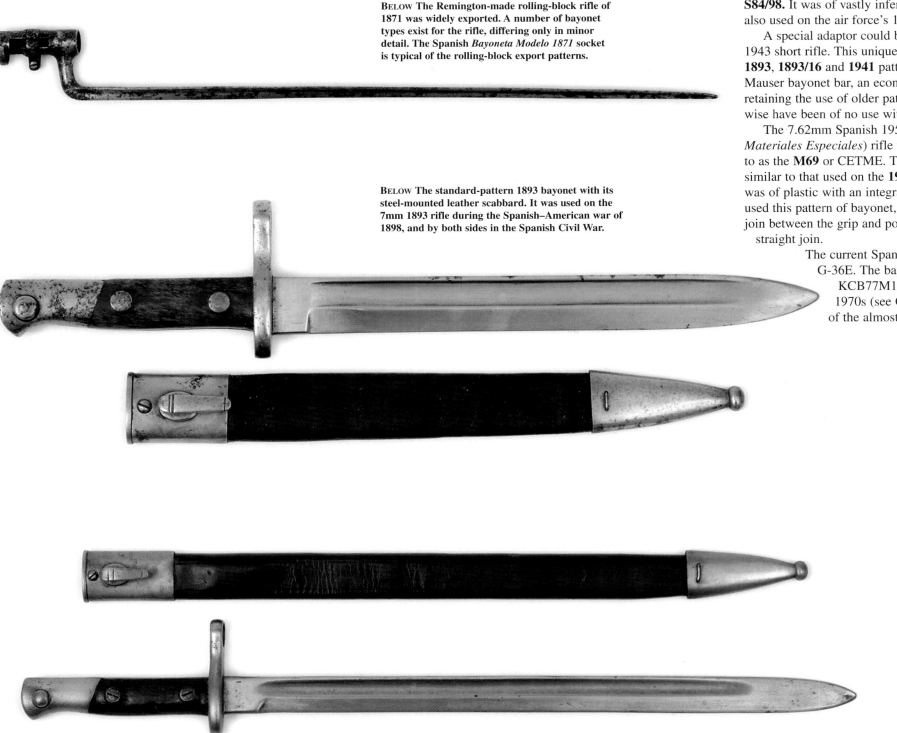

BELOW The Remington-made rolling-block rifle of 1871 was widely exported. A number of bayonet types exist for the rifle, differing only in minor detail. The Spanish *Bayoneta Modelo 1871* socket is typical of the rolling-block export patterns.

BELOW The standard-pattern 1893 bayonet with its steel-mounted leather scabbard. It was used on the 7mm 1893 rifle during the Spanish–American war of 1898, and by both sides in the Spanish Civil War.

S84/98. It was of vastly inferior quality. The **1943** bayonet was also used on the air force's 1944-pattern rifle.

A special adaptor could be fitted to the bayonet bar of the 1943 short rifle. This unique device allowed fitting of the **1893**, **1893/16** and **1941** patterns of bayonets to the standard Mauser bayonet bar, an economical and practical method of retaining the use of older pattern bayonets that would otherwise have been of no use with new rifles.

The 7.62mm Spanish 1958 CETME (*Centro de Estudios de Materiales Especiales*) rifle used a bayonet commonly referred to as the **M69** or CETME. The bayonet had a bolo blade form similar to that used on the **1941** bayonet. The modern scabbard was of plastic with an integral web belt loop. Colombia also used this pattern of bayonet, but it differed in having an angled join between the grip and pommel. The Spanish bayonet had a straight join.

The current Spanish rifle is the Heckler and Koch G-36E. The bayonet for this rifle is the Eickhorn KCB77M1/KH-JS, a design dating to the 1970s (see German section for an illustration of the almost identical **KCB77M1**).

LEFT Although a carbine version of the 1893 rifle was issued, it had no bayonet fitting. The 1893/16 short rifle was provided with a bayonet fitting, but the standard 1893 bayonet was considered too short; thus the long-bladed 1893/16 bayonet was introduced. This bayonet normally has hatched grips, worn smooth on this example.

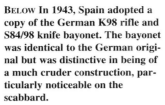

BELOW In 1943, Spain adopted a copy of the German K98 rifle and S84/98 knife bayonet. The bayonet was identical to the German original but was distinctive in being of a much cruder construction, particularly noticeable on the scabbard.

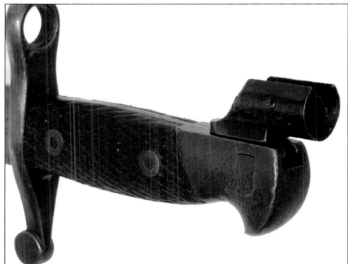

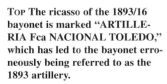

TOP The ricasso of the 1893/16 bayonet is marked "ARTILLE-RIA Fca NACIONAL TOLEDO," which has led to the bayonet erroneously being referred to as the 1893 artillery.

ABOVE A special adapter allowed the 1893, 1893/16 and 1941 bayonets to be fitted to the M1943 and M1944 rifles. For illustrative purposes, it is shown fitted to a 1941 bayonet; however, in use it was permanently pinned to the rifle's bayonet bar.

RIGHT A "bolo" blade was the distinctive trademark of the 1941 bayonet. This example has wood grips, occasionally replaced by plastic on later refurbished examples. The leather frog was also made in an identical form but of black rubber.

FAR LEFT The crossguard of the M43 bayonets are generally stamped "P.R.8."

LEFT The Spanish scabbard, at left, has no separate mouthpiece. The retaining spring is screwed directly to the interior of the scabbard throat; the screw being on the front face above the frog stud. The German scabbard has a separate mouthpiece secured using a screw at the side of the scabbard. On this example, the frog stud is plain, but hatched examples, like the Spanish frog stud, were equally common on German scabbards. The reverse is marked "42 agv."

BELOW 1941 bayonet ricasso showing the "FN" Toledo National Arsenal mark of Fabrica Nacional.

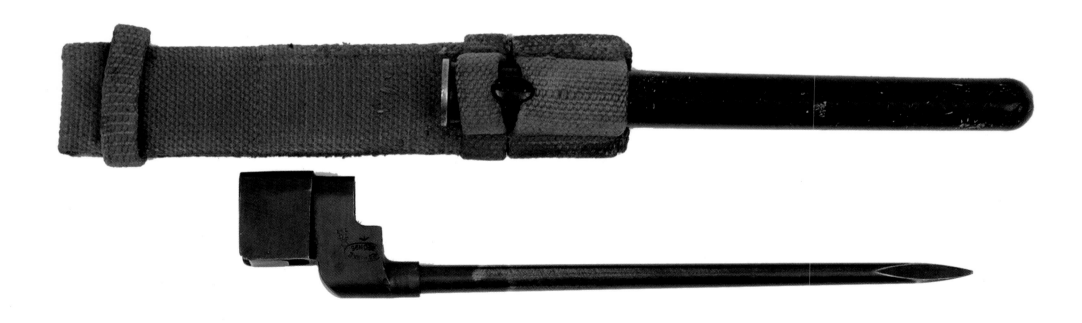

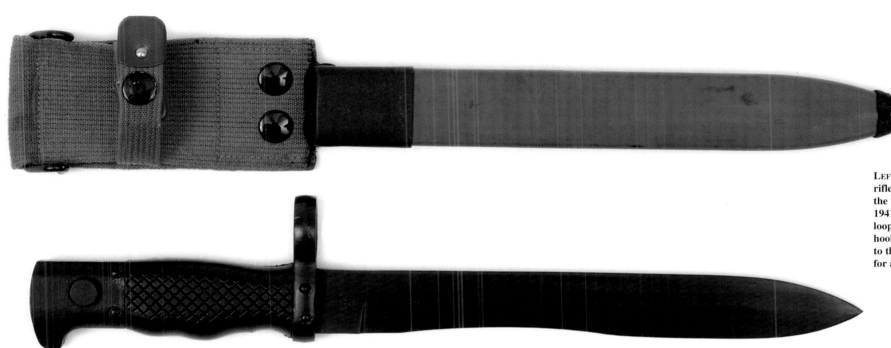

LEFT Bayonet for the CETME 69 rifle. Its blade was copied from the "bolo"-shaped blade of the 1941 bayonet. It has a plastic belt loop with U.S. M1910-type belt hook. The plastic grips are shaped to the user's hands and "hatched" for added grip.

BELOW A modern version of the old FN mark is applied to the ricasso of the CETME 69 bayonet, here with a serial number "ET 23356B."

BELOW The pommel of the Spanish M69 bayonet has an unusual rectangular mortise slot in the pommel face.

BELOW A Spanish soldier advances with his KCB77M1/KH-JS bayonet fitted to his HKG-36E rifle. The bayonet was the result of Eickhorn's self-funded commercial ventures of the mid-1970s. (Spanish Army)

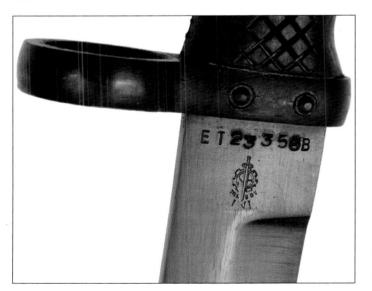

Sudan

M1958	Overall length	Blade length	Muzzle ring
	332mm	200mm	N/A

In 1820, Egyptian armies, under Ottoman command, invaded Sudan. Territorial gains were made over the following years, destroying the Sudanese nation. Following the conquest, Egypt ruled the Sudan until 1885. The start of the 20th century saw "Anglo-Egyptian Sudan" under Egyptian rule, but under the joint authority of both Britain and Egypt. Internal conflict saw Britain order all Egyptian troops out of Sudan in 1924 with the Sudanese raising their own army in 1925. Britain retained a degree of control until 1955, with Sudan gaining independence in 1956. The latter half of the 20th century saw internal strife with civil war simmering in the south of the country. The first weapons adopted by Sudan were Dutch-made AR10 rifles. The Sudanese **M1958** bayonet that accompanied the rifles was made in West Germany, but retailed by the U.S. company Interarmco, who supplied the Sudanese government. The **M1958** bayonet was based on the German S42 bayonet, produced in limited quantity during World War II. It had a combination tool in the hilt, enabling easy disassembly of the rifle, as well as a corkscrew, screwdrivers and bottle opener. The hilt and scabbard body were made from a deep red-brown plastic, metal components were heavily blued or, in the case of the scabbard throat, painted black. The scabbard was suspended from the belt by an integral metal belt hook. The **M1958** is unusual in its design and in that it was adopted only by the Sudan, with most Third World nations purchasing standard export bayonets.

RIGHT The hilt of the M1958 bayonet contained a combination tool that allowed field stripping of the weapon, as well as the ability to open beer or wine bottles!

BELOW RIGHT The M1958 bayonet was supplied with the AR10 rifle. It was based on the German S42 bayonet produced in limited quantity during World War II.

BELOW The left ricasso of the M1958 bayonet bore the Interarmco logo and "Reg.Pat." marking. The small catch at the lower left of the image is the release for the hilt tool.

Sweden

	Overall length	Blade length	Muzzle ring
1815	523mm	420mm	26mm
1860	608mm	548mm	21mm
1867	552mm	485mm	19mm
1867/89	537mm	495mm	15.5mm
1896	320mm	210mm	15.2mm
1914	460mm	330mm	15.5mm

Despite being well known for maintaining a "neutral" stance during the two world wars, Sweden was once a major European power, fully prepared to wage war to maintain a hold on Scandinavia and the Baltic and fully aware of the need for a powerful and modern army.

Sweden made every effort to equip her troops with the best and most modern of weaponry, adopting a socket bayonet as early as 1696. During the 18th century, Sweden experimented with various locking mechanisms, and produced a variety of bayonets using a screw-type wing nut locking device. The wing nut was dispensed with on 19th-century bayonets. The **1815** *bajonett*, which was similar to the 1811 that itself had been based on the French 1769, had a basal locking ring, which made it more secure than the British Brown Bess types that were also used by Sweden. In the 1860s, Sweden adopted the Wrede rifle and the long-bladed **1860** socket bayone,t but these were very rapidly replaced by the 12.7mm Remington rolling-block rifle, which had caught the eye of the ever-progressive Swedes. A number of the new rifles were fitted with sword bayonets, but the standard type was the **1867** cruciform-section bayonet. This bayonet was later adapted for use on the 1867/89 rifle, an 8mm modification of the 1867. The **1867/89** bayonet had the same blade as the **1867** but had a new socket section attached. It had a press catch of the type normally only found on knife and sword bayonets. Sweden was the only nation to use this form of press catch on a socket bayonet. The modified socket bayonet did allow use of old bayonets without any major modification to the rifle and at minimum expense. Sweden wasted little time in finding a new rifle to keep abreast of international arms developments. In 1896, a 6.5mm Mauser

action was adopted by Sweden, the first weapons being delivered by the German company Waffenfabrik Mauser in 1899. The **1896** bayonet was unusual in having a tubular steel hilt and a unique release catch that was pulled, rather than pressed, in order to release the bayonet. The design locks well, but it would not have been easy to operate in extreme cold or with gloved hands. The **1896** bayonets can be found with the markings of the three Swedish makers, "EAB" for Eric Anton Berg, the crowned "C" of Carl Gustaf and the "EJEAB" over an anchor design of the Eskilstuna plant.

The original Swedish 6.5mm 1894 carbine was not provided with a fitting for a bayonet. However, it was modified in 1914 by the addition of a bar and lug, based on that used on the British SMLE rifle, to become the 1894/14 carbine. The **1914** carbine bayonet provided a long blade for the short rifle,

LEFT Although neutral, Sweden mobilized her forces during both world wars. Here a Swedish soldier from Infantry Regiment 44 peers out from a prepared position, his *Gevar* M/96 and bayonet at the ready, during the invasion scare of 1940.

BELOW The 1815 socket bayonet had a triangular section blade, a socket with basal locking ring, and a shank of squared section. It was issued with the *Gevar* M1815, and a number of subsequent weapons based on the 1815 musket.

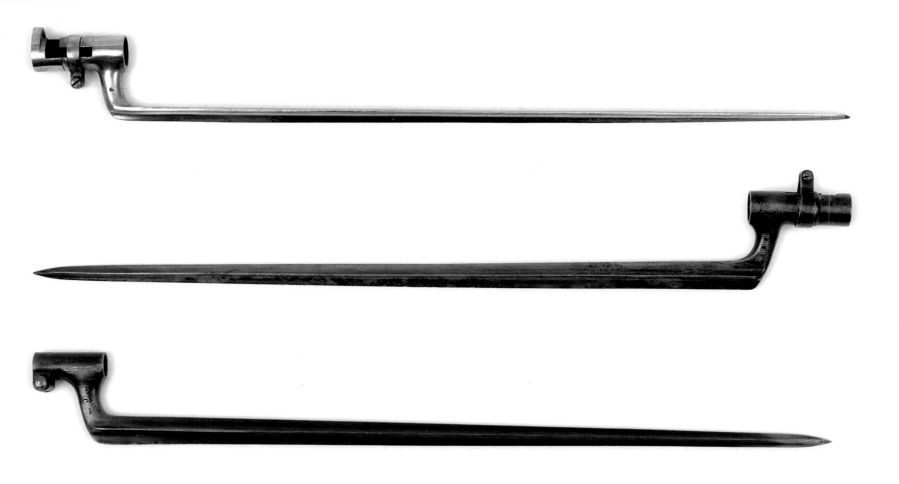

LEFT The 1860 socket bayonet for the 12.14mm Wrede rifle of 1860. The collar opening is at the top of the socket, unlike the majority of contemporary bayonets, which have an opening on the lower face opposite the shank.

LEFT Quadrangular-bladed Swedish model 1867 bayonet for the 12.17mm Remington rolling-block rifle. The locking ring is in the open position allowing passage of the rifle foresight when fixing the bayonet. The elbow is stamped "3099."

LEFT The old 1867 bayonet was converted for use on the 1867/89 rifle, with a new socket being added to the blade. The unique 1867/89 socket bayonet was the only socket bayonet to use a standard press catch release mechanism, the sole concession to bayonet development at a time when most nations were adopting knife bayonets.

giving parity between the standard 1896 rifle and the carbine. The **1914** bayonet was also used postwar on the Carl Gustaf M1945 SMG. This was quite an unusual combination as the bayonet is quite large for use on a relatively small SMG.

In 1940, a number of German K98 rifles, adapted to take an 8mm round, were acquired by Sweden, along with **S84/98** bayonets. At this time, Sweden's military looked to the German Army for inspiration, with Swedish NCO and officer cadres seen as pro-German. But the government was determined to remain neutral and the threat of invasion from Germany and Britain, both of whom needed Swedish ore, soon instilled a greater national patriotism. Sweden mobilized to defend her neutrality.

In the 1960s, Sweden took on the German G3 rifle, which was issued to Swedish troops as the AK4. The M1965 bayonet that accompanied it was made by Bahco and, apart from its grips, was identical to the German **G3** bayonet.

RIGHT Right side view of the 1867 hilt with the locking ring in the closed position. The elbow is marked "EL H ON." "EL" and "ON" are inspectors' initials and "H" represents the Husqvarna factory.

BELOW The 1889 rifle had an 8mm caliber requiring a smaller socket diameter on the bayonet. This was achieved by cutting off the old socket just above the shank and brazing on a new one, with a shorter length and smaller internal diameter. The brazed join is clearly visible at the join of the socket and the shank.

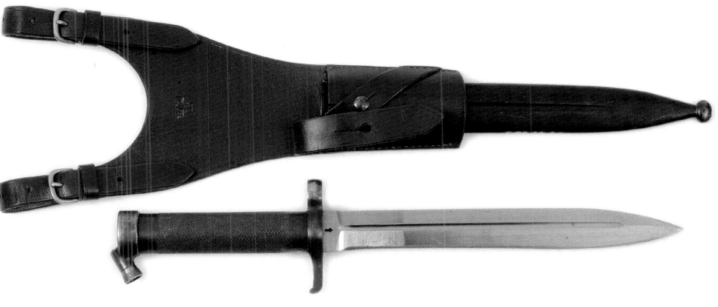

ABOVE 1896 bayonet and scabbard. The blade of the 1896 appears to be of a double-edged design; however, only the lower edge has been sharpened. The upper "edge" only appears as such because excessive metal on the blade back has been reduced to a minimum. The blade also has a narrow central fuller, further enhancing the illusion of having a double-edged blade.

LEFT A short strap passes over the crossguard of the 1896 bayonet when carried in the frog; this prevents the accidental extraction of the bayonet. This example is carried in an NCO's-pattern brown leather frog with twin belt strap arrangement.

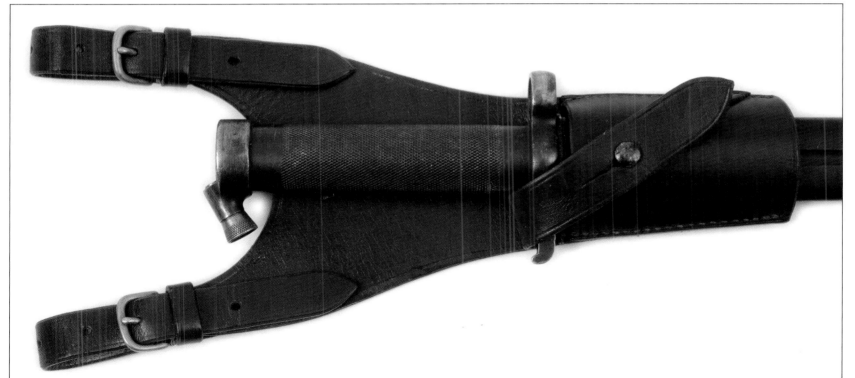

ABOVE "EJEAB" with a crown and anchor marking on the ricasso of an 1896 bayonet. This example was made at Eskilstuna.

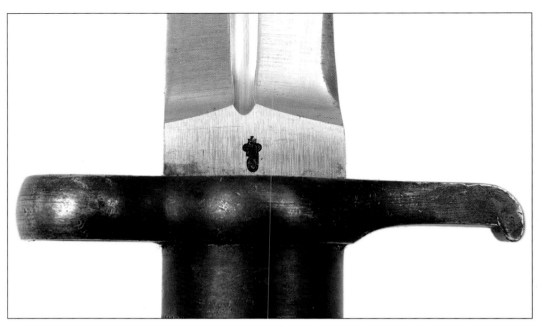

ABOVE 1896 bayonet showing the crowned "C" marking of the Carl Gustaf factory.

LEFT 1896 bayonet with scabbard secured to the bayonet using the bayonet training clip. The assembly is fitted to a 6.5mm model 1896 rifle. Thus fitted, the bayonet and rifle combination could be used to undertake bayonet training without undue risk.

RIGHT A standard 1896 bayonet fitted to the rifle. The Swedes and Egyptians used the 1896 style of bayonet release catch, but it was not particularly efficient and was difficult to operate with gloved hands.

LEFT When fitted, the flat spring of the training clip fitted over the bayonet frog stud. The upper "c" spring clip fitted around the hilt of the bayonet, just behind the crossguard, securely retaining the scabbard to the bayonet. The crossguard marking shows this bayonet was issued to the 5th Battalion, Infantry Regiment 5.

BELOW The Swedish *Gevar* M/96 in an illustration shown in a number of Swedish Army publications, *Soldatinstruktion*, and which also shows the bayonet fitted to the rifle.

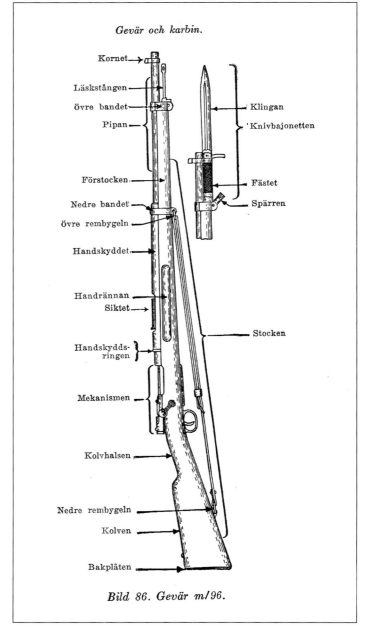

Gevär och karbin.

Kornet
Läskstången
övre bandet
Pipan
Förstocken
Nedre bandet
övre rembygeln
Handskyddet
Handrännan
Siktet
Handskydds-ringen
Mekanismen
Kolvhalsen
Nedre rembygeln
Kolven
Bakplåten

Klingan
'Knivbajonetten
Fästet
Spärren
Stocken

Bild 86. Gevär m/96.

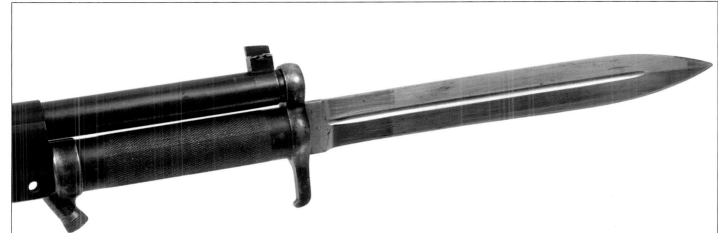

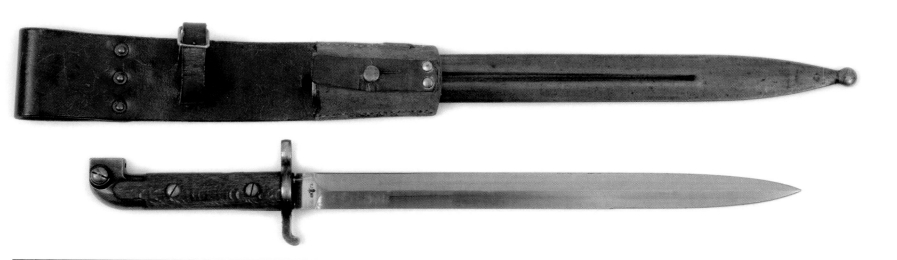

BELOW A selection of the many variations of Swedish *baranord-ningar*—belt frogs—that may be encountered by the collector. From left to right: a fine quality NCO's frog for the 1896 bayonet; frog for the 1914 bayonet with stitched belt loop; 1914 riveted belt loop; 1914 riveted belt loop with crossguard strap removed, frog stud strap repositioned vertically, and with added hilt strap; 1914 stitched back, shortened and riveted; 1896 shortened and riveted, crossguard strap deleted and hilt strap added, front of frog cut away allowing it to be used with the 1939 bayonet; 1896 shortened and riveted, hilt strap added, crossguard strap removed and with frog stud strap repositioned vertically; finally, a frog made up as the preceding example but originally having a riveted long back section. Below the bayonet frogs is a Swedish dress dagger used for walking out by NCOs and officers. This has a Germanic-style frog with hilt strap; it was not normally used with bayonets.

TOP M1914 bayonet for the 1894/14 carbine. The odd design of the hilt of this bayonet is entirely due to the fact that the original 1894 carbine had no provision for a bayonet. The unusual extended pommel mortise is the result of introducing a bayonet retrospectively; the muzzle fitting over a bayonet boss added below the barrel.

ABOVE The long-bladed 1914 carbine bayonet was securely retained in the scabbard by a press catch located just above the crossguard on the left side of the hilt. The mortise slot is raised above the pommel in a somewhat unusual placement, as shown here.

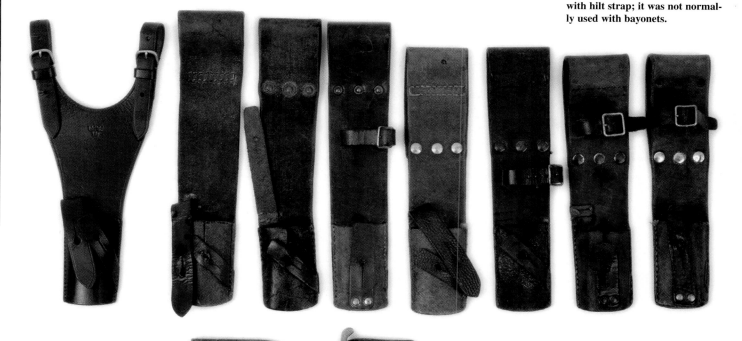

Switzerland

	Overall length	Blade length	Muzzle ring
1889	419mm	298mm	15mm
1911	419mm	298mm	15mm
1914	606mm	478mm	14mm
1918	427mm	298mm	14mm
FV4	291mm	197mm	N/A
SIG 57	368mm	241mm	22mm
540/542	277mm	178mm	22mm

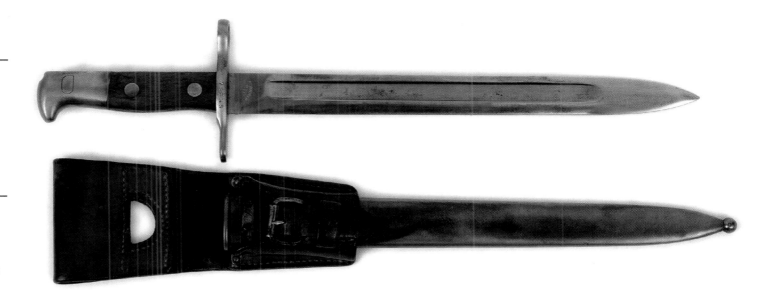

Switzerland has a long tradition of military prowess. As with many nations, all Swiss males received military training, but the Swiss proved to be natural soldiers, providing mercenaries for conflicts throughout Europe. The Swiss were the first nation to standardize the percussion rifle with the adoption of their 1851 rifle. The bayonet for the rifle was unique in that it attached to the rifle using a mortise and key device. A bayonet closely based on the British **1853** was used with the 1865 Jäger rifle. The principal weapon of the later part of the of 19th century was the 10.4mm tubular-magazine Vetterli rifle; initially fitted with a socket bayonet, from 1878 a sword bayonet was used.

In 1889, the 7.5mm Schmidt Rubin magazine rifle was adopted. The **1889** bayonet was an attractive design that was exceptionally well made. The U.S. copied it as the **1892** for the Krag rifle. The 1889/99 bayonet was a modification of the 1889; a rivet was placed in the fuller that engaged with the scabbard spring to retain the blade more securely. The **1911** bayonet was similar to the earlier patterns, but a ridge machined into the fuller replaced the rivet. The **1914** bayonet for the short rifle had a long saw-back blade, fullered only on the right side and left flat on the left. Like the other bayonets of this period, it had a steel scabbard with leather frog strap that fastened to the buckle of the leather frog. The basic **1889** bayonet styling was used for the bayonet issued with the M1911 short rifle after 1918. The **1918** differed from the earlier bayonets in having the hilt design of the **1914** bayonet and a double-edged blade. The **1918** bayonet was also used on the 1931 rifle and a series of submachine guns made during World War II.

ABOVE Made by Sig Neuhasen, this 1889 bayonet is of the original pattern. Many were later modified by having a small stud spot-welded into the fuller, with others having a rivet in the same place, that engaged with the internal scabbard spring serving to hold the blade securely in the scabbard. Modified bayonets are generally referred to as the 1889/99 pattern.

BELOW Like the 1889/99 bayonet that had preceded it, the 1911 also had a scabbard stop in the fuller. Rather than a stud, the 1911 had a ridge in the fuller that locked the bayonet in the scabbard. It was otherwise identical to the 1889 and 1889/99 bayonets. In fact, it is impossible to differentiate between the bayonet types when in the scabbard.

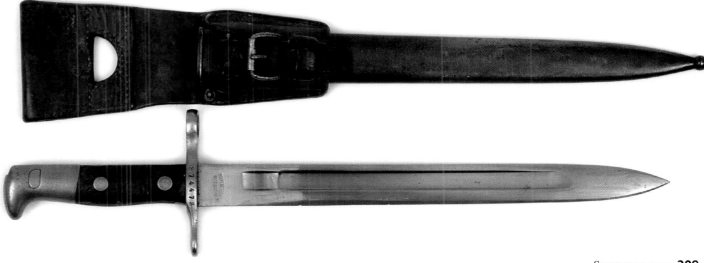

The Swiss also designed a bayonet for their post-war commercial submachine gun, the Rexim, often called the Rexim-Favor MC 4 SMG. The simple **FV4** spike-type bayonet design was a copy of the French **MAS 36** but with a short unfullered blade. It was patented by Switzerland but was not adopted by the Swiss, eventually being made in Spain at the La Coruña Arsenal after which it was named. Production ceased in 1957 as the SMG failed to appeal to the commercial arms market and sales of the 5,000 examples were poor. Most disappeared into Africa during the next few years and some were to appear in the Congo and the Nigerian Civil War of 1969.

Switzerland's move to the self-loading rifle saw the adoption of the Schweizerische Industrie Gesellschaft-made

Sturmgewehr 57 rifle. This had a very high quality bayonet with stainless-steel metalwork and a plastic grip. The unusual fixing catch of the **SIG 57** bayonet was operated by pulling down the pommel catch rather than pressing it in as was the normal practice. The high-density plastic scabbard had a metal throat and a loop through which threaded the frog strap. As well as being used by Swiss forces the SIG 57 was exported to Chile and Bolivia.

The Swiss replaced the SIG 57 with the 5.56mm Stg 90. The current Swiss Stg 90 bayonet is similar to Eickhorn's commercial **EW77SS**. The Stg 90 bayonet is wholly utilitarian in its manufacture and does not compare well with the excellent finish of the earlier **SIG 57**. Its plastic frog echoes

the earlier leather types but has considerably less appeal.

Swiss federal laws, passed in 1972, restricted the export of Swiss-made weapons. The Swiss designed a number of weapons for trials and export, including the 5.56mm Stg 540 and 7.62mm 542 rifles. As Swiss-made weapons could not be exported, Manurhin in France made both the Stg 540 and 542 rifles under license. This overcame the strict Swiss export laws whilst still providing financial gain from the license. The bayonets for the rifles were similar to the **FAL Type C** but had a plastic sleeve over the tubular hilt. The French version of the **540/542** bayonet resembled the Swiss bayonet.

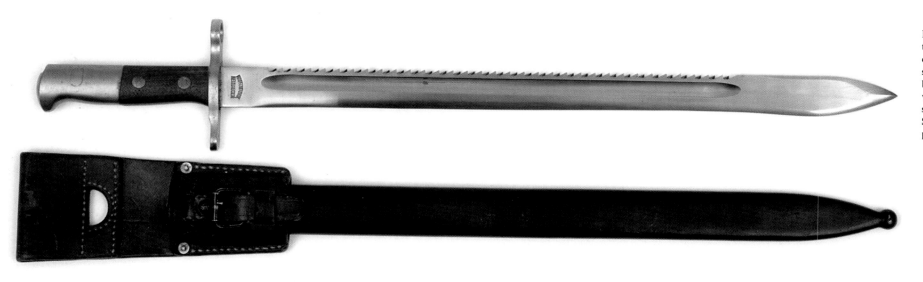

LEFT The long saw-back blade of the 1914 bayonet was fullered only on the right side. The hilt had the same shape as the earlier 1889 bayonets; however, the pommel was longer with correspondingly shorter wooden grips. As with all Swiss bayonets, it is a well-made piece.

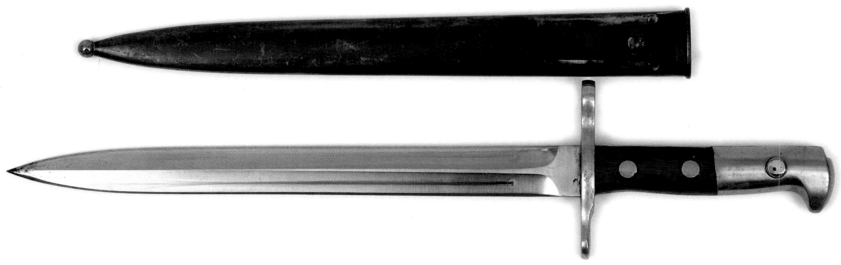

LEFT A double-edged blade was used on the 1918 bayonet, though it retained the same style of hilt as that used on the 1914 bayonet. This example has been chrome plated overall, a practice undertaken privately but condoned by the military authorities. Swiss scabbards had a frog loop with permanently attached leather fob that buckled onto the frog.

ABOVE Comparison of the 1889, 1911 and 1918 bayonets. The 1889 and 1911 have identical hilts, differing only in the detail of their blade form; the 1911 has a ridge in the fuller. The 1918 bayonet differs both in its longer hilt and double-edged blade. All three share the same scabbard type.

TOP Typical Swiss manufacturers' markings on a 1918 bayonet, "ELSENER SCHWEYZ, VICTORIA" to the left, and "WAFFEN-FABRIK NEUHAUSEN" on a 1914 bayonet to the right.

ABOVE A Swiss signaler from a carrier pigeon unit, c.1940. He is armed with a M1918 bayonet in its steel scabbard, carried in the leather belt frog.

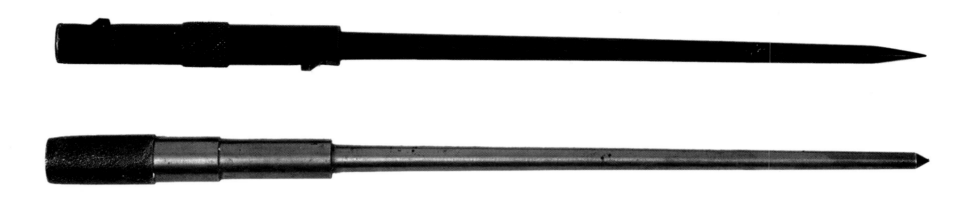

TOP The Swiss-designed FV4 bayonet was manufactured in Spain. Based on the French MAS 36 bayonet, the design received little market interest and was not a commercial success. Below the completed bayonet is an incomplete "blank" that has received basic milling to the original round steel bar, but requires considerable work to complete it.

ABOVE Made of stainless steel and exceptionally well finished, the SIG 57 bayonet was a fine example of workmanship. Whilst the Swiss may have been leading the way as far as quality of bayonet finish was concerned, the bayonet frog still relied on the well-tried and tested leather. Similar to earlier Swiss frogs, it differed in using a strap attached to the frog and mating with an alloy stud rather than a buckle.

RIGHT The SIG 57 used an unusual fixing catch that had to be pushed down away from the pommel rather than pressed in. This moved the locking bolt out of the round bayonet bar of the rifle, releasing the bayonet.

RIGHT The bayonet for the Stg 540 and 542 rifles had a single-piece steel blade and socket, over which was a plastic sleeve and an alloy pommel. Different pommel orientations can be found, as shown by the two examples of the 540/542 bayonet shown here. The scabbards are a simple plastic molding with nylon webbing belt loop. A similar style of bayonet was used with the Swiss 530 rifle, which did not see any major sales.

ABOVE The rear face of the belt loop showing the four large rivets holding it to the scabbard.

BELOW The pommel of the 540/542 bayonet showing the pivoting press catch mechanism and, internally, the locking mechanism and joint between the socket and pommel.

Thailand (Siam)

	Overall length	Blade length	Muzzle ring
1902	369mm	248mm	15.9mm
1908	406mm	295mm	15mm
1919	556mm	435mm	16.5mm

Siam was a powerful kingdom and the only nation in Southeast Asia to avoid coming under European domination. Siam was, nonetheless, forced to cede territory to France (Indo-China) and Britain (Malaya) in the 19th century. The nation remained an absolute monarchy until 1932, thereafter retaining the king as head of state. Until 1939, Thailand was known as Siam, but in that year, the name was changed to Thailand.

The 20th century saw Siam keeping abreast of small-arms development and continuing to use the universal Mauser system that it had adopted in the previous century. Having earlier adopted the German G71 rifle, a new Mauser action was adopted in 1902 and taken into service as the Type 45 rifle. The short-bladed **1902,** or Type 45, bayonet was quite modern in its appearance and, like the rifle, it was made in Japan. The wood grips were typically secured by screws with Japanese oval washers but can also be found with "flush ground" round

screw-bolts. The Thai script on the ricasso of these bayonets, "RS 121," referred to the "Bangkok year 121," the 121st year of the Chakri Monarchy's dynasty, or 1902 in the Christian calendar. The scabbard throat has a small recess so that it can be used on the blade when the bayonet is fitted to the rifle, the recess allowing clearance for the barrel. A quantity of Austrian 1888-pattern bayonets was acquired in 1903. These were termed the Type 46 bayonet.

A Japanese Arisaka-type rifle was adopted in 1908. The **1908** or Type 51 bayonet was similar to the Japanese **30th-year** type but with a short blade. Japanese 30th-year rifles and bayonets were also used by Thailand. During 1919, 10,000 British 1907-pattern bayonets were refurbished by B.S.A. and sold to Siam for issue to the "Wild Tiger Corps," King Rama VI's personal bodyguard. King Rama VI reigned from 1910 to 1925. The **1919**, or Type 62, bayonets had the British markings ground from the ricasso and a tiger's-head stamp added. A steel tube, crudely welded to the topmount and chape, later replaced the leatherwork of the original British scabbard as leather degenerated rapidly in the hot and humid climate of Siam. Siamese characters on the ricasso showed "Rama VI 2462," the monarch's name and the Siamese Buddhist year,

ABOVE 1902 ricasso marking showing the Thai script "RS 121." This indicated the 121st year of the Chakri dynasty, or 1902 in the Gregorian calendar.

LEFT Siamese 1902 bayonet (Type 45) with round grip rivet washers. The 1902 bayonet was used on the 8mm Type 45 rifle, a Mauser-action long rifle.

relating to 1919 on western calendars. The Thai Buddhist calendar follows the Gregorian but with a 543-year difference. There was also an overlap, the Siamese year running from mid-March to mid-March on the Gregorian calendar. This two-and-a-half month overlap has led to some confusion over dating, and this bayonet is often listed as the 1920; however, Thai authorities have confirmed that it was issued in 1919, the Thai date covering from mid-March 1919 to mid-March 1920 by Western dating.

Japan occupied Thailand in December 1941 and, under political and military pressure, Thailand conceded to an alliance with Japan and declared war on Britain and the U.S. The alliance was uneasy and much internal resistance was undertaken leading, at the end of the war, to British and American recognition of Thailand as an ally.

Post-war, the Danish M1947 export rifle was imported along with a quantity of **M47** bayonets, a design that was never a major success and that was to receive few buyers on the international arms market. As with much of the Far East not under communist influence, the Thais were to later use the American M16 rifle and **M7** bayonet, a combination still in use. A number of German H&K33 rifles and **G3** bayonets are also currently issued to Thai troops.

ABOVE A variant of the 1902 bayonet, this example uses Japanese-style oval washers on the grip screws.

LEFT Detail of the 1902 hilt showing a comparison of the grip attachment method.

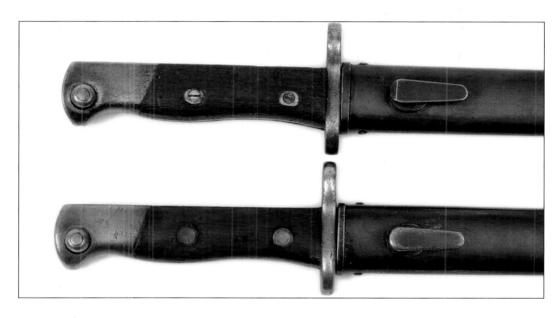

LEFT The Siamese 1908 (Type 51) bayonet has a hilt based upon that of the Japanese 30th-year bayonet of 1897. It has the standard Japanese grip-retaining oval screw washers. The scabbard has a frog stud rather than the Japanese frog loop.

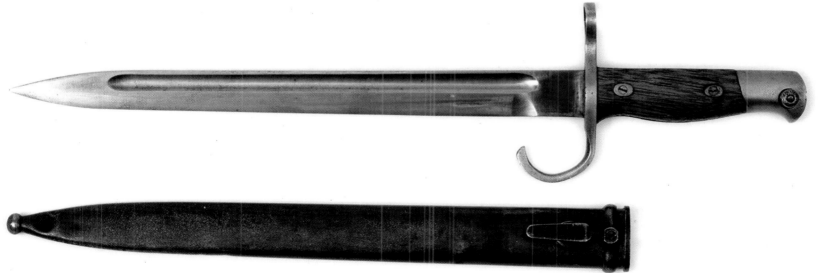

BELOW The only marking on this 1908 bayonet is the number "14" on the pommel end. Siamese bayonets can also be found numbered in Thai script.

BELOW The original British markings have been ground off of the ricasso and replaced by a tiger's-head stamp on this 1919 bayonet.

RIGHT This Thai soldier is armed with the Heckler & Koch 33E rifle and G3 bayonet. Unusually, the bayonet scabbard is shown here worn at the front left hip rather than to the rear, as is normal practice in most armies.

BELOW The Siamese 1919 (Type 62) pattern bayonet was a refurbished British 1907. The original leather body of the scabbard has been replaced by one of sheet steel. It was issued to the "Wild Tiger Corps," the personal bodyguard of King Rama VI.

Turkey

	Overall length	Blade length	Muzzle ring
1874 socket	590mm	521mm	17.8mm
1874 short	603mm	406mm	17.9mm
1890	587mm	460mm	15.4mm
1903	651mm	524mm	15.3mm
1903 short	378mm	254mm	15.5mm
1935	378mm	254mm	15.5mm
1907 short	365mm	243mm	15.5mm
G1	375mm	237mm	18mm
G3	380mm	240mm	22mm

The vast Ottoman Empire had always relied on imported weapons. During the mid-1800s, the Turks were using a variety of French and Belgian weapons as well as a large number of Enfield 1853 rifles with German-made 1856 sword bayonets, and American Springfield rifles. This hotchpotch of weaponry was to be the hallmark of Turkish armaments that continued into the 20th century. In 1873, in an effort to modernize their Army, the Turks opened a contract for .45in Peabody Martini rifles from the Providence Tool Company. The majority of the Peabody Martini rifles were supplied with the **1874** cruciform-bladed socket bayonet. As it was a breechloading weapon, the bayonet blade mounted below the barrel, but a number had provision for the fitting of a sword bayonet. The **1874** yataghan-bladed sword bayonet had black leather grips and scabbard body with steel mounts. Many of these were later shortened and had their blades straightened. The lever-action Winchester 1866 was another U.S. rifle imported by Turkey. It was issued with the Winchester **1866** socket bayonet. The American Peabody Martinis and Winchesters made a significant impact on the battle of Plevna in July 1877, when the weight of Turkish firepower broke the Russian assault and inflicted disastrous casualties. Each Turkish infantryman was issued both a Peabody, for accurate long-range shooting, and a Winchester for close-range rapid fire. The sheer firepower of the Winchester generally broke attacks before bayonet range was reached. Despite the losses suffered at Plevna, Russia was close to defeating Turkey early the following year before British intervention brought about an end to the Russo-Turkish conflict with the Russian armies

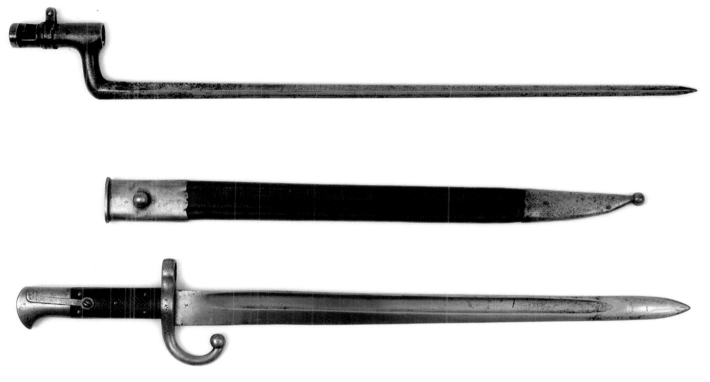

TOP 1874 socket bayonet, issued with the 11.5mm Peabody Martini rifle. The quadrangular bayonet was issued with a brass-mounted leather scabbard.

ABOVE A Turkish 1874 bayonet with shortened blade. This bayonet was issued to NCOs armed with the Peabody rifle; other ranks were issued with the socket bayonet.

LEFT Left side view of the 1874 hilt, showing the press catch and leather grips secured by five rivets. These bayonets were made in the U.S. for export to Turkey.

LEFT The 1890 bayonet was identical to the earlier 1887 but for its shorter crossguard, the muzzle ring of the 1887 being closer to the hilt. Both had a long swept-forward quillon.

RIGHT The 1903 bayonet retained the hilt of the 1890 bayonet but added to it the long blade of the German S98 bayonet. The scabbard was also of the type used with the S98. This example has had a contemporary field repair undertaken to the leather; a section of leather has been stitched near the chape to cover a jagged hole.

within reach of Istanbul (although by this stage the Russian casualties had been very high). A small number of 1870 Remington Naval rifles were also imported from America along with the **1870** sword bayonets.

The attraction of the Mauser system was not lost on the Turkish military, who adopted a 9.5mm Mauser-action rifle in 1887. However, the 7.65mm 1890 rifle rapidly superseded this. The 1887 and **1890** bayonets differed only in the muzzle ring diameter, 16mm and 15.5mm respectively, and the position of the muzzle ring, which was closer to the hilt on the 1887. Both had short wooden grips, a long hooked quillon, straight blade and steel-mounted leather scabbard. The Turkish 1903 rifle was similar to the German 7.92mm G98. The **1903** *sungu* (bayonet) also owed its design to that issued with the G98 and had the same pipe-back blade but the style of hilt as found on the Turkish **1890** bayonet. Many of the **1890** and **1903** bayonets were shortened during the interwar period, but a short-bladed version of the **1903** was also manufactured. The short version of the **1903** had a narrow blade. Its hilt was similar to that of the **1903** but differed in having a shorter quillon, and longer wooden grips that met the steel pommel at an angle. The Turks were to suffer territorial losses during the Balkan Wars, and again following defeat in World War I, during which conflicts, the bayonet saw much use.

Prior to 1928, written Turkish was a version of Perso-Arabic script called Ottoman Turkish script. In 1928, Mustafa Kemal Attaturk replaced this with the Latin alphabet in an effort to modernize Turkey and bring the nation closer to

RIGHT This brown leather frog, attached to the 1890 bayonet, has the unusual leather washer occasionally found with Turkish frogs.

FAR RIGHT This Ricasso marking on a Turkish 1890 bayonet reads "Maker VC Schilling Suhl. 1309". Turkish weapons were marked with a date based on the Turkish fiscal calendar, not the standard Islamic Hijri calendar. This calendar has an overlap with the Gregorian calendar of 2.5 months, running from mid-March to mid-March; hence, a bayonet made in 1309 relates to the Gregorian year March 1893 to March 1894.

Europe than the Middle East. Thus Arabic markings on any bayonet identify them as being pre-1928.

During the interwar years, a number of **VZ23** bayonets were supplied with 7.92mm rifles imported from Czechoslovakia. Added to these rifles and bayonets, many surplus German ersatz bayonets were bought up from the overflowing surplus arms market. Countless numbers of these ersatz bayonets were shortened from their original 310mm to lengths of around 250mm, corresponding roughly to the dimensions of the Turkish **1935** bayonet. The **1935** pattern was newly made and also converted from older types so that a number of variants exist. They were normally marked on the pommel with the Turkish state arsenal mark of "AS.FA," standing for *Askari Fabrika*, which translates as "military factory," the state arsenal set up in 1929. Whilst the generally accepted designation of **1935** bayonet has been retained in this work it is believed that the Turks actually only began streamlining their vast array of rifle and bayonet types and reworking them to a "standard" (1903-style rifles and 250mm bayonet blades) in 1938. Many other bayonet types can be found shortened and modified to fit Turkish weapons, including British **1907** bayonets.

World War II saw Turkey placed in a difficult position, attempting to maintain neutral but being coerced from all sides and surrounded by belligerents. Turkey did not take an active roll in World War II, despite extreme pressure from both the Allied and Axis governments. However, Turkey did declare war on Germany and Japan on March 1, 1945.

During the 1950s, surplus U.S. Garand rifles and bayonets were purchased in some quantity, but with the move to the NATO 7.62mm round Turkey was to adopt the FN FAL. The bayonet used with the FAL is often considered to be a conversion of World War I-vintage ersatz bayonets; however, despite its poor finish the **G1** bayonet, introduced in 1965, was purpose made. It had an all-metal ersatz-style hilt and an unusual double muzzle ring fixing. The FAL was progressively replaced in some units by the 7.62mm G3 rifle. The accompanying **G3** bayonets had a green plastic hilt and gray parkerized metalwork; the scabbard was made up of two sections with a distinct broad edge seam. It was copied from German World War I examples made by Friedrich August Gobel. If one distinction is evident in Turkish weaponry, it is undoubtedly the vast mix of weapon types used and the way in which any available bayonet was modified and re-formed to suit any weapon and current trends. This reuse of any available bayonet types not only included re-worked older Turkish bayonets but also surplus foreign weapons captured or obtained cheaply on the surplus market. British 1907-pattern blades mated with Turkish hilts as well as 1907 hilts modified to fit Turkish weaponry are just two examples of the variety that combine to make the field of collecting Turkish bayonets a particularly interesting one. The majority of Turkish bayonets also demand a considerably lower price than many of them justify.

RIGHT The "Toughra" marking of Abdul Hamid II, and the Islamic crescent stamped onto the pommel of an 1890 bayonet.

BELOW 1903 bayonet with short blade. Although standard long-bladed 1903 bayonets can be found with shortened blades, this particular bayonet was produced with a short blade. It is readily distinguished from shortened bayonets, as the fuller finishes well short of the point. Scabbards were of steel or steel-mounted leather.

BELOW This World War I German ersatz bayonet was cut down under the *c.*1938 streamlining of Turkish bayonet types. Turkey purchased countless surplus bayonets in the post-World War I period, altering them to fit weapons as required.

LEFT A further example of Turkish willingness to "make do" and improvise is this British 1907 bayonet. It has been shortened, and the muzzle ring has been cut off, with an extended crossguard section and new muzzle ring added in its place. The original scabbard has been replaced by a Czech pattern normally found with the VZ23, not a mismatch, but a further example of making best use of available weaponry.

BOTTOM LEFT Standard pattern M1935 bayonet. This was newly made, but countless variants exist, made up from a number of older Turkish and foreign weapons. This bayonet was probably not produced before 1938.

BELOW M35 pommel detail showing the marking "ASFA" for *Askari Fabrika*.

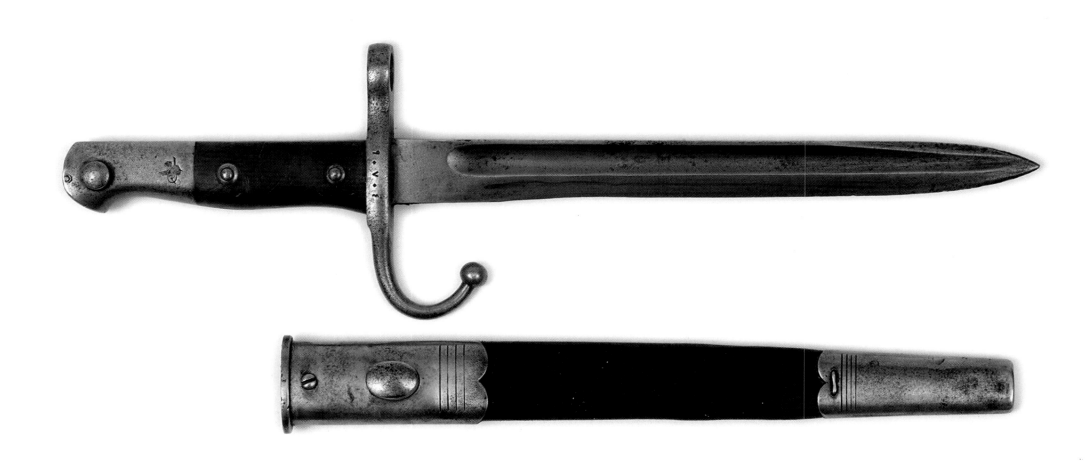

**ABOVE In keeping with the Turkish
modification of all bayonets that
took place just prior to World War
II, this 1890 bayonet has had its
blade and scabbard shortened to a
uniform length that equated closely to that of the 1935 bayonet.**

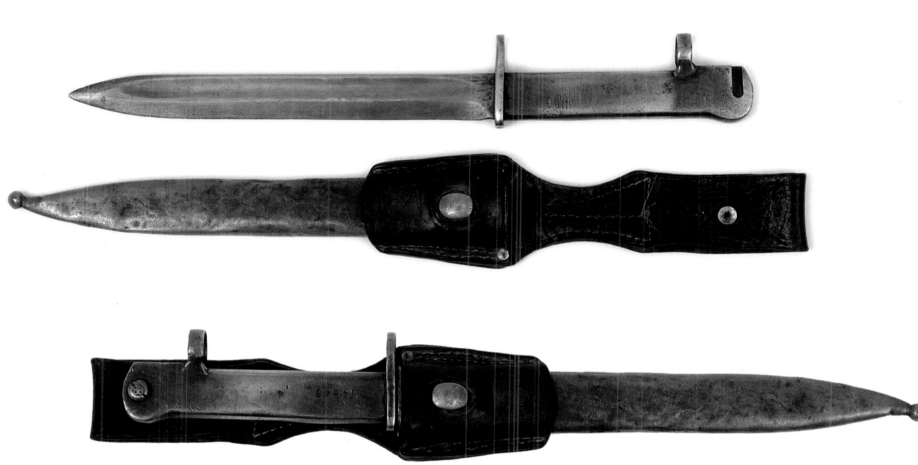

LEFT G1 bayonet. This bayonet resembles a World War I ersatz bayonet. However, it was newly made by the Turks for use with the FN FAL rifle. The leather frog has a press stud in the belt loop for securing it to the belt. Blades can be found with or without fullers.

ABOVE FN FAL G1 bayonet sheathed. The right side of the hilt is marked with the bayonet serial number "14646."

RIGHT This view of the left side of the hilt of the FN FAL G1 bayonet shows the very basic construction techniques employed in the manufacture of the bayonet and the unusual double-ring fitting method.

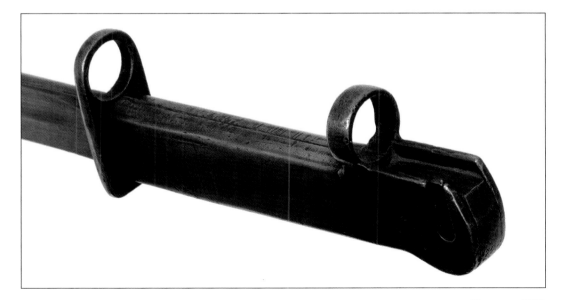

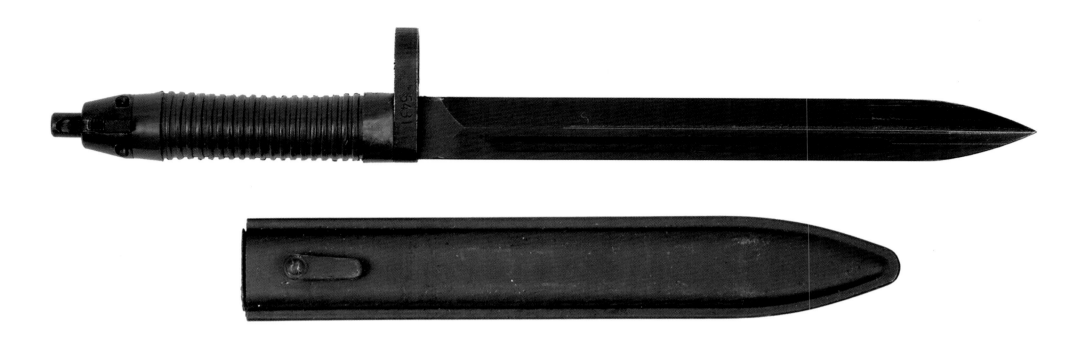

ABOVE Turkish bayonet for the G3 rifle. The blade edge is uppermost in this picture, but the bayonet would be fitted reversed, above the barrel, in typical G3 fashion. The scabbard is a copy of those made during World War I by Friedrich August Gobel, for use with German ersatz bayonets.

LEFT G3 hilt and fixing catch. The green plastic hilt is heavily ridged to provide grip. This view also shows the throat-spring retaining screw on the rear face of the scabbard, and the folded-over side seam on the body.

United States of America

	Overall length	Blade length	Muzzle ring
1816	480mm	393mm	20.5mm
1866 Winchester	450mm	380mm	15.4mm
1870	627mm	508mm	20mm
1873	530mm	457mm	19.5mm
1873 Winchester	530mm	455mm	17mm
1873 trowel	368mm	254mm	19mm
1882 generic short	518mm	450mm	18.5mm
1882 generic long	615mm	544mm	18.5mm
1885 long shank	525mm	460mm	17.5mm
1892 Winchester	533mm	456mm	17mm
1892	412mm	295mm	15mm
Cadet socket	350mm	305mm	15.5mm
1899	324mm	209mm	15mm
1903	597mm	N/A	N/A
1910	520mm	406mm	16mm
1912	486mm	409mm	19.5mm
M1917	552mm	432mm	15mm
M1942	520mm	406mm	16mm
USN Mk. I	523mm	405mm	15.5mm
M1	349mm	248mm	16mm
M4	294mm	168mm	15mm
M41	303mm	197mm	13.7mm
Ingram M6	228mm	N/A	N/A
M5	289mm	169mm	N/A
M6	229mm	171mm	18mm
M7	295mm	165mm	22mm
M9	311mm	182mm	22mm

which had first appeared in 1814, with the bridge over the slot at the collar. It was also used on the 1819 Hall rifle and remained in service until 1842, when it was replaced by the 1842-pattern bayonet. The **1816** was the last U.S. bayonet not to have a locking ring. The bayonet supplied with the 1842 muskets, the last U.S. flintlock, was the model 1835. These were based on the French Mle. 1822. Unlike previous patterns, the 1835 bayonet mounted to a stud beneath the barrel, requiring that the slot be cut on the left of the socket rather than the right as was previously standard.

During the Civil War, both Union and Confederate forces found themselves lacking weaponry. Vast numbers of muskets and bayonets were imported from Europe to compensate for the shortfall. Amongst these, British Enfield 1853 and Austrian Lorenz 1854 rifles and bayonets were imported in quantity. The standard rifle of the Civil War was the 1855 musket, which was equipped with either a sword or socket bayonet. Many of the 1855 socket bayonets were later converted to fit

RIGHT A Doughboy from an "Honor Guard" at ease with his Springfield 03 rifle and fixed 1905-pattern bayonet. The scabbard is the first pattern with leather body.

BELOW The "T"-slot 1816 bayonet, the first "standardized" bayonet type in American service. The "T"-slot lessened the likelihood of the bayonet unfixing in combat when compared to a standard "Z"-slot. But compared to the French locking ring, it was far from satisfactory. It was also used on the M1819 Hall bayonet. A number of upgraded 1816 bayonets were made during the Civil War, 1861–65.

The first true U.S. bayonet was that for the 1795 musket. Prior to this, a mix of British and French weapons had been in use. The 1795 type had a short "L" slot and no bridge, an inherent weakness in early bayonet designs. The 1808 bayonet soon supplemented this. This had the "T" slot to the socket that was better than the plain "L" type. It also added a strengthening bridge over the slot.

The **1816** bayonet was similar to its predecessors but was a minor improvement on them in that it had a "T"-shaped slot,

the 1873 rifle by cold-pressing the socket (see the **1873** bayonet).

Winchester was a well-known U.S. manufacturer of weapons and bayonets for the civilian and military markets. Some 3,000 Winchester 1866 repeating rifles and the small **1866** socket bayonets were sold to France during the Franco-Prussian war. A number were captured by the Prussians and were later sold on, many being used by the Turks. Winchester also produced the **Winchester 1873** bayonet for their 1873 repeating rifle. The last U.S. socket bayonet was made for the Winchester 1892 rifle. Very few of the **1892** bayonets were made, being produced at a time when the knife bayonet was becoming standard issue in most armies.

The U.S. Navy's requirement for a breechloader to replace their muskets resulted in the adoption of the Remington rifle. A brass-hilted sword bayonet was employed on the new rifle. The USN **1870** bayonet was made with two blade types. The first, and least common, was a semi-yataghan form, while the second, a straight double-edged blade, was one of the few sword bayonets to employ such a blade. The hilt and cross-guard were made entirely of brass, being given additional grip by the incorporation of a "fish scale" pattern. The rear of the pommel has a large hole, running longitudinally through the hilt, which accommodated the rifle's cleaning rod. The left and right side of the pommel bore the naval ordnance mark of crossed Dahlgren guns and an anchor. "USN 1870" was stamped onto the left ricasso along with the inspector's mark.

The last standard socket type bayonet adopted by the U.S. was the **1873**, issued with the Springfield .45-70in "Trapdoor" rifle. The bayonet appears identical to the 1855 and many were converted by cold pressing the socket to reduce its size. The **1873** was issued with a steel scabbard with a leather belt hanger loop. Later variants replaced the belt loop with a brass hook. Both types carried a round brass escutcheon disc. These bore the federal "US," "USN" or state markings. An innovative design of bayonet was also produced for the new rifle. The trowel-shaped bayonet was supposed to be a useful entrenching tool as well as a bayonet; however, its broad blade made for a poor bayonet and its size and style made it of limited use for digging. A further unusual feature of the **1873** trowel bayonet was its locking system. The socket had an enclosed mortise and a two-part socket that rotated 90 degrees to lock. Probably fewer than 10,000 made.

During the 1880s, the U.S. exported many Remington rifles and bayonets worldwide. The Spanish later turned these rifles against the U.S. The Remington Lee rifle was purchased by a number of nations. It was supplied with a socket bayonet that had a choice of two blade lengths. The **1882** bayonet (often

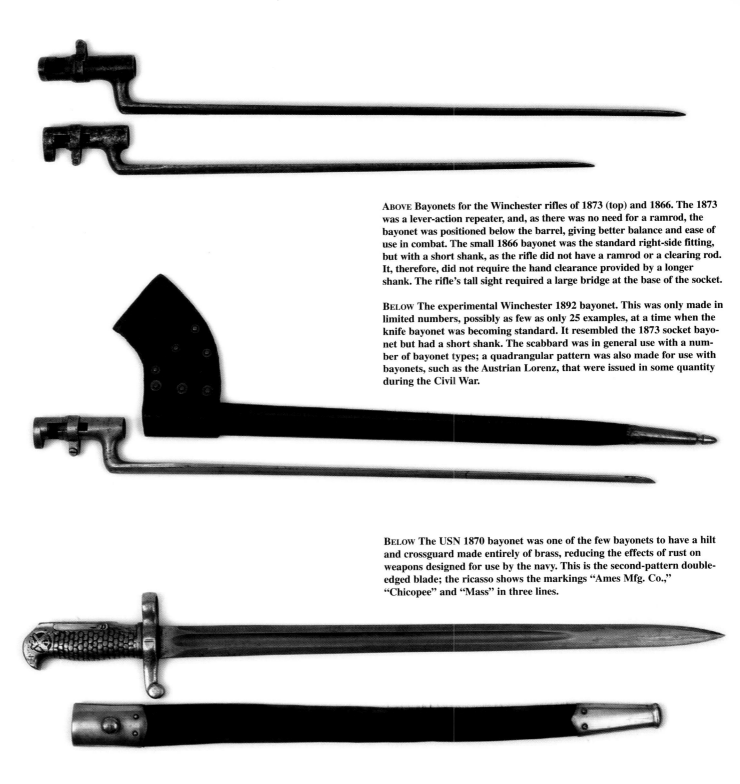

ABOVE Bayonets for the Winchester rifles of 1873 (top) and 1866. The 1873 was a lever-action repeater, and, as there was no need for a ramrod, the bayonet was positioned below the barrel, giving better balance and ease of use in combat. The small 1866 bayonet was the standard right-side fitting, but with a short shank, as the rifle did not have a ramrod or a clearing rod. It, therefore, did not require the hand clearance provided by a longer shank. The rifle's tall sight required a large bridge at the base of the socket.

BELOW The experimental Winchester 1892 bayonet. This was only made in limited numbers, possibly as few as only 25 examples, at a time when the knife bayonet was becoming standard. It resembled the 1873 socket bayonet but had a short shank. The scabbard was in general use with a number of bayonet types; a quadrangular pattern was also made for use with bayonets, such as the Austrian Lorenz, that were issued in some quantity during the Civil War.

BELOW The USN 1870 bayonet was one of the few bayonets to have a hilt and crossguard made entirely of brass, reducing the effects of rust on weapons designed for use by the navy. This is the second-pattern double-edged blade; the ricasso shows the markings "Ames Mfg. Co.," "Chicopee" and "Mass" in three lines.

called the generic Remington, as it was used on a variety of weapons) appears typically American in its design. A further Remington export bayonet was the **1885**; similar to the **1882,** it had a different socket orientation and an extremely long shank. This may not be an official Remington conversion.

The United States was a little slow in adopting a standard bolt-action rifle and smokeless powder cartridges. However, by 1890, the inadequacies of the old single shot .45-70in Springfield 73 rifle were becoming obvious, and it was conceded that a modern bolt-action rifle was required to properly equip the U.S. Army in a manner equal to contemporary European armies. The Norwegian Krag-Jorgensen was chosen as the basis for the new U.S. rifle. The Krag rifle became the U.S. standard-issue arm and saw service with American troops in the Philippines and Cuba. The **1892** Krag bayonet was the

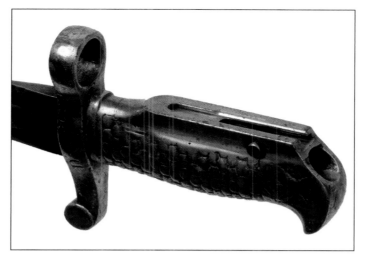 

ABOVE Dahlgren naval cannon, over an anchor, were impressed into both sides of the pommel of the 1870 bayonet. The large hole visible in the pommel end allowed passage of the rifle's cleaning rod.

BELOW Springfield 1873 bayonet. The last socket bayonet to be adopted as standard by U.S. forces, it was also the first U.S. bayonet to be blued overall. Two scabbard variants are shown, differing only in the method of suspension. Above is the early pattern with leather belt loop and brass escutcheon plate bearing "U.S." The later scabbard replaced the leather belt loop with a brass hook, the concept also being used on later U.S. knife-bayonet scabbards, including the first pattern used with the 1892 Krag bayonet.

ABOVE 1870 bayonet left ricasso showing the marking "U.S.N.," "G.G.S." and "1870:" the navy property mark, the inspector's mark and the year.

first general-issue knife bayonet in U.S. service, replacing the **1873** socket bayonet. In design, it was almost an exact copy of the Swiss **1889** bayonet, on which it was based. Interestingly, it was the first and last standard U.S. issue bayonet to use the pommel internal spring press catch release mechanism. This mechanism, almost standard throughout the world, received little interest from the Americans. The **1892** bayonet and rifle designs were short lived. However, during the interwar years, a special adapter could be purchased to enable the **1892** bayonet to be fitted to the .45in Auto Ordnance Thompson M1928 machine gun. The adaptor was advertised as an optional accessory. The **1892** bayonet was also advertised commercially for use with the Winchester 1907 police rifle.

The Spanish American war highlighted the superiority of the Mauser action used by the Spanish, when compared to the U.S. Krag. This led to the adoption of the Springfield 1903 with its vastly superior Mauser-type action. At this stage, the U.S. authorities took a step back in bayonet design as they considered the knife bayonet obsolete. The new rifle used a long "ramrod" bayonet approved as the **1903**. It was stored beneath the barrel in a manner previously used for the redundant ramrods of muzzle-loading muskets. Ramrod bayonets had previously seen service with the 1884 and other U.S. rifles. Approximately 95,000 rifles were produced before, belatedly, the ramrod bayonet was deemed of little use. Almost every major nation had by this time provided its troops with a knife- or sword-type bayonet; President Theodore Roosevelt himself stated that the rod bayonet was "as poor an invention as I ever saw."

The **M1905** bayonet provided the replacement for the inadequate **1903** ramrod bayonet, with the ramrod-fitted rifles being upgraded to take the new bayonet. Its design was based on knowledge gained in the Philippines and study of the combat experiences of other nations, including actions during the Russo-Japanese war. The hilt contained the press catch and locking bar, a lever that pivoted on the single grip screw. The press catch, located against the crossguard, also served to secure the bayonet in the scabbard. This design of locking catch had been used on the Norwegian **1894** bayonet. The first of three scabbards issued with the bayonet was the 1905; it had a leather-covered wooden body and sprung-steel belt loop. The second type 1905 scabbard was merely a modification, deleting the belt loop and adding the then newly

RIGHT 1873 trowel bayonet with the hilt rotated for fitting to the rifle.

FAR RIGHT The U.S. Patent marking on the (inverted) socket of the 1872 trowel bayonet. It reads "Pat. Apr. 16. 72."

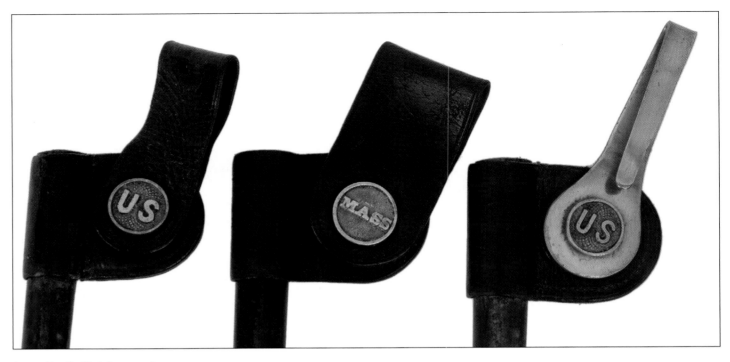

ABOVE Detail of belt hangers. A leather loop with brass escutcheon was standard (this is the federal "US"-marked type); one of the many state variants is "MASS," indicating Massachusetts, this example having a broad belt loop section. At right is the brass hook with "US" escutcheon.

RIGHT The design of the 1873 trowel bayonet was patented in April 1872. It had a unique attachment method in which the whole rear of the socket rotated to allow fixing. The scabbard was of leather with a brass tip and belt loop.

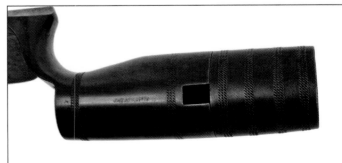

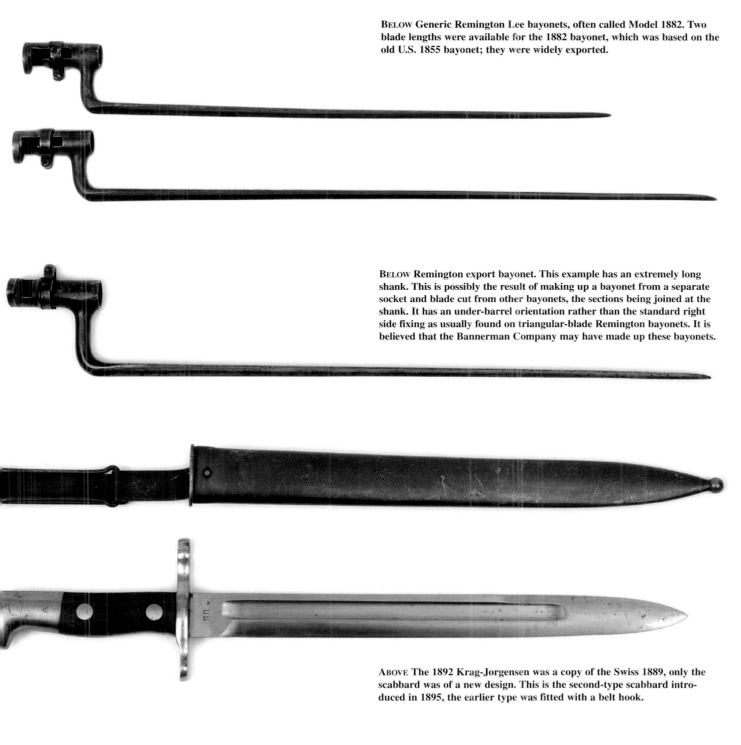

BELOW Generic Remington Lee bayonets, often called Model 1882. Two blade lengths were available for the 1882 bayonet, which was based on the old U.S. 1855 bayonet; they were widely exported.

BELOW Remington export bayonet. This example has an extremely long shank. This is possibly the result of making up a bayonet from a separate socket and blade cut from other bayonets, the sections being joined at the shank. It has an under-barrel orientation rather than the standard right side fixing as usually found on triangular-blade Remington bayonets. It is believed that the Bannerman Company may have made up these bayonets.

ABOVE The 1892 Krag-Jorgensen was a copy of the Swiss 1889, only the scabbard was of a new design. This is the second-type scabbard introduced in 1895, the earlier type was fitted with a belt hook.

introduced double-hook belt attachment device. The final scabbard was the model **1910**, it consisted of a rawhide-covered wooden body within a canvas outer sleeve, a web hanger supported the belt hook. The introduction of the **M3** scabbard in 1941 saw the **1910** relegated to limited standard.

For bayonet training, Great Britain adopted specially made fencing "muskets," with spring-loaded blades. The U.S. chose to use special fencing bayonets with sprung-steel blades attached to obsolete muskets or rifles. The first of the type was introduced in the 1850s. It had a standard socket with a sprung-steel blade ending in a large leather ball. The pattern developed into the 1906 fencing bayonet, this was the first not to use a socket for attachment. Instead, the 1906 used twin muzzle rings. The leather-covered spring blade of the 1906 bayonet allowed only for lateral movement, but it was felt that vertical movement was of greater importance. The 1906 was therefore modified by having a 90-degree twist applied to the blade, giving it the important vertical movement. This modification was adopted as the **1912** fencing bayonet.

America's entry into World War I meant that all weapon production was dedicated to providing for the U.S. forces. Thus the design for the British P14 rifle and P13 bayonet, made for Great Britain in the USA, were taken up by the U.S. Ordnance Department as the 1917 models. The rifle design was converted to the U.S. standard .30-06in from the original British .303in caliber, and the specification changed from P14 to P17. The U.S.-issue bayonet differed from the British pattern in having U.S.-issue markings and in having a clearing hole in the pommel. The M1917 bayonet retained the grooves cut into the grips. In British service, these had served to provide an instantly recognizable method of differentiating between the P13 and 1907, two otherwise very similar bayonets. The grooves were superfluous in U.S. service as the 1907 was not used. The M1917 was issued with modified British-type scabbards, the first pattern having a swiveling leather fob, with U.S. belt hooks, attached to the topmount. The second pattern had the belt hooks attached directly to the topmount. Unlike British scabbards, the American type had a small drain hole drilled in the bottom of the chape. Some Remington-made M1917 bayonets produced in 1918 bore the stamp "1918" on the ricasso rather than 1917. It is believed this was undertaken to follow the standard practice of date-stamping U.S. bayonets. The 1917 mark was actually a model designation rather than the year of manufacture; thus Remington was ordered to discontinue the 1918 stamp and revert to marking the bayonets "1917." In 1940, over 1,000,000 rifles and M1917 bayonets were sent to Great Britain as war aid. They were issued to the Home Guard and other Allied troops. Even after World War II, the bayonet design still had some service life left. During the Vietnam War, the M1917 bayonet was again put into production. The new manufacture had a poorer overall finish, with checkered plastic grips and a plastic scabbard based on the old M3, though it had a longer topmount. The longer topmount was necessary as the M3 plastic body was too short for the longer 1917 bayonet. It was designated "Scabbard M1917" and, along with the new bayonets, was for issue with trench shotguns. France purchased surplus 1917 bayonets after World War II. They were cut down to fighting knives and had a leather belt loop attached to the scabbard topmount.

America's unexpected entry into World War II, on December 7, 1941, brought with it a major requirement for arms. The **M1905** bayonet was rapidly put back into production after a manufacturing break of some 20 years; however, the opportunity of modernizing the design was also taken. The bayonet was given new black or red-brown ribbed plastic grips and the canvass-covered scabbard was replaced by one made of molded plastic that had a metal topmount and belt hook section. The new scabbard was designated the **M3,** with each of the new scabbards costing 75 cents. The **M1905** bayonet reintroduced to service during WWII is commonly referred to as the **M1942**, although this is a collector's term. Orders for 1.5 million were placed during 1942/3.

In 1943, The U.S. Navy adopted the unusual **USN Mk. I** bayonet. This plastic training bayonet was required due to the extreme shortage of rifles at the beginning of the war, particularly within the U.S. Navy. The Navy procured around 300,000 dummy rifles and **USN Mk. I** bayonets. Intended for ceremonial, drill and bayonet training, they allowed the release of an equivalent number of Springfield 03 rifles to the active fleet. Ideal for drill, they were not so well suited to physical bayonet training; the weak blades broke easily and were sufficiently strong to cause injury in a direct stabbing assault. Nonetheless, the bayonets did allow training to be undertaken, they used little metal and cost only around $1.70 each. The end of the war rendered these bayonets obsolete.

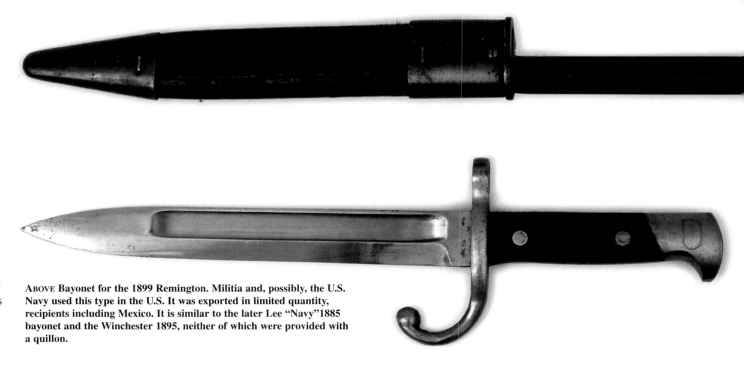

ABOVE Bayonet for the 1899 Remington. Militia and, possibly, the U.S. Navy used this type in the U.S. It was exported in limited quantity, recipients including Mexico. It is similar to the later Lee "Navy" 1885 bayonet and the Winchester 1895, neither of which were provided with a quillon.

ABOVE The 1903 Springfield rifle was initially provided with a rod bayonet. The 1903 pattern was the last of this type that had seen use on earlier weapons. It is surprising that, after the clean lines of the Krag 1892 bayonet, the all-but useless rod was adopted. Its service life was short, as the M1905 bayonet soon replaced it.

LEFT The 1903 rod bayonet tip, the cut-out recess connected with a spring in the rifle, holding the bayonet when it was in the stowed position, whilst the depression immediately behind the point allowed a finger grip for withdrawing the bayonet from the rifle's stock.

FAR LEFT Illustration from U.S. Infantry Regulations 1911, showing the "low parry."

The scabbard used with the **USN Mk. I** bayonet was a copy of the **M3**; it differed in not having the ordnance flaming grenade on the topmount and was instead engraved "USN MK 1" over two lines.

The **M1905** and **M1942** bayonets were found to be somewhat long, especially when compared to the bayonets in use with Germany's K98 and the British No. 4 rifle. In August 1942, the Cavalry Board made a request for a short bayonet that would be easier to carry when in a vehicle or mounted, and would provide a better handheld weapon than the **1905** bayonet. In early 1943, a number of cut-down **M1905** bayonets and scabbards were provided for trials as the **M1905E1**. They proved well suited to the requirement and were officially adopted as the **M1** bayonet in the spring of 1943. All cut-down bayonets are commonly referred to as the **M1905E1** by collectors. However, in U.S. Ordnance terminology, there is no differentiation between shortened blades or newly manufactured ones; all were issued as the **M1**. The designation **M1905E1** was only applied to the original bayonets that were used for the trials. As the original bayonets had a variety of fuller styles, a number of different point styles exist on cut-down bayonets, the point being cut to provide maximum strength for any given fuller type. By the end of the war, over a million **M1905** bayonets had been modified to **M1** type at an average cost of around $1.36 per blade. Most modified bayonets carried the mark of the company responsible for the work, a typical marking being "PAL-MOD," showing modification by the Pal Blade and Tool Company. A new scabbard was required for the shortened blade; it was identical to the plastic **M3** scabbard but reduced in length to suit the new bayonet. It entered service as the **M7**. The now obsolete **M3** scabbards proved an ideal basis for conversion to the new type; however, it was found the tabs that secured the metal topmount into the depressions on the scabbard side broke when the mount was removed for shortening of the scabbard body. Shortened **M3** scabbards converted to **M7** are thus instantly recognizable by the absence of the tabs on the topmount and lack of depression in the sides of the scabbard body; the topmount being crimped into place on the shortened scabbard body. All of the **M3** scabbards in QM stores were shortened as were scabbards withdrawn from troops or returned to depots. For ceremonial use, the USMC used a white duck cover. It resembled the web cover of the **M1910** scabbard but had an integral belt loop. It is still in use with ceremonial units using the **M1** bayonet. The **M7** scabbard was slid into the cover and the scabbard's belt hooks tucked behind the integral belt loop. The standard U.S. belt hook device attached to U.S. scabbards fit the M1910 and subsequent cartridge belts, and the M1912 and M1936 pistol

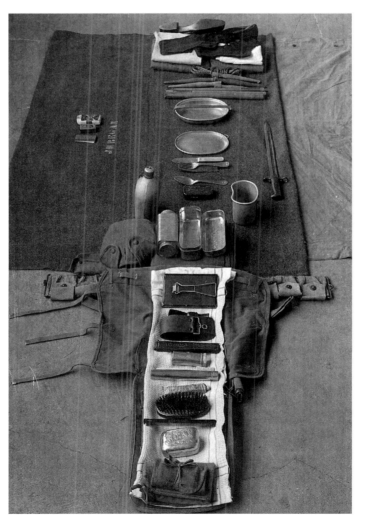

Top U.S. cadet socket bayonet based on the French 1770's styling. This diminutive bayonet was produced commercially for the many cadet organizations that flourished in the late 1890s; scabbards were either leather or shortened versions of the 1873-type steel scabbard.

Left A U.S. Doughboy's kit layout, this includes the M1905 bayonet.

Above The socket of the cadet bayonet showing the locking ring and open collar ring for the fixing stud.

belts. It also allowed the scabbards to be carried on a variety of U.S.-issue packs including the M1910, M1928, M1943, M1944, M1945 and the USMC M1941 pack. It did not, however, allow attachment to the enlisted man's leather garrison belt, and to enable the use of the bayonet when the garrison belt was worn a small leather slider was provided. It consisted of a leather loop that slid over the belt and two reinforced holes on the lower edge, which allowed attachment of the scabbard's belt hook. A similar webbing loop was made for use with the M1910 webbing garrison belt.

In the postwar years, the M1 Garand was supplied to many nations, along with the M1 bayonet. A number of countries produced their own versions of the M1 bayonet, amongst these were Denmark, Indonesia, Iran, Italy, Japan, Korea and Taiwan.

The .30in M1 carbine was a substitute weapon for many troops previously armed with the .45in M1911A1 pistol; it was not originally provided with a bayonet attachment. As the carbine had no provision for a bayonet, many troops carrying the weapon were issued the **M3** knife. The knife was well designed. It had a short 172mm blade and leather grips and was carried in the all-leather **M6** scabbard. This was later replaced by the **M8** scabbard, which had a plastic body and steel throat, similar to the **M7** scabbard, but with an integral webbing belt loop. It was soon deemed that a bayonet would be required for the carbine and design of such was instigated. The **M3** knife was chosen as the basis for the new bayonet, it required a new pommel and crossguard with muzzle ring. It was approved for issue in July 1944 as the **M4** bayonet. Originally the **M4** bayonet had leather grips, but these were found to be prone to rot, particularly in humid tropical regions. The problem was rectified shortly after the Korean War when, in 1954, a new contract for the **M4** bayonet authorized the use of plastic grips. The new bayonets also had a slightly wider crossguard as it had been found that the earlier type had been prone to cracking. The M1 carbine had no provision for the attachment of the bayonet, but this was rectified by the manufacture of a new forward barrel band and sling mount incorporating a bayonet bar; this was easily added to the weapon enabling it to take the bayonet. The **M8** scabbard was initially issued with the **M4** bayonet, but the improved **M8A1** scabbard later replaced this. The updated scabbard differed in having a longer belt loop section and a wire belt hook. The belt hook was not a component of the earlier **M8,** but it was retrospectively fitted to many scabbards.

The **M41** bayonet for the Johnson self-loading rifle was unique amongst U.S. bayonets. A recoiling barrel on the rifle meant that the bayonet had to be as light as possible. It consisted of a simple triangular blade formed by an extension of the single-piece forged hilt. The hilt was merely a flat steel section, with no grip or pommel, a simple attachment mechanism

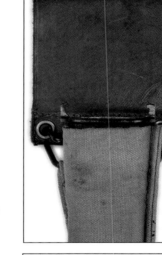

LEFT The enlisted-issued garrison belt provided no means of carrying the bayonet scabbards fitted with 1910 belt hooks. In order to do so, a russet leather slider was issued. It fitted to the belt and allowed the M1905 bayonet to be attached to the eyelets using the M1910 scabbard's M1910 belt hooks. A web slider was also manufactured.

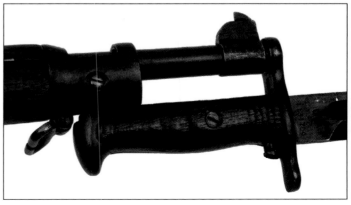

ABOVE A leather scabbard was first issued with the M1905 bayonet. This example has the third pattern of scabbard, the M1910. It has a canvass outer cover within, which is a hide-covered wooden body.

RIGHT The wood-gripped M1905 bayonet attached to the Springfield M1903 rifle. The "Krag"-type release mechanism is one of the most efficient and easy to use; however, when excessively worn, the bayonet can lock on the rifle, necessitating stripping of the grips in order to unfix the bayonet.

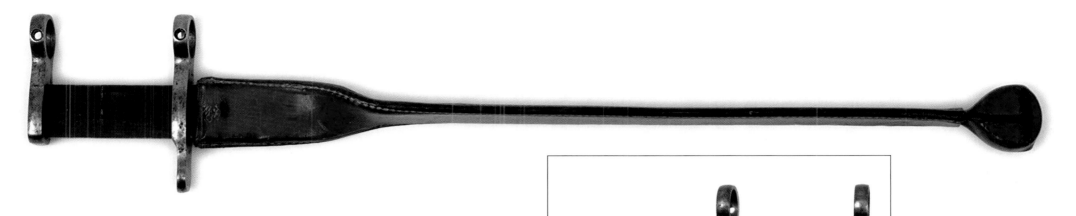

and a muzzle ring. It was similar in style to the Austrian World War I ersatz bayonets. The equally simple all-leather scabbard had an integral belt loop and hilt strap with brass stud fastener. Of the U.S. forces, only the USMC used the Johnson in small numbers, but it was also issued to Dutch forces, being used in the Netherlands East Indies in the immediate post-war period. Its designer, Captain M. Johnson, patented the bayonet in December 1943.

The Ingram M6 submachine gun was a commercial venture by the Californian Police Ordnance Co. First produced in 1949 the **Ingram M6** spike bayonet that accompanied the SMG is probably the shortest of any bayonet type ever made, measuring in at a total of only 229mm. It was certainly long enough to kill, but its effectiveness when attached to the gun was undoubtedly limited, and it was all but useless as a handheld weapon. The design was sold to Cuba, Peru and Puerto Rico, but it was not used in the U.S.

In 1955, the U.S. Ordnance introduced a new bayonet to replace the **M1** type still being used on the M1 Garand rifle. Using the **M3** blade, the **M5** knife bayonet used a locking system design based on the well-tried Krag-Jorgensen **1894** bayonet used on the **M1905**. Unusually, the **M5** had no muzzle ring, but instead a small rearward-facing stud protruded from the crossguard. This engaged with the rifle's gas plug, ensuring a secure fitting. This method of attachment was patented, as was the locking system. The attachment mechanism of the early bayonets was found to be faulty, resulting in the adoption of a modified **M5A1** bayonet, which was externally identical. For unknown reasons, some manufacturers marked the modified **M5A1**-type bayonets as M5-1, but they were identical to the **M5A1**. A commercial copy of the **M5** was made in Japan for the U.S. company Kiffe. It has a leather belt loop rather

ABOVE **1912 fencing bayonet.** The sprung-steel blade of the bayonet allowed vertical movement in a thrust. This movement, and the ball tip, lessened the chance of injuring an opponent, who, nonetheless, would have been wearing protective clothing.

LEFT **Markings** on the left side of the leather covering show that this fencing bayonet was made in 1914 at the Rock Island Arsenal.

BELOW **Bayonet training** Camp Shelby USA 1941. This color postcard was sold on the camp for recruits to send home, showing family and friends some of the aspects of training.

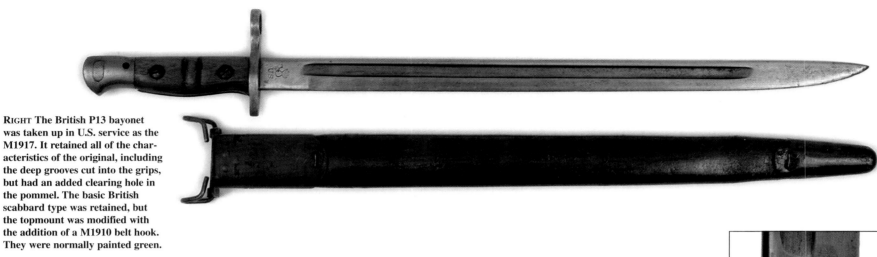

RIGHT The British P13 bayonet was taken up in U.S. service as the M1917. It retained all of the characteristics of the original, including the deep grooves cut into the grips, but had an added clearing hole in the pommel. The basic British scabbard type was retained, but the topmount was modified with the addition of a M1910 belt hook. They were normally painted green.

than the normal webbing. Although the majority was sold on the commercial market, it is believed that a number did see military use in South America.

The United States' commitment to NATO required the adoption of a rifle using the standard NATO 7.62mm ammunition. The new rifle, adopted as the M14, utilized the Garand action but with a 20-round magazine feed and half stock. It was provided with a short knife bayonet with **M3** blade and black plastic hilt. The barrel of the M14 differed from the Garand in that it had a flash eliminator, which meant that it was impossible to use the **M5A1** bayonet because of its unusual attachment system. Otherwise identical to the **M5A1** bayonet, the **M6** therefore deleted the stud from the crossguard and returned to a conventional muzzle ring system of attachment. Adopted in 1957, the **M6** bayonet was in production until 1963 and is still in use with chromed metalwork for use on the M14 rifle as a parade and ceremonial arm.

The **M8A1** scabbard was found to have a weak tip that was easily damaged, with many used examples in private collections having splits to the plastic tip. Effective repair of the plastic was difficult, but the problem was remedied by the introduction of a steel tip reinforcement sleeve that fitted over the end of the scabbard. The tip, which incorporated a hole for a tie down cord, was introduced in 1955. It was added to all new-production **M8A1** scabbards from 1963. A tab on the entrenching tool cover of the M1956 field equipment allowed the attachment of the **M8A1** bayonet scabbard as an efficient means of carriage, keeping it clear of the belt. The scabbard continued in service with the **M7** bayonet for the M16 rifle.

Utilizing the well-proven **M3** blade, the **M7** hilt returned to the locking system used on the **M4** bayonet to which it was quite similar, differing only in the size of the muzzle ring and in having checkered plastic grips. The standard **M8A1** scabbard was used with all U.S. bayonets from the **M4** to the **M7**.

Although occasionally found together, the hilt strap of the older **M8** scabbard was often too short to fit around the bulky hilt of the **M5** and **M5A1** bayonets. A modernized black plastic scabbard with nylon belt loop was authorized as a replacement for the **M8A1**. Officially approved in 1970, the **M10**

ABOVE Armed with a M1917 rifle, this American Doughboy also carries the M1910 pack with M1917 bayonet attached to the left side, an ideal position for the carriage of a long bayonet. The fact that he also has a bayonet attached to his rifle suggests it was borrowed for the photo.

ABOVE LEFT Right ricasso markings of the U.S. M1917 bayonet, showing the "US" stamp and ordnance flaming bomb with the "eagle" inspector's stamp. British P13 bayonets taken up by the U.S. had the British inspector's marking hatched out.

LEFT 1917. American soldiers undertake bayonet exercise prior to shipping out to the conflict in Europe.

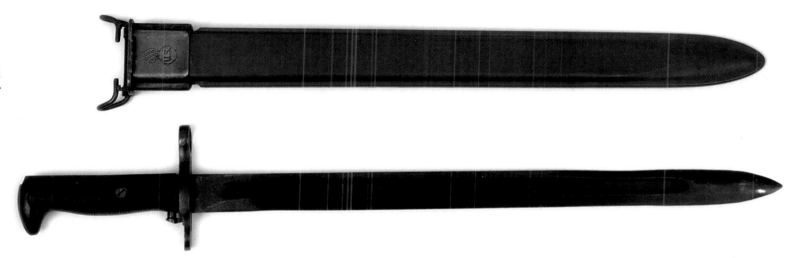

RIGHT The outbreak of World War II saw the U.S. short of everything, including bayonets. The M1905 bayonet was rushed back into service, the WWII model commonly being referred to as the M1942 by collectors. It differed from the M1905 in having plastic grips, which were also added to newly refurbished M1905s. A new plastic-bodied scabbard was introduced as the M3; it replaced the old canvas M1910 model.

scabbard was not manufactured in any quantity until the mid 1980s. It has a one-piece molded body and throat. The throat section is embossed "M10" and has an integral loop for the black nylon belt loop. A black tie down lace is fitted at the scabbard tip.

The bayonets **M4, M5, M5A1, M6** and **M7** were officially listed as "Bayonet-Knife" in U.S. service, indicating the perceived dual role as either bayonets or general-purpose knives, allowed by the **M3** blade form. Bayonets produced between the mid 1950s through to the mid 1960s often carry a small U.S. Department of Defense acceptance stamp consisting of a boxed stylized eagle surmounted by three stars. This replaced the old flaming grenade. Normally stamped onto the guard, it can occasionally be found as a white paint stamp.

Phrobis designed the rather large and awesome-looking M9 bayonet. It was initially manufactured under contract to the Buck Knife Company and later Lan-Cay. It was envisaged as a utility knife, saw, wirecutter and bayonet. It had green plastic grips and scabbard, with a clip-point blade and a serrated back edge saw. As with the Russian AK bayonets, to which the **M9**

RIGHT This GI wears the M1905 bayonet attached to the left side of his M1928 pack. This was a convenient method of carriage and prevented the long scabbard interfering with the legs, as was common with the British 1907 bayonet.

FAR RIGHT An emotive World War II patriotic poster calling upon the civilian population to give their blood to the transfusion service, to help the nation's soldiers who were spilling their blood on the battlefield. A Springfield 1903 rifle with fixed M1905 bayonet provides a temporary support for a bottle of plasma administered to a wounded GI by a medic.

HE GAVE HIS BLOOD...
WILL YOU GIVE YOURS?

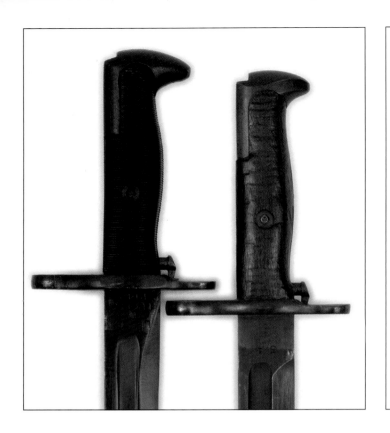

ABOVE LEFT The M1942 bayonet hilt, this example with red-brown grips, compared with the wood-gripped M1905 (right).

ABOVE Detail of the ricasso markings. An M1942 by Utica Cutlery in 1942, and an M1905 made at Springfield Armory in 1920.

LEFT The plastic USN Mk. I bayonet was introduced as a contingency measure during the early stages of World War II, when production of the M1942 bayonets was insufficient to meet the needs of the Army. This left the Navy short of bayonets. The USN Mk. I allowed training in rifle drill and bayonet use to continue until production of the M1942 met the demand.

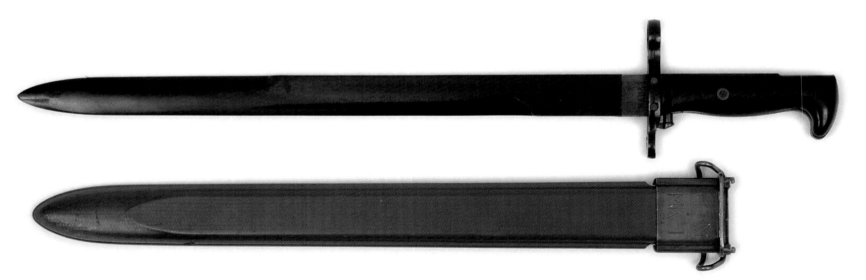

concept owes much, the blade fitted to the scabbard to form a wirecutter. The early Phrobis/Buck bayonets are readily identifiable, as they have a blade fuller; the bulk of Lan-Cay models have a plain blade. The Ontario Knife Company also made a number of **M9** bayonets with light-green grips. The accompanying high-density plastic scabbard has an unusual spring-type belt clip produced by Bianchi holsters, and a "Fastex" clip. This fastener allowed the scabbard section to be separated from the belt clip when using the wirecutter. A sharpening stone is permanently attached to the rear of the scabbard. A small removable nylon pouch, in which a penknife can be carried, attaches to the front. In addition to the standard green plastic grip and scabbard, the **M9** can be found in black, white, and desert tan, with an orange option also available on the commercial market. The **M9** bayonet has also been supplied to Australia and Abu Dhabi and vast quantities have also been produced to fuel the commercial market.

The United States Marine Corps was not particularly happy with the **M9** bayonet and has adopted a similar, but simpler, design without a wire-cutting facility and with a saw edge along the first part of the cutting edge. The first contract for just fewer than 100,000 of the new **OKC3S** bayonets was placed in 2003.

FIGURE 42.—To fix bayonets.

ABOVE RIGHT "Fix bayonets" as illustrated in the manual *FM21-100 Soldiers handbook*, 1941.

RIGHT Throat marking of the USN Mk. I scabbard. It is almost identical to the M3 scabbard, differing only in the markings. The bayonet ricasso is stamped with the navy stock number, "NXSO-17249," and the maker's marking, "PBC," for the Prophylactic Brush Company, who had previously made toothbrushes.

FAR RIGHT A comparison of the hilts of the USN Mk. I and M1942 bayonets show the difference in construction. The USN Mk. I fit a special training rifle procured at the same time as the bayonet.

LEFT U.S. GI's head for Normandy. M1 bayonets, cut down from M1905s, are fixed to their Garand rifles.

ABOVE The initial batch of M1 bayonets were shortened M1905 and M1942 blades. The cut-down bayonets are readily identifiable by the fullers that run through to the point, as shown on the lower example. Production of the M1 bayonet was quickly underway with new short-bladed bayonets being produced well before many of the long-bladed bayonets were cut down. Allied Fork and Hoe Company of Geneva, Ohio, made the lower example; Victory Plastics made the scabbard.

RIGHT A UFH-made M1 bayonet fitted to an M1 Garand rifle. The absence of the grips gives a clear understanding of the locking mechanism that pivoted on the grip screw. The attachment system used on the M1 bayonet was based upon that used on the Krag Jorgensen.

ABOVE Originally made by Springfield Armory in 1918, this M1905 bayonet was modified to an M1 as shown by the "U.C.-MOD." marking on the ricasso, indicating conversion by the Utica Cutlery Company of Utica, New York.

RIGHT A bayonet-training dummy designed to train soldiers in the thrust and parry. This illustration is from the American World War II bayonet-training manual, *FM23-25*, 1943.

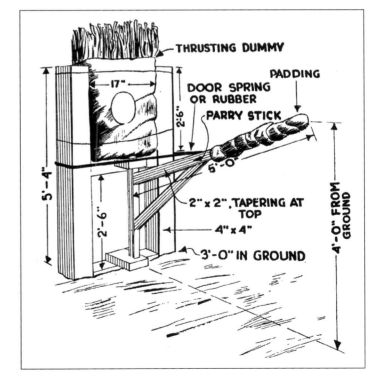

THRUSTING DUMMY
PADDING
DOOR SPRING OR RUBBER
PARRY STICK
17"
2'-6"
5-0"
5'-4"
2'-6"
2" x 2" TAPERING AT TOP
4" x 4"
3'-0" IN GROUND
4'-0" FROM GROUND

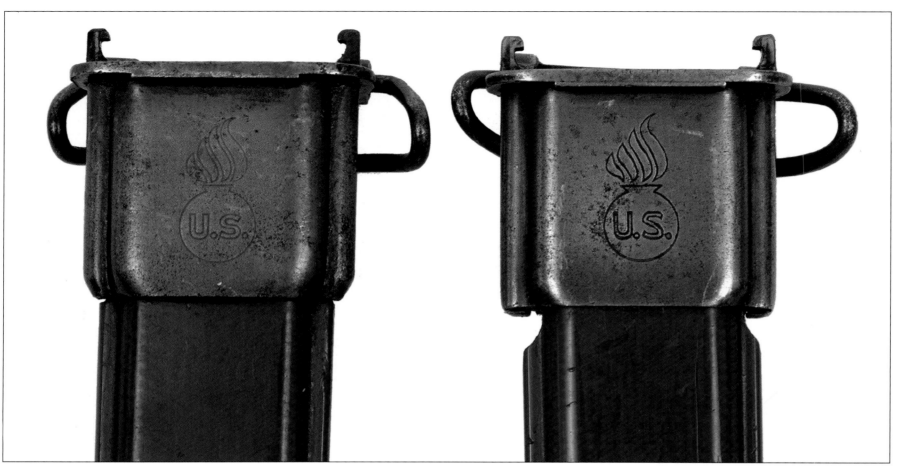

LEFT The first M7 scabbards were cut down from the longer M3. It was found that once the topmount had been removed to allow the body to be shortened, it was not possible to re-fix it using the tabs originally used. It was therefore necessary to crimp the bottom edge of the mount to secure it in place. New-production M7 scabbards used the original tab method of securing the topmount. At left is a cut-down M3 using the crimped locket fixing; at right, a newly made scabbard with tab fixing, as also used on the M3. Note the distinctive cut-out on the newly made scabbard body that allowed the folding in of the tabs, clearly shown here. The topmount was stamped with the ordnance department's flaming grenade.

BELOW LEFT After the introduction of the short M5 bayonet, the old M1 remained a limited issue for quite some time until production of the new bayonet met demand. However, a quantity of M1 bayonets were retained in many units as a ceremonial arm. With white painted scabbards, and often with the bayonet's metal parts chromium-plated, they provided a smart spectacle during arms drill. White duck covers with black leather tips were also provided for ceremonial use. The cover, a copy of the original M1910 cover used with the M1905 bayonet, slipped over the original M7 scabbard.

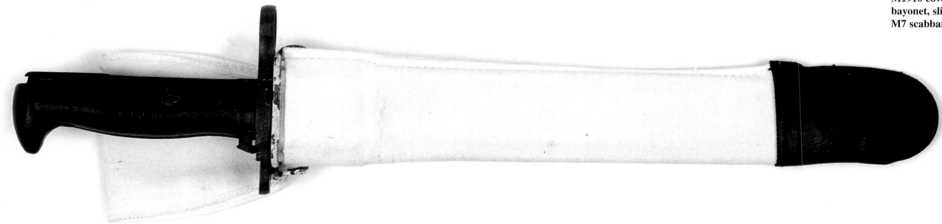

ABOVE The M1 Garand bayonet was widely copied in the post-war years. Typical variants are shown here alongside U.S. examples for comparative purposes; Danish M1950; Italian M1; Taiwanese M1; U.S. M1, cut down from an M1905; U.S. M1; U.S. M1 and duck cover.

LEFT The U.S. manual *FM 23-25, Bayonet*, 1943, shows the method of disarming an assailant in a bayonet attack. Easy to illustrate but requiring some degree of skill and courage to actually perform.

RIGHT Non-U.S. manufacture M1 bayonets may look the same as the original item; however, closer examination will reveal their non-American origin. Initially identical, closer inspection of the Taiwanese M1 shows minor differences in detail. Whilst overall quality of manufacture is high, the ricasso lacks U.S. markings, as does the scabbard throat. The scabbard body is molded from a dark-green plastic, unlike U.S. examples.

BELOW The M3 knife was for issue to troops armed with the M1 carbine or M1911A1 pistol who were not issued with a bayonet. It is illustrated here, as it formed the basis for US bayonet development for the next 20 years, with the blade design being used on the M4, M5, M5A1, M6 and M7 bayonets. The all leather M6 scabbard was only used on the knife.

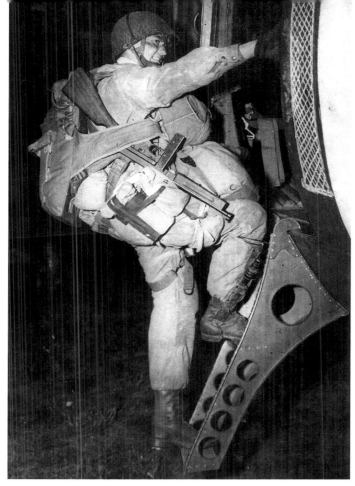

ABOVE June 5, 1944. An American paratrooper boards a C47 enroute for Normandy. Strapped to his right ankle is an M3 knife in its M6 scabbard, the predecessor of the M4 bayonet and a blade form used on the post-war M5, M6 and M7 bayonets, as well as countless other bayonets and knives worldwide.

LEFT The ricasso of the Taiwanese M1 is marked "60-6," possibly indicating June 1960 manufacture. The segmented wheel marking is that of Combined Logistics Command, Taiwan. Such markings serve to prevent any confusion with original U.S. M1 bayonets.

ABOVE RIGHT Although not envisaged as requiring a bayonet, the fitting of a modified forward barrel band to the M1 carbine allowed the use of a bayonet. Shown here is the original carbine with the replacement barrel band with bayonet fitting that was to be standard on the later M2 carbine and retrospectively fitted to the M1. The M4 bayonet was based on the M3 knife with a new crossguard that had a muzzle ring and a modified pommel with attachment mechanism. The scabbard is the M8, designed as a replacement for the M6 and issued with the M4 bayonet.

RIGHT A late-production M4 bayonet with plastic grips. Other than the diameter of the muzzle ring, the plastic-grip version of the M4 bayonet is very similar to the M7.

RIGHT The Johnson bayonet had a simple all-leather scabbard with integral belt loop. A short hilt strap secured the bayonet in the scabbard.

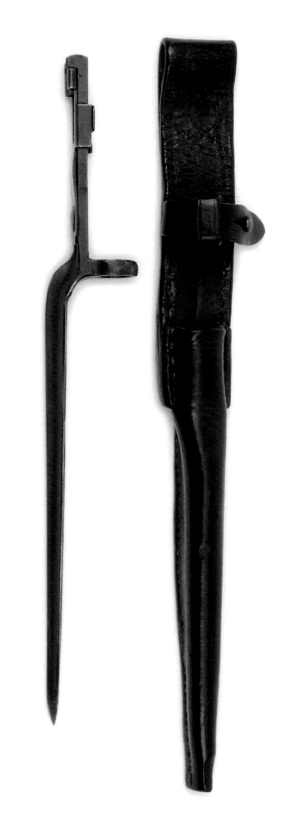

LEFT M41 bayonet for the Johnson self-loading rifle. The rifle had a recoiling barrel, which meant that the bayonet had to be as light as possible for the weapon to function satisfactorily. It was a simple forging with triangular blade, flat tang and spring locking device. It was issued in limited numbers to the USMC and Netherlands East Indies forces. Chile also purchased a number in 1941.

ABOVE Crossguard marking on the late-production M4. "U.S.M4" over "TMN" indicates that this bayonet was made by Turner Manufacturing.

LEFT The rudimentary hilt of the M41 had a flat spring locking mechanism; it was similar to those used on World War I Austrian ersatz bayonets.

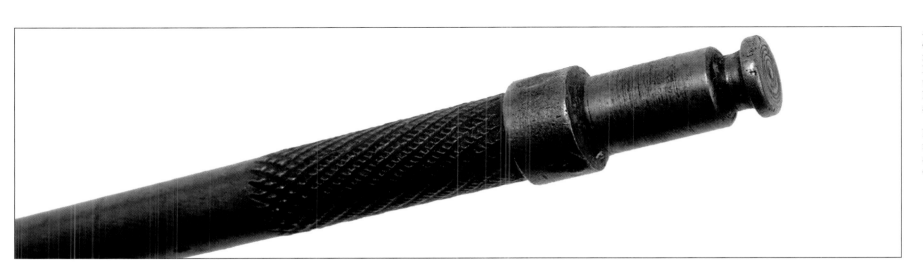

ABOVE The Ingram M6 spike bayonet is among the shortest and most impractical of any bayonet. It was made in the U.S. but not used there, being purchased in limited quantity by Peru, Cuba and Puerto Rico.

LEFT The simple fitting mechanism of the M6, with a knurled grip section for ease of attachment.

LEFT The U.S. M5 bayonet (above) replaced the old M1, for use on the Garand rifle, in 1955. It was unique in not having a muzzle ring but rather a small rearward-facing stud that fit into the rifle's gas plug fitting. The M5 bayonet was replaced by the improved M5A1 (in scabbard). It was externally identical and, without removing the grips, was only distinguishable by the designation stamped into the crossguard and a slight difference in the press catch. The scabbard is an M8A1 made by Beckwith Manufacturing.

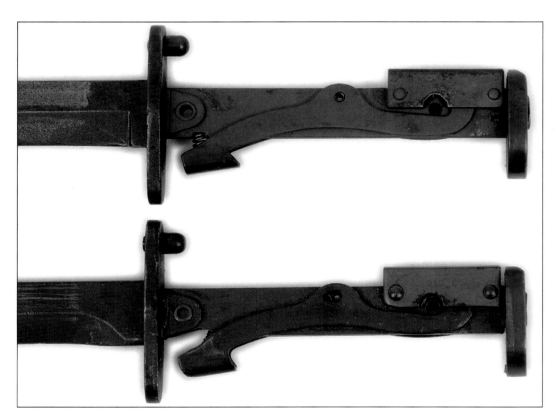

LEFT The U.S. government Department of Defense acceptance mark stamped into the underside of a U.S. M5 bayonet crossguard manufactured by Imperial, based in Providence, Rhode Island. Some markings were stamped in white paint, which soon wore off. The stamp consists of a stylized eagle surmounted by three stars. This replaced the old flaming grenade from about 1955 and was in use until the mid 1960s.

LEFT With the grips removed, the differences between the M5 (above) and M5A1 are evident. The M5A1 (below) differs in having the lever spring fitted at a sharper angle and in having an oval recess in the "latching lever." The modifications were undertaken because field reports indicated that the M5 bayonets release catch could be difficult to operate, and some bayonets were found to have a loose fit on the rifle. The M5 bayonet fitted to the M1 Garand rifle. Unlike the original M1 bayonet, which used the muzzle ring over the barrel, the M5 and M5A1 used a small stud that fitted into the gas plug.

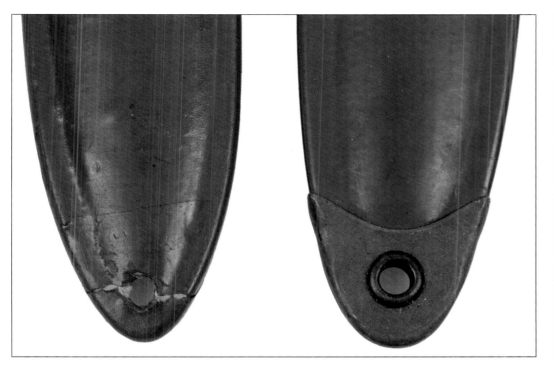

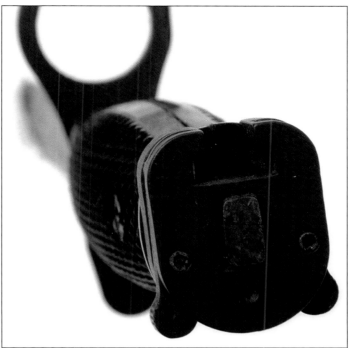

FAR LEFT U.S. M8 and M8A1 scabbard tips. The early scabbard shows typical signs of damage to the internal fiber reinforcing to the plastic body. This was rectified on late-production M8A1 scabbards by the addition of a metal tip.

LEFT Pommel of M7 showing press catches ("bayonet release" in U.S. terminology) and mortise for the M16 rifle's bayonet bar.

LEFT The M16 rifle was issued with the M7 bayonet, which was very similar to the original M4. Its main difference was the larger muzzle ring required to fit over the flash eliminator of the rifle. It is shown here with the M8A1 scabbard, which is stamped "M8A1 PWH."

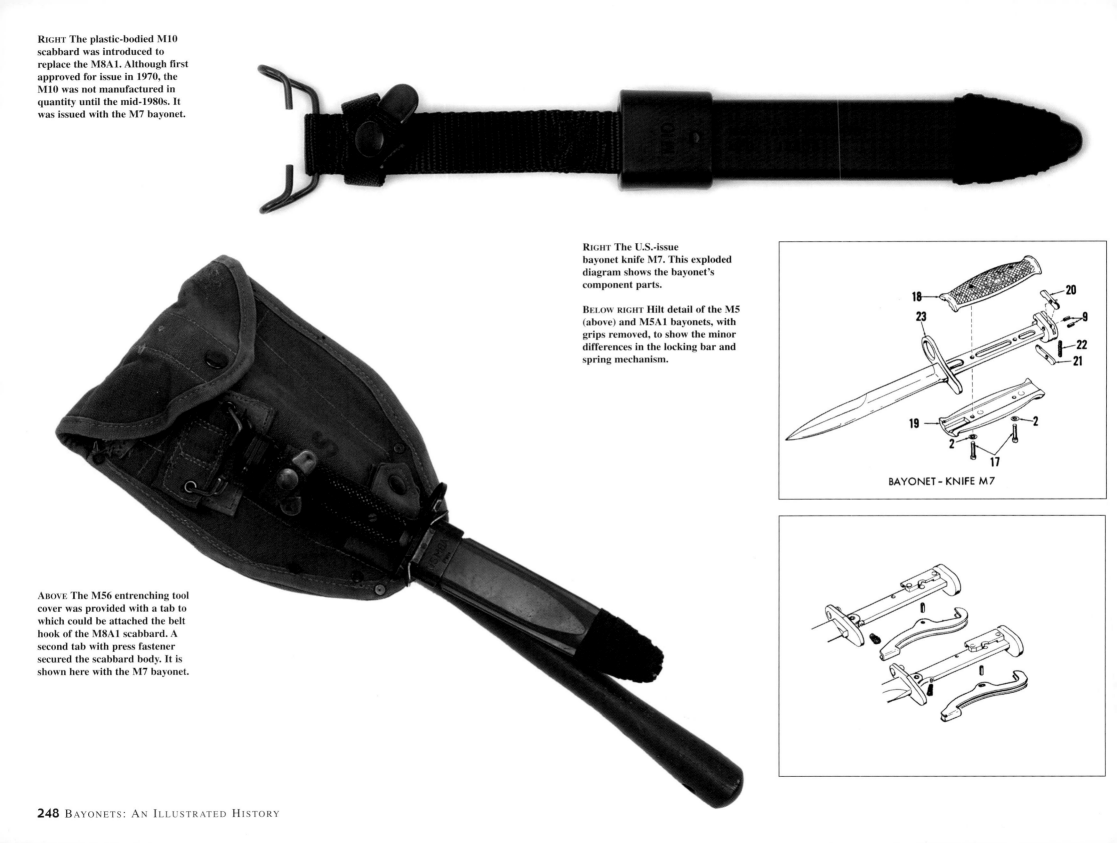

RIGHT The plastic-bodied M10 scabbard was introduced to replace the M8A1. Although first approved for issue in 1970, the M10 was not manufactured in quantity until the mid-1980s. It was issued with the M7 bayonet.

RIGHT The U.S.-issue bayonet knife M7. This exploded diagram shows the bayonet's component parts.

BELOW RIGHT Hilt detail of the M5 (above) and M5A1 bayonets, with grips removed, to show the minor differences in the locking bar and spring mechanism.

ABOVE The M56 entrenching tool cover was provided with a tab to which could be attached the belt hook of the M8A1 scabbard. A second tab with press fastener secured the scabbard body. It is shown here with the M7 bayonet.

BAYONET - KNIFE M7

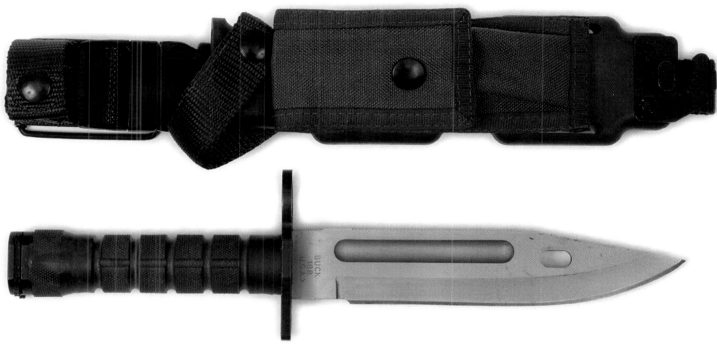

ABOVE The ricasso of this M9 is marked "BUCK 188 U.S.A.>" in three lines. The right-facing arrow indicates 1987 manufacture; this symbol-type year coding was soon abandoned. The cutting edge and reverse of the blade-back saw-tooth edge is also evident in this view.

ABOVE RIGHT The current U.S. bayonet is the M9, designed by Phrobis. This is a departure from the standard knife bayonet and provides the U.S. soldier with a combination field knife and wire-cutter. It has saw teeth to the blade back, a wirecutter and screwdriver point to the scabbard; an oilstone is inset into the rear of the scabbard and a utility (pocket) knife pouch is fitted to the front of the scabbard. It is quite a heavy combination.

ABOVE The patented belt clip on the rear of the M9's scabbard was designed by Bianchi. It incorporates a quick-release spring clip that enabled the whole assembly to be removed from the belt without any disassembling of the equipment set.

Uruguay

	Overall length	Blade length	Muzzle ring
1908	410mm	280mm	15.5mm
M1937	432mm	298mm	14.9mm

Uruguay, aided by Argentinean troops and ratified by Great Britain, became a nation in 1815 after years under Spanish and then Brazilian domination. Initially, the Brown Bess and a version of the French 1822 style of bayonet, the *Bayoneta de Cubo de rifles de Avancarga, Percusion*, was used. The British **1853** was employed, the bayonet being converted for use on the Mauser 1870 as the *Bayoneta de Cubo Los rifles Mauser Mod.1870*. The generic Remington (**1882**) was used on the .433in Remington rolling-block 1869–70. This was called the *Bayoneta de Cubo Los rifles Remington "Rolling Block"* in Uruguayan service.

In 1895, a Belgian Mauser was adopted. The 1895 bayonet was similar to the Belgian 1889 but had a steel-mounted leather scabbard. A copy of the Brazilian 1908 rifle was purchased by Uruguay just prior to World War I. The bayonet was much simpler than the Brazilian type, the Uruguayan **1908** being of the standard Mauser export pattern. During the years after World War I, Uruguay imported the Belgian-made FN 1924 rifle and standard **1924** export bayonet. The FN was later supplemented by the export version of the Czech VZ24 rifle, Uruguay being one of a number of nations to import weapons from Czechoslovakia. In Uruguayan service, the VZ24 was called the 1937 short rifle. The **M1937** bayonet was very obviously of Czech origin. It was a copy of the Czech **VZ24** but had a standard blade orientation with the sharpened edge on the lower side of the blade. The Uruguayan bayonet bore the national "sunburst" marking on the crossguard and the frog stud.

BELOW Uruguayan 1908 bayonet with steel scabbard. The 1908 rifle was based on the one supplied to Brazil. The bayonet is of the ubiquitous Mauser type produced in many minor variants and supplied to armies worldwide during the early 20th century.

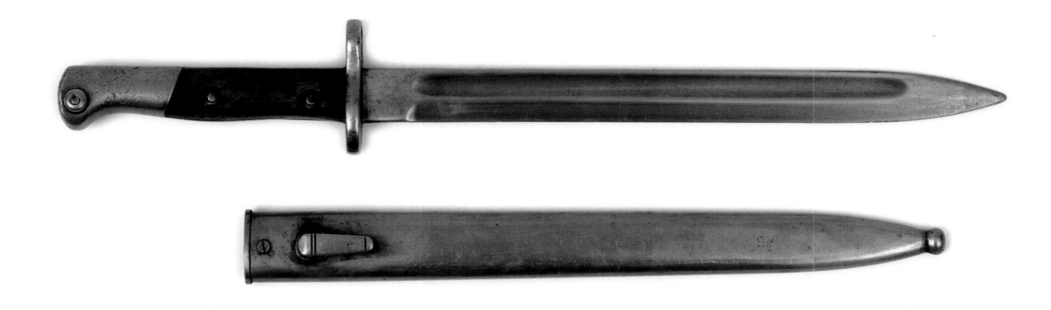

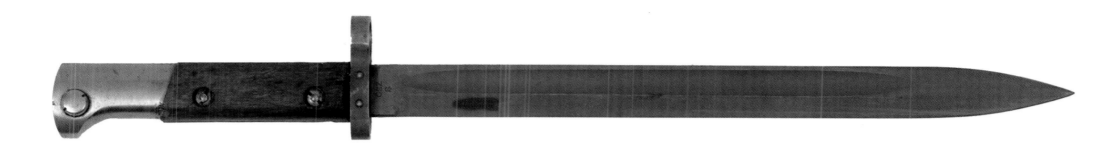

ABOVE This export version of the Czech VZ24 bayonet was supplied to Uruguay as the 1937 bayonet. The blade is orientated in the standard position, with the edge opposite the muzzle ring, rather than uppermost as on Czech VZ24s.

LEFT Uruguayan 1937 bayonet showing the "sunburst" marking on the frog stud and crossguard.

Yugoslavia

	Overall length	Blade length	Muzzle ring
1924	378mm	246mm	15.3mm
M1956	286mm	176mm	14.5mm
244	590mm	512mm	18mm
209	585mm	512mm	17mm

Serbia had been under Ottoman rule until 1878 when independence was gained. The army rapidly re-equipped with the best weapon then available, the Mauser 1871 modified as the 1878/80 rifle. The Balkan War of 1912–13 saw the Serbs using the 1899 rifle, based on the Chilean 1895 Mauser. The conflict led the Serbs into World War I where, despite fighting gallantly against the Austrians and Germans, they were rapidly defeated. A variant of the Mosin-Nagant **1891** was made for Serbia by the U.S. company Plumb. An example has been noted dated "1915." At the end of World War I, the state of Yugoslavia was founded as a monarchy, consisting of Bosnia, Croatia, Herzegovina, Kosovo, Macedonia, Montenegro, Serbia and Slovenia.

During the years prior to World War II, the Yugoslav Army was equipped with a variety of similar weapon types, the Belgian FN 24 and 30 rifles, and the Czech VZ24 rifles. The Kragujevac Arsenal also made the FN 24 under license along with the **1924**-pattern bayonet. The Yugoslav pattern is identical to the Belgian export FN **1924**, although Yugoslavian-made bayonets have a distinctive grip bolt head that requires a special bifurcated tool to remove them. In April 1941, Germany, Bulgaria and Romania attacked and soon defeated the Yugoslavs. The end of World War II left a political void that was rapidly filled by the Communists under Tito. The Communist government continued to use the pre-war rifles, supplemented by large quantities of German arms and the new 1948 rifle, a copy of the German K98. This rifle also used the **1924**-type bayonet.

Many post-war Yugoslavian bayonets are marked with Cyrillic lettering, not Russian but Serbian. Typical Serb markings during the Communist regime read "Enterprise 44," in this instance representing State Factory number 44, not the year

1944. Factory 44 was located in Kragujevac, the seat of the Yugoslav arms industry. The marking "AT3" is often encountered and was applied by the state arsenal in Kragujevac on bayonets produced prior to World War II.

The Communist government soon looked to Russia for small arms. The Soviet SKS carbine was adopted as the Zastava M59. It was fitted with a copy of the SKS folding-blade bayonet. Due to the rifle's fixed grenade launcher, the blade is noticeably longer than the standard SKS type; it also has no muzzle ring. The AK47 was later adopted and called the

M64, with a modified version known as the M70. Yugoslav-made **AK47** bayonets and **AKM** bayonet types were used on these weapons.

A small 7.62mm SMG was introduced in 1956, resembling the World War II MP40 *Schmeisser*. It had provision for the attachment of a bayonet. The plastic-gripped **M1956** bayonet measures in at just 286mm total length. It had a unique method of retaining the blade in the scabbard, whereby a spring steel extension of the frog stud passed through the scabbard face and a small stud engaged into a depression in the blade.

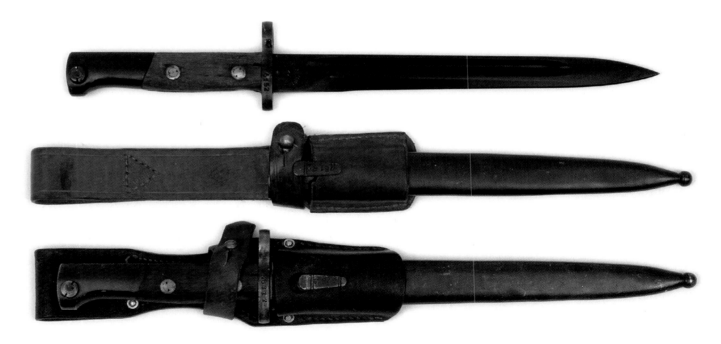

ABOVE 1924 bayonets. These are the standard 246mm blade examples; a pre-World War II variant has the longer 382mm blade. The 1924 bayonet was both imported and made in Yugoslavia. The Yugoslavian-made bayonets have distinctive grip bolts, as can be seen on these examples. The upper example is a post-war bayonet made in State Factory 44 at Kragujevac. It has the standard brown leather bayonet frog. The lower bayonet is of pre-war manufacture, but the frog is a post-war modification of the German S84/98 frog with an added hilt loop. The post-war bayonet was made for the 1948 rifle.

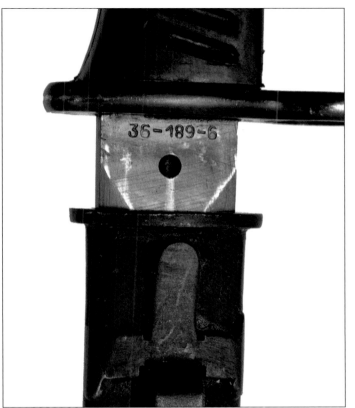

FAR LEFT A Cyrillic inscription on the right ricasso of a communist-era M1924 bayonet shows that it was made in State Factory 44. Of note is the distinctive Yugoslav grip bolt. At right is the standard-pattern M24 frog with the "BT3 VTZ" and eagle marking believed to stand for the Kragujevac Arsenal.

LEFT M56 SMG bayonet showing the ricasso marking "36-189-6" and the recess that engaged with a stud on the inner face of the frog stud extension, passing through the scabbard body to retain the bayonet in the scabbard.

BELOW LEFT The M56 bayonet for the 7.62mm M1956 submachine gun. The simple attachment mechanism is not dissimilar to that used on the Swiss SIG 57 bayonet, consisting of twin catches that pushed down away from the mortise.

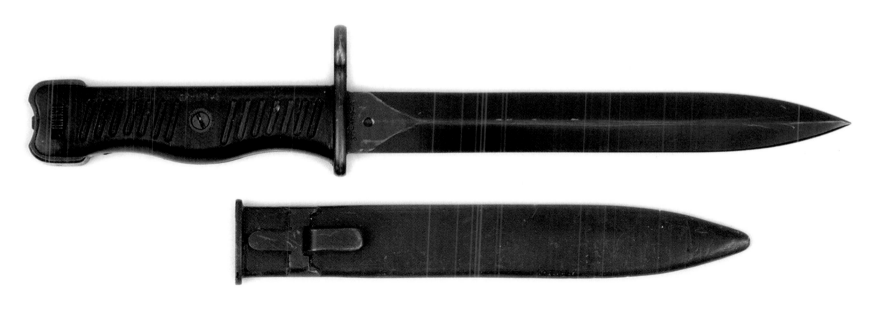

Index

ABOVE A French infantryman from the 85th RI photographed c.1915. He wears an 1886 bayonet at his left side. Of interest is the very rare Mills webbing belt and webbing bayonet frog used to suspend it. (RF Stedman collection)

ABOVE A Japanese infantryman shows the Type 30 bayonet to good effect in this portrait shot taken in Manchuria. (RF Stedman collection)

RIGHT Iraq, 1991. A Royal Marine of HQ 3 Commando Brigade puts his L3A1 bayonet to good use clearing mud from the tread of his boots, a practice not listed in the bayonet manual.